TRIGGER MARSHAL

The Story of Chris Madsen

BOOKS OF THE WEST

by HOMER CROY

JESSE JAMES WAS MY NEIGHBOR

HE HANGED THEM HIGH

OUR WILL ROGERS

WHEELS WEST: THE STORY OF THE DONNER PARTY

LAST OF THE GREAT OUTLAWS

THE LADY FROM COLORADO

TRIGGER MARSHAL: THE STORY OF CHRIS MADSEN

TRIGGER MARSHAL

The Story of Chris Madsen

BY HOMER CROY

DUELL, SLOAN AND PEARCE
New York

Library of Congress Catalogue Card Number: 58-10436

First edition

MANUFACTURED IN THE UNITED STATES OF AMERICA

VAN REES PRESS • NEW YORK

Contents

Illustrations

Foreword

CHRIS MADSEN was a greater peace officer than Wyatt Earp. As a matter of fact, Wyatt Earp spent more years gambling than he did bringing peace to the land. And his part in the O. K. Corral fight, under the cold inspection of history, does not show up very well. The men he helped kill that dark day had better reputations than the Earps had; besides, the victims were unarmed and had their hands in the air. The affair was a feud between the two groups, starting over mule stealing, and was not at all the matter of bringing law to a wild land. Wyatt Earp is a great hero and will go galloping along for years to come, but that is because he played in luck. He teamed up with Doc Holliday and Doc helped immortalize him.

Chris Madsen had no such luck. If he'd had a Doc Holliday to help him out, and a bit of luck in a few other places, he would be as great a hero in the public mind as Wyatt Berry Stapp Earp.

Chris brought in far more bad men than Wyatt Earp ever did. He brought them in from hay crossings and outlaw dugouts in Oklahoma instead of from publicized Dodge City, Ellsworth, and Tombstone. And now I expect all the Earp fans will want to bring me in.

It would seem that Wyatt Earp, as a peace officer, served six years and three months, or seven years, if one counts his deputy United States marshalship in Tombstone, of which there is no record. Chris Madsen, as peace officer, served twenty-five years.

Chris's story has never been told, that is, except in the newspapers. This is the first book that has attempted to set it down.

I had the good fortune to meet up with Chris's son Reno, and he began to tell me about his father. He hauled out an ancient, brass-bound trunk—it was full of doubloons. Chris had written his life story, and there was the manuscript smiling up at us. And he'd written many pieces for the Oklahoma papers about his adventures—and there they were, too, beaming at us. And there was a whole armload of papers. Seemingly the man never threw away anything—thank goodness! I itched to get my hands on them and when I did I was as happy as a boy in a watermelon patch.

I want to thank Reno Madsen for his great help. Half the time he thought I was crazy—he might have a point there—so many questions and demands for verification did I throw at him. He grumbled but he came through. And here it is, in your hand.

I think of the story as bigger than one man. I think of it as the history of an era—the Outlaw Era—in a section of Indian Territory that was trying very hard to grow up into a state.

I am glad to pass on to those interested in Americana this story of the making of one corner of America.

—The Author

TRIGGER MARSHAL

The Story of Chris Madsen

CHAPTER 1

A Danish Boy Arrives in America to Fight Indians. He Gets to Fight 'em. Sees Buffalo Bill Kill Yellow Hand.

NOT TOO LONG ago a Danish youth named Chris Madsen landed in New York to fight Indians. At this time, in Denmark, the favorite reading for young people was about Indian fighting in the "Wild West." One way and another Chris saved up enough money to come to America to help kill the bloodthirsty Indians who were scalping and murdering innocent white people. That is the way he thought of the Indians—"bloodthirsty"; for that matter, that was the way almost everybody thought of them—downright savages; the sooner they were killed the better.

Chris arrived in New York in January 1876—the year of the Battle of the Little Big Horn. He was a short, stocky lad with a barrel chest, hands as big as snowshoes, and an accent as thick as a coffeecake. And blue eyes.

He didn't know it, but he had come at exactly the right time and to the right place. The great Indian campaigns were on and they were not doing well. So greatly did the United States Army need recruits that it was signing them up in New York. Sergeants walked the streets; when they saw a young man who might develop into a fine Indian fighter they would go up to him and tell him about the glories of Indian fighting. The last thing they would mention was the rate of pay—fifteen dollars a month. Nor did they mention the chance of being scalped. But the young men of New York thought for themselves and said, in effect, that they didn't want to kill Indians, however much the Indians deserved to be killed.

This was where young Christian Madsen came in. The books and magazines he had read in Denmark made him eager to help the West get rid of the painted devils. He met a sergeant and said, "Where is eet peoples sign oop to kill Indians?"

"What did you say?" asked the sergeant, so thick was Chris's accent.

Chris repeated what he had said.

The sergeant smiled. "You come with me," he said with great cordiality. "I think we've still got a few places open."

Chris marched off happily.

The two arrived at a rough, crude office at the top of a wooden stair. Three or four dejected creatures were sitting in the room—evidently the bottom of the man barrel. "Sit there and wait your turn," said the sergeant, then went out in search of other Indian fighters. One by one the men were called, and they shuffled into a back room. After a while they reappeared, but left by a side door; whether they had been rejected or had signed up, Chris didn't know.

At this time a person didn't have to have a passport to come into the United States. He got off the boat and he was in the United States. Nor did a person have to be a citizen to be enrolled into the Army. The Civil War had been over ten years; the people knew the grim realities of war and wanted none of it. It was hard scratching for the Army to get recruits; it took what it could get—especially for the western campaigns. And here was young Chris Madsen pining to sign up.

A man poked out his head and called, "Next."

It was Chris's turn and he got up joyfully. His first step to become an Indian fighter! He was shown into a side room. "Take off your clothes," said an orderly.

Chris got out of his clothes. In a few minutes a doctor came. "How old are you?"

Chris told him.

"What do you do?"

"I am a surveyor. I can survey."

This was noted.

"Bend forward and touch your fingers to the floor without bending your knees. Bend backward. Now pretend you are running, but stand in the same place." Chris ran delightedly, standing in one place. The doctor put a stethoscope to his chest and listened. Everything was ticking right. "Now hop from one foot to the other."

Chris obliged.

The doctor looked closely. "You've got a wound on your left ankle."

"Yes, sir."

"Did you get it from the police?"

"I got it at the Battle of Sedan."

"Where?" said the astonished doctor. "Where do you claim you got it?"

"At the Battle of Sedan in France."

"When was the Battle of Sedan?" asked the doctor cleverly.

Chris told him.

The doctor went behind a partition and talked in a low voice to some other person, then came back. "Who was in command of the French forces?"

"Marshal MacMahon."

The doctor studied Chris again, looking at him even more closely. "Are you a Frenchman?"

"It is I am a Dane. I was borned in Schleswig-Holstein."

"Where did you learn English?"

"I have studied in school a leetle."

Chris told how he had fought in the Danish Army, when he was fourteen, against the Germans, and how the Danes had lost. Then how he had joined the French Foreign Legion and been assigned to the Chasseurs d'Afrique and sent to Algeria. He had been serving with his unit, in the province of Oran, when the Franco-Prussian War broke out, and he had returned with his outfit and fought the Germans at the Battle of Sedan. Things had gone a little wrong; he had been wounded, captured, and put in prison. But not for too long. He had escaped and returned to France where he had fought with the guerrillas and other irregulars. Then out of a clear sky the war was over and Chris had been sent back to Algeria where he had completed his five-year enlistment in the French Foreign Legion.

"Good land!" said the astonished doctor when Chris finished. "Didn't you fight any other place?"

"No, sir," said Chris apologetically. "I fight in only t'ree countries."

"You were really a member of the French Foreign Legion, then?"

"It ees zo."

"It was a pretty tough bunch of men, wasn't it?"

"But goot soldiers. I was mustered oudt an' I come to Amerika an' now I want to fight Indians."

The examining doctor made some notes. "Did you know, when you came in, that we were enrolling men to join General Custer?"

"General Custer!" Chris's face glowed. "No, sir, I do not know eet. I have a goot piece of luck, is it not zo?"

The doctor said it was zo. He made some more notes, then said, "I think we want you. You will not have to be trained. We are enrolling men now for the Seventh Cavalry, and we can start you out West at once."

"Dot is goot. I am pleased," said Chris, delighted with his fine luck.

There was a wait of three days and then the men who had been enrolled were put on a train. Chris was told by the recruiting officer that ninety men had come up for examination and that he, Chris, was the only one to be accepted. But Chris now was on the train and speeding across the country. On the train, however, new orders were received. Instead of being whisked out West to General Custer, one hundred of the men were transferred to the Fifth Cavalry, Chris among them.

The men were taken to Fort Hays, Kansas, to drill. The first day Chris got there he heard two men talking. One said something about Boot Hill.

"Where is eet, dis boots hill?" Chris said.

The men glanced at each other and smiled. "North of town. Go out there and you'll find it."

Chris walked out by himself, looking for what he thought must be old army boots piled up to make a hill. At last he came back and said, "I don't see any boots." The men had a laugh and Chris learned his first bit of western talk.

From his reading in Denmark, Chris had thought that, in America, Indians were as thick as cloves on a ham, but here he was in the middle of America—and not an Indian. It was plumb discouraging. What had happened was this: there had been Indians around Fort Hays, but the government had moved them further west. On the other hand, there were buffaloes. If he got on his horse and rode out into the country he could see buffaloes. What a strange and complex country he'd got into!

One day good news came through. The company was to mount. Young Chris was tremendously excited. He would not only see an Indian, but he'd slay him. Then came a more detailed report. The soldiers were to chase horse thieves in Texas. Up until 1879 the United States Army could be used as a posse to help civil authorities run down horse thieves and organized lawbreakers. It was Boots and Saddles—away to catch a pack of low-down horse thieves. The soldiers rode here and they rode there, and at last rounded up twenty sorry-looking human beings who were accused of lifting horses and turned over to the civil authorities. Then the soldiers rode back to camp. Nary an Indian.

The days moved along. Then came exciting news. The troop was to be sent to Wyoming where Sitting Bull was making a nuisance of himself. Chris was thrilled. On June 5, 1876, the men were put on a train and the train started west. Chris's heart pounded like a broken wheel. The train went less than fifty miles, then stopped for supper. The men piled out, hunted up firewood, and started to cook outdoors, real soldiers now. Just at this unhappy moment a Kansas cyclone came roaring along, knocked over tents, pots, equipment, food, men, everything. The men picked themselves up, but no sooner had they done so than the whistle tooted and back into the cars the men had to go, hungry as coyotes and using language this writer will not shock his readers with.

The train rolled on, arriving finally at Fort D. A. Russell. Here indeed were preparations for an Indian campaign; excitement was in the air. There was to be a battle, the soldiers said. They would cover themselves with glory. They would twist Sitting Bull's tail. They would make him paw dirt.

That afternoon Chris saw something on the company street that made him blink. There came swinging toward him the most gorgeous human being he had ever seen. He wore black velvet trousers with a lacework of gold strings, a belt with enough silver ornaments to fill a store window, a hat that looked like something used by the freshman class in a high-school play, and hair to his shoulders. The extraordinary gentleman marched on by, his chin in the air, speaking to no one. After the apparition had gone by, Chris edged over to one of the men and said, "Who vas that?"

"That was Buffalo Bill."

"What does he do?" asked the puzzled Chris.

"He's an actor, but now he is going to be our scout."

And that was the way Chris got his first glimpse of the immortal boy from Iowa. Buffalo Bill's dress was not completely absurd. He was appearing in Wilmington, Delaware, in a play called *Scouts of the Plains*. Besides, the costume had been designed by his wife, who was "artistic." He was in his fancy costume, dressed to make an entrance, when a telegram was handed him from General Phil Sheridan asking him to come to Wyoming and act as chief of scouts for the Fifth Cavalry Regiment. Without changing his clothes, he rushed to the railroad station and was soon speeding West, braid, hair, and all. And here he was now, walking down the company street, dressed in his stage costume.

The troop Chris was with was moved here and there, getting ready for a big battle, where and when no one knew. Finally the troop got to Fort Laramie, Wyoming, and there Chris saw his first Indian—Spotted Tail, a chief. He looked the part of a great warrior, and Chris was thrilled. When Chris found that Spotted Tail didn't believe in fighting, Chris was disappointed. He'd come across the ocean and waited all these days, and the only Indian he'd seen wouldn't harm a fly.

One morning the trumpet blew and orders were read. The Fifth Cavalry (to which Chris had been assigned) was to prepare for active duty. That was more like it. Then Chris found that the cavalry was merely to chase reservation Indians back on their land. What a letdown! But bad luck can't dog a person forever. He was assigned to work with the scouts. And the chief scout was Buffalo Bill. The two sized each other up. Chris knew nothing about scouting, but he felt that Buffalo Bill knew his business and was favorably impressed by him.

Chris was told to learn the wigwag system, and set to work with great enthusiasm. He was to accompany the advance scouts and wigwag messages back to headquarters. And so, with Buffalo Bill leading the party, Chris set out on the trail of the damned Indians.

Then came news about General Crook. He had met Crazy Horse in what became known as the Battle of the Rosebud, and Crazy Horse had made a monkey of him. It was not long before even worse news arrived. General Custer had been killed, and with him every man in his command. It shook Chris. What were these Indians, anyway?

But the Fifth must chase Indians. That was the order. The Indians had retreated to the northwestern corner of Nebraska, near a place now known as Montrose, Sioux County. The country was as barren and worthless as any that could be conjured up, but the Indians had to be taught a lesson.

On July 15, a little after midday, the column started out to find the Indians and deal with them. The march became famous in military history as a fast one over impossible terrain. On the evening of July 16 the column reached War Bonnet Creek. (Note: Chris, in talking of the place, always called it Hat Creek, but the location has gone down in history as War Bonnet Creek.) Shortly before daybreak next morning, Buffalo Bill took Chris with him and went to what was described as a "little conical mound" at the edge of a series of flatlands. Nearby was War Bonnet Creek, a thin trickle of water in this sandy good-for-nothing soil. From the crest of the little hill Buffalo Bill, Chris, and two or three others in the scouting party could look down on what was going on below. Chris was left on the little hill with his wigwag flags to send messages, when the time came, to the officers. Two couriers were sent on horseback from Fort

D. A. Russell to take the news to General Merritt. Seven Indians were moving silently along a dry wash when they saw the two couriers. Ah! they would gobble them up. To do this, the Indians would have to pass the hill where Buffalo Bill, Chris, and the others were waiting. A new element entered. The men looking from the hill saw a lone Indian leading the other Indians, with mischief in his manner. The Indian saw Buffalo Bill coming, rode toward him, and the two faced each other. The moment had come. The two fired almost simultaneously. Buffalo Bill's bullet went through the Indian's leg and into the Indian's horse, killing the animal and throwing the Indian to the ground. Buffalo Bill's horse stepped into a prairie-dog hole and Buffalo Bill found himself on the ground, fifty feet from the Indian, his rifle flung from his hands. The Indian had not lost his rifle and, as he was taking aim for a second shot, Buffalo Bill got in some of the quickest work of his life. He snatched up his own rifle, knelt, took careful aim, and fired, killing the Indian. And then Buffalo Bill darted forward, whipped out his knife, and scalped the Indian then and there. Picking up the Indian's elaborate headdress of feathers and quills, he waved it and shouted words that have become famous in the history of the West: "The first scalp for Custer!"

No one knew who the Indian was, but they soon found out. He was Yellow Hand, a Cheyenne now known by name to all who read Western history. In later years Chris repeatedly had to tell the story of the encounter. One part he had to scotch was that there had been a duel and that Buffalo Bill and the Indian had fought each other with knives. Chris always said the meeting between the two had been accidental. Chris, on the hill, witnessed the scalping. This became important later when certain people tried to discredit Buffalo Bill.

Today, in the Buffalo Bill Museum, at Cody, Wyoming, there is a painting of the event by Robert Lindneux. Lindneux was a good painter, but sometimes a bit hazy on details. In this painting he has Buffalo Bill in a buckskin suit with as many fringes as on a chorus girl's panties. He was not correct in this, for, according to Chris, Buffalo Bill had on the black velvet, gold-laced suit he had been wearing on the stage when he received the telegram from General Sheridan.

Chris had seen his first Indian killed. He was shocked by what Buffalo Bill had done and spoke to him of it. Buffalo Bill's defense was this: when he came up to the Indian he saw that the Indian had an American flag around his middle and between his legs; also that he had a white woman's scalp at his waist. This so enraged Buffalo Bill that he whipped out his knife and whacked off the Indian's scalp. Buffalo Bill proudly sent the scalp to his wife who was living in Rochester, New York. The legend is that she would not let the scalp stay in the house overnight. She sent it to Buffalo Bill's friend, Moses Kerngood, who ran the Kerngood Cigar Store and Sample Room at 49 East Main Street, Rochester. He put the scalp in the window; it sold a lot of cigars for him.

Here is a descriptive tidbit from the Rochester *Union and Advertiser*, July 27, 1876: "Yellow Hand's scalp consists of a piece of skin about three inches square, to which adheres a switch of straight, jet-black hair nearly two feet long. This is neatly braided to the tip, and is more ornamental than useful. The scalp is not yet dry." (Note: The scalp now reposes in the Buffalo Bill Museum, on Lookout Mountain, Colorado, completely dry.)

The killing of Yellow Hand had some military importance: it helped the Fifth Cavalry keep eight hundred Cheyenne warriors from joining Sitting Bull. Even more important was its psychology. It showed the Indians—still rolling the Battle of the Little Big Horn under their tongue—that the white man had dry powder.

Chris and Buffalo Bill were thrown together day after day; each studied the other with interest, for Chris had never before seen an Indian scout, and Buffalo Bill, it developed, had never before met a Dane. One day Buffalo Bill said, "I'd like to cross the Big Pond, but I don't suppose I'll ever get to."

The Fifth Cavalry, under General Merritt, had received orders to join General Crook. The Fifth joined General Crook, at Goose Creek, Montana, near the Custer battlefield, August 3. On August 5 Chris reached the Custer battlefield itself. The smell of death still hung over it. The bodies of General Custer, Tom Custer (his brother), and Boston Custer (another brother) had been picked up and buried. Chris was told by the men who had remained on the battlefield that the bodies of the Custers had not been scalped. One of the men Chris heard mentioned was Captain Myles Keogh, who had been buried near his general. Even after this many days the battlefield was strewn with guns and bits of saddles, bridles, and war matériel; no sabers, for they had been discarded. Also here were Indian guns that had been thrown aside for the better weapons of the dead soldiers.

One body was found some distance from the battlefield proper, evidently overlooked by the burial detail. This body Chris and some of the men in the squad buried. Chris said that during the digging of the grave and the burial of the body the men hardly spoke, so moved and stirred were they by the tragic death and sad burial of the soldier. The battle became more and more vivid to Chris and more and more depressing. He thought about the Indians he had come to America to kill. Had he done right?

Indian bodies still lay on the field. This was unusual, for Indians almost always return to remove their dead. Even the squaws had not claimed them, or carried them off to wail over. This seemed to indicate that, although it had been a great

Indian victory, the Indians wanted to get out of this section before another wave of white troops could be launched against them. And well they might, for there were twelve regiments of cavalry in this area searching for them when the Indians had fallen on Custer's command.

Chris's papers showed that he was a surveyor, and this would indicate that he could make a map. He was approached by John Finnerty, war correspondent for the Chicago *Tribune,* to make a map of the battlefield. With three Crow Indians, supposed to be friendly, Chris started to make the map. He worked alone, except for the Indians, who were sullen and uncommunicative. When he told them to do anything, they pretended not to understand, then would go about the task resentfully.

When night came, he prepared to make camp. The Indians walked off to one side where they talked in low tones, glancing from time to time at him. Finally the leader came up to Chris and said they did not want to sleep on the battlefield.

"Why?"

"Evil spirits."

"We have to stay here whether we want to or not," said Chris.

Again the Indians went off by themselves and conferred. Then one came back and said they would camp on the other side of the Little Big Horn. Chris was relieved. Alone on the battlefield, Chris spread himself out in his blankets and tried to go to sleep. The next morning he woke with a start, the way an apprehensive person will, and there standing silently a few yards away were the three Indians.

"What do you want?" he demanded.

"Eat," they said.

During breakfast the Indians talked in their native language, now and then throwing a glance at him.

The night of the second day Chris went to his command and

stayed with them. The Indians again went back on the other side of the river where there were no evil spirits.

It took three days to make the map. The map was lost; there is no record of it in the files at the War Department. Another map, however, was published in the Chicago *Tribune*, July 7, 1876, over the caption, "Scene of the Slaughter of Custer's Command."

Frederick S. Barde, the Oklahoma historian, went to see Chris, in Guthrie, about April 20, 1923. Chris gave this interview which Barde wrote down:

"The bodies of our soldiers were frightfully mutilated. This mutilation was performed by the squaws with war clubs. Sitting Bull told me afterward that Custer and his immediate companions took their stand on a knoll which was too small for both men and horses. The troops turned the horses loose in the hope that the Indians would follow them, thereby giving Custer a chance to escape. The Indians, however, paid no attention to the horses, but bore steadily down upon the knoll, and the horseless soldiers, unable to take flight, were slain to a man.

"In July, or August, 1877, General Sheridan came out and I accompanied him as an orderly to the battlefield. There were a number of foreigners in his party. It was my duty to point out the particular places. Upon our arrival, the battleground was covered with such a luxuriant growth of tall grass that often it was difficult to see a man riding ahead of you. A tornado struck the spot during our stay and literally whipped it bare of vegetation. To our surprise we found in remote ravines and depressions and in sagebrush thickets a number of bodies that had been overlooked by the burial party. There were skeletons in faded uniforms that had been mauled and dragged about by wolves. General Sheridan ordered that all the bones be buried.

"I shall never forget a pest that came from the carcasses of the dead horses. These insects were half the length of a man's finger, and resembled ants, though they had wings. They attacked our horses like hornets; it was almost impossible to control a horse as long as these pests were on him.

"I'll never forget a conversation I overheard while standing with the officers on the spot where Custer fell. Somebody asked General Sheridan the direct question:

" 'Could Custer have done any better, or avoided the disaster?'

" 'No, Custer could not,' replied Sheridan.

" 'Could anybody?'

" 'Yes.'

" 'Who?'

" 'There is one man that I believe could have done it—Wesley Merritt,' said General Sheridan, with much deliberation. 'Merritt was in command of my cavalry in the Civil War and I never saw him get into a place he couldn't get out of.' "

The first published account of the massacre was in the Bismarck *Tribune*, Bismarck, Dakota Territory, July 6, 1876. Chris's name was given as having fallen. Chris didn't know about this account. He learned later, and it caused him trouble.

CHAPTER 2

Chris Gets All the Indian Fighting He Wants. His Troop Is Sent Back to Fort Riley, Kansas, Where Chris Becomes a Dancing Master and Meets Maggie Morris. Ah!

BACK IN Denmark it had seemed easy to kill Indians. The savages were not very smart; they wouldn't stand up and fight. But Chris was beginning to find that fighting Indians was just about the hardest kind of fighting there was. First, you had to find 'em. At this game the Indians were better than the white man. They could disappear like prairie dogs. And then, like prairie dogs, pop up behind you. It was maddening.

And so now Chris started to find 'em. In one campaign he rode horseback fourteen hundred miles and never got shot. Where did they obtain their food? How could they travel so fast? And disappear so completely? Especially since they were not very bright. It was perplexing.

Also he discovered that the Indians were exceedingly brave. As fighters, they had two weaknesses. One was that they attacked at dawn. So the whites were prepared. A second weakness was that they didn't fight as a unit; instead, they fought individually, each man his own captain. In some ways this individual effort helped the Indians, but generally it worked against them. The white men, fighting as a unit, could worst them.

The great and wise War Department, comfortably situated in Omaha, sent word to Fort D. A. Russell to "get" Dull Knife. It developed that Dull Knife did not want anybody to "get" him. Chris and the men in his troop were sent to bring him in, dead or alive, take your choice. Dull Knife, it was found, had gone with his warriors to northern Nebraska and to the lower part of what became South Dakota. It was winter; the thermometer had crawled into winter quarters. The men did not have enough blankets to keep warm. In one temporary camp, half the men spent the night marching in a circle in the snow, one man behind the other, until they made a trench. At midnight the rest of the command was awakened, and the men who had been marching crawled into their blankets, and the new men got into the snow trenches and started to march around and around. The Indian chasers stayed out three months, during this time they did not see one single Indian. The commander of the company sent word to Omaha that the Indians had been "dispersed." That was Indian fighting as Chris was seeing it. It certainly wasn't what he'd imagined in Denmark.

Chris had an experience that he had never dreamed of back home, and this was with a "contract doctor." In the Indian campaigns at this time the United States Army let out contracts to private doctors. The Army got the bottom of the barrel. The incident happened at a camp on Clear Creek, Wyoming, the site on which, later, Fort McKinney was established. Not far away was Buffalo, Wyoming, which later became the central point in the bloody Johnson County War, famous in Western history.

Here the soldiers were supposed to be knocking over Indians. As a matter of fact, the soldiers couldn't even find the Indians.

In such a situation even the most experienced Indian fighter can accomplish nothing.

General Merritt left on a scouting expedition. Chris did not go with him, for he was not feeling well. Shortly after General Merritt left, Chris became dangerously ill with "mountain fever" and was taken to one of the company tents. The contract doctor was sent for. He was a drunken character and had no interest in this man who had turned up on the sick list. "You've got a touch of fever," he said. He went to the supply tent where there was a huge medicine chest filled with bottles, each with a number printed on it. The numbers ran from 1 to 10. The sicker the patient got, the higher the number of medicine he was given. When he returned, the doctor said, "Take a dose of Number 1 twelve times a day."

"What kind of medicine is it?" asked Chris.

"It tells you on the bottle—Number 1."

The bleary-eyed doctor looked around, studying the tent. "I need this tent. I'll requisition it; you can move to the dog tent at the end of the company street." The doctor reeled out.

Chris dragged himself to the dog tent. After Chris had left, the doctor had Chris's tent set up in another location for himself. The doctor wanted the best of everything for himself so that he would not get sick and be unable to attend his patients.

When General Merritt returned, he was shocked to find Chris in such a sorrowful tent, ordered the doctor into another tent, and Chris to return to his own tent. Chris and two other men, suffering from mountain fever, were put into an army ambulance and started to Old Fort Reno, on the Powder River, in Wyoming, a distance of about forty-five miles. The two others died in the ambulance. Chris was carried, unconscious, into the temporary field hospital where the fort doctor examined and prescribed for him. After a time Chris began to mend. The fort doctor told Chris that if he had taken the medicine—quinine—

it would have killed him. Under the ministrations of the fort doctor Chris became better; in a month he was on his feet.

In September 1879 Carl Schurz, Secretary of the Interior, arrived at Fort Russell. The troops were drawn up and paraded before this government official. When the inspection was over, Carl Schurz had thrilling news to tell the men. He said that the Indian wars were over, that peace would reign forever between the white and the red man, and that the weary soldiers could soon go home. The soldiers shouted with delight. He said that he had just come from talking with the chief of the Utes at the Ute agency on the White River, in northwestern Colorado. He said that the Utes had not had trouble with the whites in twenty-five years and that the chief of the Utes—a noble man—had assured him there always would be peace between his people and the whites. Then the great man went back to Washington, D.C., to direct Indian affairs.

Carl Schurz had hardly got back to his desk before the Utes went on the warpath. Three troops of cavalry from Fort Russell, under command of Major T. T. Thornburg, were rushed to quell them but were ambushed at Milk Creek, twenty miles from the Ute agency. Major Thornburg was killed at almost the first volley. In fact, almost one third of the command was killed or wounded. (This is sometimes called the "Meeker Massacre," after N. C. Meeker, who was in charge of the agency. This engagement is considered an important one in the history of the Indian wars.)

Finally the Utes were quelled and the able-bodied soldiers got back to camp. Carl Schurz, in Washington, was harmed in no way. When the whole affair was over, he gave out an interview in which he said that the Utes betrayed a trust. Also he said he was thoroughly shocked.

At last the "Indian campaign" was over. The Indians had had their heads knocked together. The whites were all, more or less, professional soldiers, but they had made no better showing than the poor, untutored Indians. If the Indians had had as many men and half the equipment, they would have brought the great United States Army—of twenty-five thousand men at that time—to its knees. And so it goes. There was no better fighter than the Indian.

By this time Chris had been fighting Indians four years. But in all that time, so far as he knew, he had not killed a single Indian. He had shot at many, but he had no proof that he had killed even one. But he need not feel bad. Buffalo Bill himself had killed only one after July 16, 1876. Buffalo Bill was now in a Wild West show and was a dauntless hero to millions.

Plaguing thoughts flitted in and out of Chris's mind. Sometimes he felt that the whole so-called Indian campaign was unnecessary. If the white man had lived up to his treaties and agreements there might well have been no wars. But the ruthless white man wanted land; the Indian was on it. Get him off. It was that simple.

Another thing in Chris's mind was that the Indian was not a "noble red man," as some of the books called him. He was, Chris came to believe, a human being who had to live under trying conditions and managed the matter very well indeed. Sometimes the Indian was admirable; sometimes he was completely impossible—like a white man.

Here is Chris's military record as shown by the United States Government records:

Campaigns engaged in against the Indians:

Sioux and Cheyennes	1876
Nez Percés	1877
Bannocks	1878
Cheyennes	1878
Cheyennes (second campaign)	1879
Utes	1879–1880

Battles:

Hat Creek	July 17, 1876
Slim Buttes	September 9–10, 1876
Milk Creek	October 5, 1879

But at last the campaign was over. The whites, with only a few thousand more men than the Indians, had won a glorious victory. There never would be any more trouble. (No one ever dreamed there would be Wounded Knee, in 1890.)

Came May 4, 1885. On this day orders were issued for the troops to return to Kansas. "We have won," said the officers. And so the men marched out of Camp Washawkie, where they had been so long, and started to Fort Casper, Wyoming—quite a jaunt in itself. After staying there a few days the troops marched to Fort Fetterman, another jaunt. From there they marched to Fort Laramie—lots of marching now, no fighting; the Indians had been laid low. After a few days at Fort Laramie the troop started down the valley of the Platte River, along the great Oregon Trail, and came, finally, to Fort Kearney, Nebraska. After a few days there they started again, and on July 3, 1885, arrived at Fort Riley, Kansas, having covered in two months the astonishing distance of two thousand miles.

But no sooner had the troops got comfortably settled than word came that the Cheyennes and the Arapahoes, in Oklahoma, were on the warpath. The settlers were flying to the forts with ghastly tales of scalping and looting. The great General Nelson A. Miles was rushed to the scene. He was said to be the greatest Indian fighter since Custer and Custer wasn't fighting any more Indians.

The men wearily buckled on their guns and started out again. Would this sorry business never end? The troops went into camp on the Cimarron River between Fort Dodge, Kansas, and Fort Supply, Oklahoma. In a few days came orders to march to

Oklahoma and slay Indians. The veterans knew this was going to be harder to do than it seemed, but they'd try it. And so again the Fifth Cavalry got under way, as it had done so many times before. They marched here and they marched there, but they didn't find any Indians—only settlers who told them shocking stories they'd heard. They themselves hadn't seen the Indians, but they knew it was true because somebody had told them it was and, for God's sake, hurry. The Fifth Cavalry hurried.

After a time the troops came upon the Indians—on their reservations. The Indians were astonished when told they were on the warpath. And so the soldiers marched back to Camp Riley, with nary a scalp but lots of saddle sores and bunions. (A cavalryman was punished in those days by being made to walk and lead his horse, a humiliating indignity.) And now, having conquered the Cheyennes and the Arapahoes, the men again settled down to camp life. Chris by this time had risen to regimental quartermaster sergeant, the highest noncommissioned office in the command. Pay, twenty-nine dollars.

One day a messenger came hurrying down the street with a telegram for Chris. When Chris opened it, his eyes got as big as duck eggs. It was from the great General Nelson A. Miles asking him to come at once to New Kiowa, where Miles was stationed. It wasn't every day that an enlisted man got a telegram from a general. At last promotion! Hopping a horse, Chris hurried to New Kiowa.

"General Miles is waiting," said an orderly, and Chris was taken to a room in the wooden barracks which was serving as headquarters.

"How are you, Sergeant?" asked General Miles warmly. "I don't mind telling you I'm glad to see you."

"T'ank you, General," said Chris modestly.

"The paper work here is a disgrace," said General Miles. "I want you to take hold of it and straighten it out."

Chris's heart went down. Paper work! With his ability at penmanship and with his understanding of army accounts, he had been doing this job for his own troop. General Miles had heard of this and had sent for Chris. Until this matter had come up, General Miles had never heard of Chris.

"I will do ze best I can, General," said Chris like a true soldier. It took Chris four months to untangle the accounts. General Miles then sent him to Fort Riley, Kansas, to straighten out matters there. And this Chris did; two months this time.

Chris returned to Fort Supply, feeling pretty proud of himself. But he had hardly put his foot on the company street before the adjutant stepped up to him. "Sergeant Madsen, you are under arrest."

"Vot is it I am under arrest for?"

"For absence without leave," said the jealous adjutant.

What kind of country had he got into? Recovering his composure, Chris explained he had acted under General Miles's orders.

"That makes no difference," said the adjutant. "The record shows you have been absent without leave. Come on."

And forthwith the stunned Chris was marched off to the guardhouse. Chris was able to get permission to send a telegram to General Miles. In it he said that he was under arrest and reminded the general he had been acting under orders. Two hours later the cold and frosty adjutant came in. "I have orders to release you," he said, and that was all he said. It was one of the inscrutable ways of the army.

Shortly after this Chris was ordered to go to Camp Martin, Kansas, to straighten out the supply department. The matter took a month. When it was over, Chris got ready to return to Fort Riley, which he could do by railroad at a cost of six dollars. He applied for a ticket, but the man said there was no money for sending a soldier by train. Chris found that in another department there was money by which a soldier could go by horseback. Onto a horse went Chris, headed for Fort Riley. He had to buy feed for the horse and food and lodging for himself. The trip took six days and cost the army twenty dollars. This was a small matter, of course, but showed another one of the problems an Indian fighter had to go up against.

A new kind of life opened for Chris at Fort Riley—life in an army fort. No Indians, no marching, no starving, no freezing—it was the life of Riley.

One thing brought very vividly to him the Battle of the Little Big Horn. The only creature to escape alive from the battlefield was Comanche, the horse ridden by Captain Myles Keogh. The horse had been caught later by soldiers and, finally, had been sent to Fort Riley where Captain Keogh had first gotten him. And here was the horse, when Chris arrived—a living link with that ill-fated battle. (Note: The stuffed skin of the horse is in the Museum of Natural History, University of Kansas, Lawrence. And there today you may see it if you wish.)

One of the problems of a fort during peacetime is to keep the men "happy and content"—as if any soldier ever was. The commander of the fort thought up a way to bring about this delightful state of mind. He would institute a series of dances. What he didn't realize was that most of the men had been recruited from the streets in New York, and were rough and tough. Dancing was sissy—the last thing they wanted. Liquor, women, gambling, fist fights. Those were a real man's life.

The commandant, however, went on with his plans; he'd get a dancing teacher who would show them how to glide gracefully across the ballroom floor. The perverse men said they didn't want to glide gracefully across a ballroom floor, but that made no difference to the commandant. Who was going to teach 'em? He had the men questioned; maybe a dancing teacher would show up in the troop—a forlorn hope, if there ever was one. None showed. But it developed that the unfortunate Chris had learned to dance back in Denmark and that he had gone to dances put on by the French Foreign Legion. The commandant was delighted. If Chris had danced with the crack French Foreign Legion, he was good enough to be a teacher in Kansas.

Chris didn't look much like a dancing teacher; he looked more like a wrestler. He was short and had a chest as big as a bushel of wheat. His feet were as big as cushions and his hands hung at his sides like hams from the rafters in a farmer's smokehouse. However, there was something to be said on the other side. He was light on his feet, he had an ear for music, and had, after all, a kind of lumbering grace. Anyway, there Chris was and there were the men who were going to be taught to dance whether they liked it or not.

The commandant sent for Chris. "I am going to open a company dancing school, Sergeant, and you are to be the teacher."

Chris was flabbergasted. "I never teach nobody to dance yet," said Chris.

"You will begin tomorrow."

The next day the men assembled in a barracks room where they stood in sullen, resentful groups. Chris clopped out in front and, taking a pose, explained a few simple steps. "Now dis ist the vay you backwardt go." He glided backward, moving his hands gracefully. "Undt now we go forwardt again." He glided forward. "Now iss it you understan'?" The men changed their chewing tobacco to the other cheek and said they understood. "Now the lesson ve vill commence. One, two, t'ree."

The band struck up. Each man danced as he thought best, each with a resentful expression on his face.

"Now I vill a girl be," said Chris, and he tied a handkerchief on his arm. "You vill the gentleman be and lead me." One of the troopers stepped out and danced with the girl. "Ach!" said Chris. "It is more ve vill have to practice, is it not?"

The men chewed silently. After a time handkerchiefs were tied on the arms of half the men, and away went the merry-makers.

The men had a few lessons, then word was sent out to the people in the village and on the farms that free dance instruction would be given at the fort to all the girls who wished it. The girls wished it, indeed, for there was nothing more dreary than living on a farm. The girls came rushing to the fort as if pursued by Indians.

They were escorted to the barracks room and were seated in chairs along the wall—as fine, corn-fed specimens as anyone would want to see. The girls' parents were pioneers and had licked wind, storm, blizzard, and grasshoppers; the girls would now lick dancing. They had the stuff heroines are made of.

Professor Madsen took his place in front of the girls. "Ze band vill make musique," he said. The band made music.

Chris picked out one of the girls and, using her as his partner, showed the others how the matter was accomplished. Then he chose another and showed her, explaining, as they clumped across the floor, that she did not have to watch her feet. The girl tried it, and found it was exactly as the professor had said.

The mass instruction was a success. Girls danced who had never danced before. Now that the girls had had a little practice, the doors were opened and the men came in—men who hadn't seen girls in nine years. *Ah!* Why, the girls were all beautiful. The band struck up. The ex-Indian fighters seized the girls and dashed across the floor with them as if saving them from bloodthirsty savages. The girls liked it and were glad to be saved by the chivalrous gentlemen of the Fifth Cavalry.

The girl Chris was dancing with was a pretty creature, with

black hair and brown eyes, and a nose just a little tipped up—very becoming, thought the dancing master.

"What is eet your name?" he asked.

"Maggie Morris."

"Where is eet you live?"

"On a farm, six miles out of town."

"You mean you come six miles twice to dance?"

"My sister Annie and my girl friend here and I came together," said the brown-eyed miss.

Chris looked at her again. She was as lovely as a Kansas sunflower. "Ve need practice," he said.

They proceeded to glide across the floor. Suddenly Chris felt his arm gripped by a powerful hand and, when he turned, a man with a black beard was looking at him fiercely. "Let go of my daughter!" said the man. "Let go, I tell you!" Chris was shocked by the ferocity in the man's tone.

"I haven't done anyt'ing," said Chris.

"I tell you to let loose!" shouted the man. Taking hold of the girl, he drew her away, glaring at Chris as he did so.

The music stopped; everyone was watching the little drama on the dance floor.

"This is my father," said the girl, and then, after an awkward moment, explained that her father thought dancing was "work of the devil." The girl stood hesitating; it was almost unheard of, at this time, for a girl to oppose a parent, especially her father. "Father, I want to learn to dance. Please let me," she said in a choked voice. The fierce old patriarch studied her, meantime looking Chris up and down.

"Please, Father." And now her mother, coming up, urged the girl's father to relent. The old man couldn't give in all at once—not with all the people watching.

"Well," he said at last, "all right. But"—and here he turned fiercely to Chris—"don't you hold her close."

It was an awkward moment for the girl, and for Chris, too, but the old farmer was so sincere, so earnest, so determined to protect his daughter that Chris did not resent the fierce assault upon him. Chris danced again with the girl, holding her as if she were a roll of barbed wire.

It was a lovely, exciting, thrilling evening. "I will tell the commander ve need another dance for practice," said Chris, and this was brought about.

And now, as the days went by, Nature took her course. How beautiful, how exciting, how thrilling Maggie looked to the Indian fighter. And how brave was he, she thought, this man who had seen Buffalo Bill scalp Yellow Hand. The man who had helped bury the dead after the Battle of the Little Big Horn. The man who had surveyed the battlefield. The man who once had marched two thousand miles in one whoop. The man who had heard General Sheridan talk about General Custer. On top of this, how handsome and graceful he was. The girl again gazed at the square, block-faced man, her heart swaying like an oriole's nest.

Chris, who had associated so little with girls in his life, was timid. One day, however, he got up his courage to ask her if he could come to her home. She said she would be pleased. He wanted to take something especially nice to treat her with—no chocolate candy in a brown paper bag. By this time, he was assigned to the commissary department. Something new had come in—green olives—meant for the officers. Chris had never tasted olives, but if they were good enough for the officers, they were good enough for him. He signed for a bottle.

He requisitioned a horse and, with the bottle in his pocket, set out across the prairie to Maggie's house. He was greeted by the family, the father still watching him like a hawk. Chris would show him that he was a fine, gallant young man—an acquisition to any family.

After a time the two went into the parlor, reserved for the most part for funerals, and there Chris fetched out his surprise.

"What is it?" said Maggie.

"Olives!" said Chris proudly.

He took his knife and pried the cork out of the wide-mouthed bottle. It would hardly do to fish the olives out of the bottle with fingers, so Maggie went to the kitchen and came back with an ivory pickle fork—a two-pronged affair that just then was considered the top of fashion.

Taking the fork Chris delicately stabbed an olive. "You first, Maggie," he said gallantly. She took the olive and politely held it in her fingers. "Taste it," he urged.

It was the saltiest, bitterest thing she had ever gone up against in her life. But she couldn't tell him she didn't like it. "It's delicious," she avowed. He tried one and gave a shudder. "How do you like it?" she asked.

"Fine," he said as he gnawed the cursed thing.

"Have another."

He took another and ate it with a great pretense of enjoying its subtle flavor. And she, seeing how he liked his, took another and ate it with tremendous relish, smiling at him for having brought her such a fine tidbit. He was so bashful and sensitive that he could not say that he hated the salty, bitter thing. Nor would she admit she could hardly choke it down. The two nibbled on, delicately putting the pits aside.

Mr. Morris, with his great black beard, came in to talk to Chris and get better acquainted with this young fellow who wanted to be a soldier and not a farmer.

"Won't you have an olive, Mr. Morris?" asked Chris hospitably.

"I dunno but what I will." He studied Chris coldly.

Chris speared an olive and held it out to the tough old

farmer, who clawed it off and put it in his mouth. His eyes got big. "What is this you've given me?" he demanded.

"An olive, Mr. Morris," Chris said. "Don't you like it?"

"I do not. It's rotten and unfit for human consumption." Getting up, he stalked out of the room, banging the door. Constraint fell over Chris and Maggie, but after a time—so deeply were they interested in each other—it wore off.

Some of the better-to-do families in Kansas owned organs, and now Maggie sat down and played for him. It was the sweetest music he'd ever heard. She looked lovely perched on the stool, her feet pumping, her fingers flying.

Her mother came in with a bowl of popcorn balls made with white sugar—a rare treat. Chris and Maggie took a ball each and ate, chatting and looking into each other's eyes. When they'd eaten all they wanted, they delicately wiped their fingers on a wet towel.

Finally the two went into the living room where the family was. There they were ill at ease. The golden moments in the parlor were gone. To show them how important he was, Chris began to talk of his war experiences. Mr. Morris listened glumly. Finally he said, "How much do you get?"

"Twenty-nine dollars a month."

The old man was silent. It was some moments before the conversation could be started again.

The evening wore on, Chris and Maggie talking bashfully in the presence of the family. Sometimes they ran out of things to say. At last Mr. Morris yawned. "If you'll excuse me, Mr. Madsen, I'll go to bed. Farmin' is hard work, but a man's his own boss." He wound the clock, threw the key back in, and stumped off to bed. After he had been gone a moment, he put his head back inside the room. "You needn't bother with the stove, Maggie. I'll get up and fix it after he's gone."

One by one the family went to bed. At last Chris and Maggie

were alone. It was better now; conversation came more easily. The clock, with weights to run its gears, ticked on, the sound growing louder, now that the family was quiet.

"Well," said Chris at last, "I must be going."

"Won't you have another popcorn ball?" asked Maggie.

"I t'ink I vould."

Maggie dampened the tea towel and passed the bowl. The two sat crunching and enjoying themselves. A little heap of hard, uncracked grains that no one could eat collected in the bottom of the bowl—chicken feed tomorrow.

At last Chris stood up. "I t'ink I vill haf to go."

At the door he kissed her and started on the long trip back to the fort. It had been a wonderful evening and Maggie was a wonderful girl.

CHAPTER 3

Chris Pins on His Silver Star

After the way of the army, the Fifth Cavalry was sent to Fort Reno, Indian Territory. Four miles from the fort was a settlement; to distinguish this from the fort, the town was called El Reno, and El Reno it is today. The Indians were getting obstreperous and needed taming; in fact, all of the Indian Territory was getting obstreperous. Outlaws were flocking into this haven. The soldiers, however, could have nothing to do with them unless the outlaws made free with government property or knocked soldiers around. The old days when a troop of United States cavalry had been sent to chase horse thieves were over; let the state or the territory chase 'em. That was the new idea.

Chris was depressed that he had to leave Maggie. Then came exceedingly good news: Mr. Morris moved his family from Kansas to a farm near Fort Reno and Chris began to see Maggie again. She looked bewitching.

Nature took its course and in December 1887 Chris and Maggie were married in what later became Oklahoma City. There was no Oklahoma then and no Oklahoma City; the section was an expanse of red clay and sandy soil laced together by blackjack timber. This settlement was a few houses huddled together like cattle in a storm. They "set up housekeeping" on the fort grounds, in rough soldiers' quarters, and here happiness came and made its abode. Oh, to be young and in love! Oh, to be getting twenty-nine dollars a month!

There came news that intrigued Chris very much. Buffalo Bill had succeeded amazingly as a showman, and had been ordered to give a command performance of his Wild West Show before Queen Victoria. He was now a world figure. The Yellow Hand scene had been dramatized, but, as Buffalo Bill played it, it was not quite so simple as it had been in the sand hills; in the dramatization, it was a fearful hand-to-hand struggle, rifles cracking and knives flashing, with Yellow Hand finally getting what he so richly deserved.

So great was Buffalo Bill's popularity in England that once in one of his shows Buffalo Bill drove the Deadwood Coach with the Prince of Wales beside him on the seat. Inside the coach were four kings: the King of Greece, the King of Saxony, the King of the Belgians, and the King of Denmark—all this just eleven years after Buffalo Bill had told Chris he never expected to get to Europe.

But all the sugar wasn't on Buffalo Bill's slice of bread. Chris was happily married. Buffalo Bill was married....

And then into Chris's life came two little mouths to take nips out of that twenty-nine dollars. And what big bites little mouths can take! The little mouths were named Marion Morris Madsen and Christian Reno Madsen. (The latter is my guide and mentor in telling this story of Chris Madsen.) The child was named Christian Madsen, Junior, but the soldiers at the post called him Reno, after the fort, and pretty soon everybody was calling him Reno, and Reno he was, Reno he is.

On top of this, when Chris had to move his family, he had to pay the expenses himself. There was no kind Uncle Sam to say, "Here, son, let me do this for you." And so the cookie jar got lower and lower.

Meantime something was happening that was to change

Chris's life. The Indian Territory had now become a happy hunting ground for outlaws. There were more bandits, horse thieves, cattle thieves, counterfeiters, whisky peddlers, and train robbers per square mile in Oklahoma than in any other place in the United States. Travelers disappeared and were never heard of again. A good example of what was going on at this time centered around a country store near Caddo, in the Choctaw Nation. The store looked as innocent as a Sunday-school room. Inside, it was a bit different, for there was what was called The Shelf of Skulls. On it were five skulls the proprietor had picked up in the woods back of the store. He said he took only the skulls that hadn't been crushed.

The reason there were so many dangerous characters in the Indian Territory was that there was, broadly speaking, no law. If a man was an Indian and a member of the Five Civilized Tribes he had to be tried by an Indian court; no white court could touch him. (Before the Opening in 1889, all of what is now Oklahoma was Indian Territory. After the Opening it was divided into Oklahoma Territory and Indian Territory. In 1907 it became the state of Oklahoma.)

Here is a simplification of the way Oklahoma was born:

Old Oklahoma—the Opening—April 22, 1889.

The Cherokee Outlet—the Run—September 16, 1893.

The Kiowa, Comanche, and Caddo Reservations—the Lottery—August 6, 1901.

The trial in the white court, before the Opening, had to be a federal one, for there was no state law; in fact, there was no state. The only federal court near was the one at Fort Smith, Arkansas, presided over by Judge Isaac C. Parker, who "took care" of the outlaws in a big way; in fact, during his days on the bench he hanged eighty-eight men. (I wrote a book about him. It deals with a bit of Americana that will make you blink.)

So dreaded did the court become that it was called the Court of the Damned; the gate that opened into the prison was the Doorway to Hell, and the basement, where the prisoners were kept, was Murderers' Row. This was where the outlaws from Oklahoma were going. But those who were arrested and sent there were but a breath on the mirror compared to the number that roamed what is now the state of Oklahoma.

On top of all this, the cowboys were turning outlaws. Many of the great ranches were being broken up; barbed wire was coming in, cowboys were going out. All they knew was ranching; many of them were without jobs. A cowboy, after having spent years in a saddle, wasn't going to follow a plow, or stand behind a counter and sell carpet tacks; nor was he going to put a comb behind his ear and cut hair. He would continue his outdoor life and would keep to the saddle where a man belonged. And so, easy as slipping into sin, many of the cowboys became train robbers and outlaws. They knew the territory; they could hide in a prairie-dog hole or disappear into the brush like quail.

The United States Attorney General, sitting in Washington, D.C., decided to tame Oklahoma. But who was going inside that lion's cage with only a chair in one hand and a blank pistol in the other? Not me, said Cock Robin.

Living in Kingfisher, Oklahoma, was a businessman named William Grimes. One day he received a telegram from President Harrison asking him to come to Washington, D.C., "for a talk." When he got there, President Harrison said that he wanted Grimes to accept the post of United States marshal for Oklahoma.

"What do I have to do?"

"Clean up the outlaws," said the President. "Make Oklahoma a peace-loving state."

"How many men can I have?" asked Grimes.

"You can have twenty deputies."

Twenty! It sounded like a lot. The young man left with

springs in his shoes. It wouldn't be long until Oklahoma would be as peaceful as a wheatfield. However, by the time he got back to Oklahoma, he realized that twenty men would not be very many for the number of square miles that would have to be covered. And where was he going to get them? The deputies would have to face the most desperate men in the Indian Territory—most of them dead shots, all with criminal careers. The possible deputies he approached explained they didn't have time to take over the job.

At the fort one day word was brought to Chris that a man was waiting in the barracks reception office to see him. Probably some old soldier who had got out of the army and was drifting around, thought Chris.

A little stout man of medium height, redheaded and with a ruddy complexion and a reddish mustache, was waiting.

"Are you Chris Madsen?"

"Yah. I am. Who is it speaks?"

"I'm William Grimes. I've been appointed United States marshal for Oklahoma."

"Zo. Won't you have the seat?"

After a few words of preliminary conversation Grimes said, "My office is in El Reno. Your officers here at the fort have told me about you. I want to talk to you about becoming a United States deputy marshal."

"'A United States deputy marshal!'" repeated Chris in surprise. "I am a soldier, not a policeman."

"A United States deputy marshal is a high office. You would be working for the United States Government."

"I vill have to talk it over mit Maggie. How much is it I would get for mine pay?"

"I have been authorized to pay my deputies two hundred and fifty dollars a month."

"How much you say?" asked Chris.

Grimes repeated what he had said.

"I t'ink I vill take it," said Chris, with just the right amount of hesitation.

"I will remind you that your district will be about half the size of Rhode Island and that you will have to police it by yourself."

"I vill take it."

Chris had had fifteen years in the United States Army, five years in military school, and five years in the French Foreign Legion—a total of twenty-five years; now he was starting a new career. In his Indian campaigns he had been exceedingly lucky; he'd been shot at many times, but had never been wounded. Now he was going up against an entirely different kind of enemy.

However, there was a good deal to be said in Chris's favor. He had been the champion marksman of his regiment. Reno, his son, told me this: "My father said he had shot away a carload of ammunition, practicing, when he was in the army. In the cavalry he had been taught to shoot every kind of weapon, and from every conceivable position. The cavalry taught its men to shoot with a revolver from a running horse. First, Father would ride by a line of six targets the size of a man, and fire at each. Second, he would ride his horse at full speed, shooting first on the right side, then on the left. After he had gained some proficiency at this, he was drilled to see how many bullets he could fire into one target, the horse running as fast as it could clip. Then he was taught to fire with either hand. He was an expert penman and I think this manual steadiness was of great help to him. I can remember, when I was quite young, seeing him have tomato cans tossed in the air. After the can had left the thrower's hand, my father would draw and fire twice at the can. I cannot recall that I ever saw him miss. Once, when I was older, I asked my father if he shot by instinct. He answered, 'I could hit a man at close range by shooting from my hip. But

I could not hit a small target without seeing the gun sights.' His shooting skill had been acquired by having handled guns all his life; this developed a coordination of hand and eye that was quite extraordinary. My father never engaged in the foolishness of 'fanning.' It was not just a chance shot when my father, at close range, knocked a gun out of a man's hand. He knew there were some extraordinary shots among the outlaws, but he was willing to take a chance in order to save the other man's life."

In no time at all Chris was out of the Fifth and had a silver star pinned on his vest. He was sworn in January 21, 1891, as field deputy in the United States marshal's office operating out of El Reno, and thus became a "trigger marshal."

One day he was sitting in his office in Guthrie when a tall, rather good-looking man entered and said, "Is this United States Deputy Marshal Madsen?"

"It iss," said Chris with the prolonged hissing sound he had for *s*. "Who iss it wishes to know?"

"I thought I would come in and make your acquaintance," said the tall man. "I'm Heck Thomas."

Chris got to his feet, and the two men met for the first time. His real name was Henry Andrew Thomas, but since boyhood he had been called Heck and as Heck Thomas he has gone down in history. He was born in Athens, Georgia, and was a year older than Chris. The two men were vastly different in looks. Heck was tall and thin and Chris dumpy—there is no other word for it. Already Thomas had had a fabulous career. He was being educated to be a Methodist minister when, at the age of twelve, he'd run away from home to fight the damnable Yankees and had joined the Stonewall Jackson Brigade as courier. As courier he remained till the end of the war. Too late to go to school then. More adventure. That was what he wanted.

He got a job with the Houston and Texas Central Railroad

as express messenger. His duty was to guard the money in the express car—a sizable job. One night the train was held up at Hutchins, Texas, eleven miles south of Dallas, by the notorious Sam Bass. Some years later Heck dictated an account of the affair to his wife, Matie Thomas, who took it down in longhand. It is now printed for the first time:

"On the night of March 18, while I was running as express messenger for the Texas Express Company, our train was held up at Hutchins, Texas. The express car and the engine were run forty yards down the track. The engineer, fireman, railroad agent, and others were forced to stand in front of the express car door to keep the messenger within from firing on the robbers. The door was smashed in with an ax. The robbers had been firing through the car and I was hit twice—one bullet entering my neck, the other passing under my eye. I had previously fixed up some decoy packages and had put them in my safe, fixing them like regular money packages. When I saw the robbers, as the train pulled into the station, I took the real money packages, containing twenty-two thousand dollars, from the safe and hid them in the ashes of the stove. I left the decoy packages in the safe and a small stack of silver amounting to about eighty-nine dollars. The outlaws entered. I was forced to unlock the safe and put the decoy packages and the silver into a grain sack which the leader held. When the matter was over, the robbers galloped gaily away, their grain sack held tight."

For this fine work the express company gave Heck two hundred dollars for saving twenty-two thousand dollars—hardly an overwhelming burst of generosity. The case attracted so much attention that Judge Isaac C. Parker—the "Hanging Judge"—sent for him and again Heck strapped on his holster.

In no time Heck was a deputy United States marshal working out of Judge Parker's court in Fort Smith, Arkansas.

After some general talk with Chris, Heck said that he was being transferred to the United States marshal's office in Oklahoma. And now the two men looked at each other with double interest, Heck and Chris.

Another man was to come into Chris's life and into history—William Matthew Tilghman, now known to the world as "Bill" Tilghman. The name is pronounced without the *g* and *h.* It shakes down to Tillman, and there you have it. He was the aristocrat of these border days, for he had a family tree that went back, in England, to the year 1344. If you had asked the average man in Oklahoma at this time if he had a family tree, he would have looked at you queerly and got away as fast as he could. But Bill Tilghman really had it. The writer of these lines has seen it. It was framed and hanging on the wall in his widow's house and looks as big as a maple. In fact, it gave me an inferiority complex, for our family tree is a bush. (Bill's name in old English meant "the man who tills," or the "till-man.")

Bill was born in Fort Dodge, Iowa, and was three years younger than Chris and a good many inches taller. When Bill was still a boy his family up and moved to Kansas and into about the wildest spot you could put your finger on. He was in Dodge City when the town was surveyed. He became an Indian scout but did not kill an Indian; it was his duty to find 'em, not to kill them. The first thing he knew he was elected city marshal of Dodge City and began bringing in the bad boys. He was city marshal for three years, which would seem to be enough for any man, but he liked to be where things were happening, and so allowed himself to be elected sheriff of the county where Dodge City was located. And there he brought in more bad men. There Bill stayed until the Cherokee Strip opening. Then he took a whack at Oklahoma and soon was city marshal of Perry,

Oklahoma, which fancied itself tough. But it wasn't, at least compared to Dodge City where the old ring-tailed ripsnorters were. Things were too tame for the young peace officer, so he got a job with Colonel E. D. Nix as deputy United States marshal where he hoped things would be a little more lively. His hopes were fulfilled.

And so now Chris had these two men: the tall, soft-talking southerner who had beaten Sam Bass at his own game; and Bill Tilghman, full of aristocracy and courage.

I asked Reno Madsen to give me a description of Heck Thomas and Bill Tilghman. Here it is:

"I knew the two men well, of course. Heck was six feet, weighing in the neighborhood of one hundred and seventy. He had black hair, a mustache, and black eyes. Also a Roman nose, and he was a little dark complexioned. He was a neat dresser and, with his fine carriage and swinging way of walking, made feminine eyes pick him up. I never heard him swear in my life and I don't think he ever indulged in that kind of language. He was friendly, but when business came up, he was all business. He carried his .45 in a holster at his right side, hanging from a leather cartridge belt. The holster did not show below his coat, and it was never tied to his leg the way the Fancy Dans in TV have them. There was no safety strap on his holster. He was fast on the draw and an expert marksman. When he pulled down on an outlaw he meant business, but I never heard of him mistreating a prisoner. He was a wonderful friend and loved his family deeply.

"Bill Tilghman had brown hair and brown eyes, a straight nose, and regular features. His weight would run about one hundred and sixty-five. He was fair complexioned but was out in the open so much that he had a tanned appearance. He was considered handsome. Was always well dressed, a little on the fancy side. He carried his gun like Heck and they were the same caliber.

"Most men creased their hats; Bill Tilghman was an exception. He wore his with the crown filled out, no dents. He never drank, used tobacco, or swore. Which was quicker on the draw? I don't know . . . nobody knows. Being quick on the draw depends on so many things that there is no legitimate comparison between the two men.

"Here's a story about Bill you might like. He was appointed chief of police in Oklahoma City. Oklahoma was a dry state. It was better to be caught in a bank at midnight with a dark lantern than to be caught with a bottle of whisky in your possession. One day Bill was taking on a new patrolman to help him keep the town dry. This new rookie was a green-looking and -acting fellow from Kentucky. Bill explained how the new man could search a suspect for a pint and, if he found it, he could taste it to see if it was redeye. Bill then handed the greenie a corkscrew and said, 'Here, carry this with you and use it when you need it.' 'Thank you, Chief,' said the rookie, 'but I always carry one of my own.' And with that he reached into his pocket and came out with a corkscrew big enough to open a Kentucky still. Bill used to tell this story and laugh."

Comparative dates:

Chris was born February 25, 1851.

Heck Thomas was born January 6, 1850.

Bill Tilghman was born July 4, 1854.

Chris waited for his first assignment, his eyes shining, his silver star glistening.

CHAPTER 4

Chris's First Assignment as a Peace Officer. Chris Meets the Dutchman.

CHRIS'S FIRST ASSIGNMENT was not long in coming. Instead of having to mount a horse and chase an outlaw over hill and dale, the assignment was to be carried out in the fort itself. Certain rough characters had been selling whisky to the Indians in Fort Reno where there were two companies of Indians. Selling whisky to Indians was against the federal laws; you could kill a white man with an ax and not get in as much trouble as if you slipped an Indian a bottle of whisky. If a man was caught doing this he would be sent to a federal penitentiary before he could say, "Old Granddad."

This was the way it was done: the Indian would hand over his money; the whisky peddler would tell the Indian where to go, later. In this particular case, the place was under a wooden bridge. When all was quiet, the Indian would go down to the bridge, feel around in a certain spot, and lo! there would be the life-sustaining firewater.

That night Chris crept to the bridge as silently as an Indian's shadow. Suddenly there was a bloodcurdling whoop and five Indians came rushing toward him, firing right and left. They had been there hiding, expecting just this to happen. The whoops didn't seem quite like the ones he had been hearing for fifteen years. The ex-Indian fighter pulled out his pistol and fired; the Indians fired back. It was like old times.

"Stop!" Chris cried. "Stop shooting or I vill kill you."

The Indians stopped. But when Chris got up to them, he found they were white men dressed up as Indians, hoping this would frighten him. But Chris had seen too many real Indians for this to make him take to the hills. The Indians surrendered, using words that would have shocked Hiawatha to the core.

Chris marched the five would-be Indians to the cantonment, where they were put in the post guardhouse. Three of them were civilians, two were white soldiers. It was a nice little capture for him, but after all they were whisky peddlers and not bandits.

When he got back to his quarters at the fort, Maggie was sitting up, anxiously waiting for him to return.

"I heard shots," she said. "Were they shooting at you?"

"Yah, kind of. But it's all over now."

The civilians were tried in court at El Reno, and the soldiers tried by court-martial, and all got sentences. There was satisfaction in having done something to uphold the law. This satisfaction grew when he found that his arrest of the whisky peddlers put an end, for the time being, to the sale of whisky to Indians at Fort Reno. He was proud of that.

It wasn't long till he got a whack at a real outlaw.

The Dutchman was so called because of his German accent. He was a horse thief who, now and then, took a fling at cattle. A horse was a man's most valuable property, far more valuable than, later, a car came to be. If a man's horse was stolen, he could not farm, he might not even be able to earn a living.

Oklahoma and the Indian Territory were peppered with horse thieves. Usually they worked in a group of three or four. The Dutchman was different. He operated by himself. He stole horses, he drove them off, he hid them, he sold them—all most unusual. He stole them in the Chickasaw Nation, drove them across the Canadian River, and sold them in Oklahoma. The country was filled with shady characters who didn't ask where a man got the horse; the only question they asked was how much.

The Dutchman terrified people, especially men traveling alone. He carried on his horse a Winchester, with two revolvers in holsters. And he would use them; there was no doubt of that. He had one peculiar trait. When he met a person on the road, he would pull his Winchester out of its saddle holster, curse the man, and tell him to get out of the way. The man always took the hint. Then, with his rifle nestled in his arms, the Dutchman would ride silently by. The Dutchman was not a pleasant character.

The local police officers were afraid to try to arrest him. Finally three police officers swept down on him and arrested him. Now that they had him, what to do with him? That was the question. They shackled him and took him to the Oklahoma County jail, in Oklahoma City, which was considered one of the safest jails in the Territory. The three officers rode thankfully away, having had all of the Dutchman that they wanted.

The Dutchman was in sour mood and began terrorizing the jail. The first day he had three fist fights. The prisoners were so afraid of him that they asked the sheriff to get the Dutchman out of the jail as quickly as he could. This word was conveyed to Marshal Grimes, who sent Chris a telegram, telling Chris to go lonehanded to Oklahoma City, pick up the Dutchman, and take him to the federal jail in Guthrie.

The moment the Dutchman saw the Dane he suspected why he was there, and he began cursing Chris.

"Ve vill go to Guthrie," said Chris. "But first ve dress up." He put a pair of handcuffs on the man, then dropped the key in his own pocket. The Dutchman watched silently. Chris marched him to the train and into the passenger coach where he took off the handcuffs and put on leg irons. The prisoner could sit in the seat with his arms free; anyone seeing him would not realize that the man was a prisoner.

(Comment from Reno: "I think it might be worth while to put in here how prisoners were handled, so far as leg irons are concerned. If a prisoner had to be walked, handcuffs were used. If a man was really dangerous, both articles of adornment were put on him. When prisoners were marched in groups, they were shackled in pairs. The prisoners could walk in step, but if they started to run away, they didn't do so well. I have seen a few mean ones led by a dog chain attached to their handcuffs. This was to prevent a man from making a break in a crowded place like a railroad depot. No officer wanted to shoot in a crowded place.")

Chris took his place in the seat behind the Dutchman. Leaning forward, he said, "If you make one false move, I kill you."

They had not gone very far when Chris saw the man slip his hand down his leg to the shackles. Chris punched him in the back with his gun. "It is soon you vill be dead." The man straightened up.

Chris got him to Guthrie and turned him over to the jailer. In three days the Dutchman escaped from the tightest jail in Oklahoma. He stole a horse—nothing new to him—and was a free man again. His clothes had been torn in the fights he'd had in the jail in Oklahoma City, so he decided to break into a store and get a suit that would make him presentable. Arriving in Norman, Oklahoma, he broke into a clothing store and was helping himself when a town policeman, who didn't know who the notorious prisoner was, walked in and told him to throw up his hands. The Dutchman had not the slightest idea of doing this, for he was a courageous man, and he pulled out his pistol. It snapped twice. Something—possibly a matchstick—had become wedged under the hammer. This was a lucky thing for the policeman, who drew his own gun and shot the Dutchman in the abdomen. In spite of his wounded condition, the Dutchman dashed past the policeman and escaped. Again he was a free man.

Chris got another telegram from Marshal Grimes. "Go and get the Dutchman." In no time at all Chris was in Norman.

What the Dutchman had done was truly amazing. The slug had driven a large metal belt buckle into him and had opened up his abdomen. Holding his intestines in his hand, he had walked to the South Canadian River, a distance of three miles. But finding the river filled with drifting ice, he turned and walked back to Norman where he planned to steal a horse and make good his escape. That walk really took fortitude.

The loss of blood, however, was too great, and at the edge of town he collapsed and fell in the road. He was picked up and carried into a barn, and, while he was lying there, Chris arrived. Opening his eyes, the Dutchman recognized Chris and gave him a cursing. His breathing became heavier. "I'll send for a priest," said Chris. The man's eyes flickered open again. He was his desperate, violent self till the last.

"I don't want a priest," he said. "He would switch me to purgatory and I don't want that. I want to go straight to hell." In a minute he was where he wanted to go.

That was the kind of men that Chris was going to have to deal with. Chris, however, was getting his hand in. He was made chief deputy United States marshal for the Territory of Oklahoma, May 26, 1892.

It was not long till he was operating out of Guthrie—an up-and-coming town if there ever was one. Almost in the middle of the town, where Second Street and Harrison Avenue crossed, there were four saloons, one on each corner. This corner was populated by more bad men per square yard than any other similar space of ground in the United States. Dodge City, Kansas, also an up-and-coming town, had its share of bad men, but the bad men there were not so thick as on this lively corner. Tombstone, Arizona, had them, too, but not so many as hovered about this Guthrie corner.

Chris didn't know it then, but he was going to do a lot of business on that corner. The saloons had picturesque names:

Southeast corner: Old Moses' Place. No one knows how it got such an odd name. This saloon and gambling house was owned by Big Dave Sidenbender who had quite a name himself.

Northeast corner: The Blue Bell Saloon. This was more than a saloon; it was the habitat of many charming girls.

Northwest corner: The Reeves Casino. Some uncouth people called it The Reeves Honkeytonk. Here also could be found girls who loved the world and had smiles for everyone.

Southwest corner: The Palace Hotel. It was a respectable, high-class place. It soon got into financial difficulties. It was the home of the smooth dice-box artist.

I asked Reno what a "smooth dice-box artist" was. This is his answer: "He is a person who uses loaded dice. The dice are loaded on one side with metal so that certain numbers turn up more often than others. Recently, at Las Vegas, Nevada, I saw people—young and old—paying a fancy price to learn what I'm telling you free. Since you are young and gullible, I suggest you keep away from the smooth dice."

Here's as good a place as any to set down the names of some of the customers on that popular corner:

Black-faced Charlie Bryant
Red Buck
Bitter Creek Newcomb
Tulsa Jack
Dynamite Dick
Arkansas Tom
Red Horse Hays
Big Sinch
Eat-'Em-Up Jake
Skeeter Dick
Zip Wyatt
Bee Dunn

(As to the latter, this was his real name; he was the brother of Rose Dunn, the Rose of Cimarron. As we go along, we will meet others of this strange crew.)

The corner was also patronized by men who didn't have picturesque names but had picturesque careers. Among them:

Bill Dalton	Bob Dalton
Grat Dalton	Bill Doolin
Dick Broadwell	Charlie Pierce
Jim Casey	Ol Yantis

And poor, little, overestimated Al Jennings, the make-believe bandit.

CHAPTER 5

The Law Comes to No-Man's Land. A Whiff of the Bone-Hauler.

AN UNEXPECTED TURN came. It had to do with a strip of land that extended from the west side of old Oklahoma, shaped like the handle of a frying pan. And that was what it was called—Oklahoma Panhandle. There was enough of this land to make three counties—pretty worthless land, most people said. But of course the people who had settled there said it was God's country, which was the way of our pioneer. The place he lived might be the leftovers after Creation but to him it was a garden spot; he'd even proclaim this when his family hadn't enough to eat. This spirit carried the early settlers through—their belief in the land they had chosen. They needed this high and soaring belief—what with outlaws, storms, crop failures, blizzards, and cancerous mortgages.

There was another class that thought this section wonderful. The outlaw. It was his happy home. There was no state law, little or no federal law; there was only the Indian tribal law which the outlaw didn't bother his head about. An outlaw would raid and rob in Texas, Kansas, or in Oklahoma, then get to this section as fast as buckskin could take him. Here he was safe, a member of the club in good standing. Some of the outlaws who called the Oklahoma Panhandle home had picturesque names, as witness these, all of this section, all ornery: Red-licker Sam, Slough-foot Nell, Six-gun Pete, Daredevil Dick. (Note: I must confess that I was most intrigued by the second one on the list. I tried to run down her history, but *alas!* there is nothing in the Oklahoma Historical Society about her. I know she must have been a delightful lass.)

There was another class that called this home—the bone-hauler. He was far down in the social scale—Slough-foot Nell wouldn't have given him a pleasant look, for he was the man with an old dilapidated wagon who roamed over the country picking up buffalo bones and hauling them to a railroad where they were shipped to St. Louis. Here they were bought by firms who ground them up and turned them into carbon. He was a sorry-looking specimen and had an odor that kept him from being socially prominent. In fact the lonely bone-hauler was so important in this section that a poem was written about him by Orange Scott Cummins, who had once been a bone-hauler himself. He is supposed to have written it with a bullet on the bleached shoulder blade of a buffalo. Just how he could get a poem of this length on a shoulder blade is more than I can understand, but that's the way it was told to me.

Here's his delightful poem:

SONG OF THE LONELY BONE-HAULER

I pass by the home of the wealthy,
And I pass by the hut of the poor,
  But none care for me,
  When my cargo they see,
And no one will open the door.
Oh, think of the poor bone pilgrim,
Ye who are safely at home;
No one to pity me, no one to cheer me,
As o'er the lone prairie I roam.

There's a place, as we journey to market,
Where the Minneescah River doth flow;
There we camp on the strand
And fill each skull with sand
To make up the shrinkage, you know.
Oh, think of the poor bone pilgrim,
Ye who are safely at home;
No one to pity me, no one to cheer me,
As o'er the lone prairie I roam.

Orange Scott Cummins—a delightful name—was quite a character in his own right. He hauled buffalo bones to Wichita, Kansas, and often was out alone for days. For a time he lived in a shanty in Barber County, Kansas, where he had a sign posted which read Last Chance Cabin. It meant this was the last chance people traveling westward would have to sleep under a roof. Some of them accepted the opportunity. When Orange Scott was at home they didn't stay long. (This information about the sweet singer of the buffalo bones was given by his nephew George Vincent Cummins. The latter lived at 900 Fifth Street, Alva, Oklahoma. He was very devoted to his colorful uncle.)

Three states were quarreling over the panhandle strip of sand and sagebrush: old Oklahoma, Kansas, and Texas. Each wanted it annexed to its own state, a strange urge. Once it had belonged to the prairie dog and the buffalo; some people said they could have it back, and welcome. But not the people who had settled on it. No, indeed. Someday it would be flowing with milk and honey, they thought.

The people who lived there wanted it to be called Cimarron Territory and to have the rights and privileges of the Indian Territory. These people wanted to be independent, make their own laws, elect their own officials, and govern themselves. There was so much trouble and so many heads were knocked about that the strip came to be called No-Man's Land, as fine a descriptive title as you'd want.

It was prairie-dog country. The prairie dogs would dig their holes, then the rattlesnakes would promptly move in, the prairie dogs moving out even more promptly. This left the rattlesnakes in possession of fine winter homes. We have learned that the greedy do not always triumph, and so it was here, for along came the prairie owls and moved in on top of the rattlesnakes. The rattlesnakes—seemingly not liking feathers—let them stay. This was the land three states were fighting over.

There were three counties: Cimarron, Brown, and Beaver. (Brown County is now Texas County.) The principal county was Beaver, and Beaver City was its seat. So earnest, so sincere, so determined were the people that the first commission to a city officer read: "Beaver City, N. S. I. T." The latter two letters stood for Indian Territory; the first two for Neutral Strip.

The agitation became so great that a commission of local people went to Washington, D.C., to ask Congress to create Cimarron Territory. Congress said that it could not, out of a hat, create a territory, and sent the patriots back home. The Supreme Court pondered the matter and in 1891 ruled that the land belonged to Oklahoma. On top of this great indignity it was announced that the law was to be administered by a United States judge—John H. Burford. The people were shocked. A judge taking them over! Well, they'd continue to run things their way. To perdition with this fancy judge from goodness knows where.

The man who was walking into this situation, Judge John H. Burford, was from Indiana. (Everybody at this time was from some place else, so new was Oklahoma.) When he got the appointment, he called up Chris. "How'd you like to go with me to Beaver City and hold court?"

"I'd like it," said Chris.

CHRIS MADSEN IN 1891

A prairie saloon. Chris watched these carefully to see who was there . . . quite often good picking. This lively establishment had a four-piece orchestra. Very fine. ([A.P.] Swearingen Collection, University of Oklahoma Library)

Chris often stopped "to eat and ask" at just such a place as this. The "hotel" is comparatively simple. . . . (Swearingen Collection)

Chris often stopped just such men as this one to ask if they had seen the outlaws he was chasing. But he never used such a man as this as a deputy: no saddle, poor horse, courage unknown. (Swearingen Collection)

"The Club Theatre," in Guthrie, which Chris attended. The orchestra made lovely music. (Swearingen Collection)

Chief Whirlwind greatly admired Chris. When the Chief died, he willed his family to Chris, and they moved in . . . what a time that was!

In the upper row, four marksmanship medals won by Chris. In the lower row, two of his deputy badges. The one he was most proud of is on the left, made of gold.

Chris often stopped at such a scene as this to ask about men he was pursuing. Many of the outlaws came from just such outfits as this, after the range closed.

The kind of saloon that Chris took many a man out of. The picture was taken early in the day, before things livened up. A light swings from the ceiling . . . an inspiring target.

Bill Tilghman, one of the "Three Guardsmen," who worked with Chris in bringing in the outlaws. This is a posed picture showing how he captured "Little Dick" West, leader of the Jennings Gang.

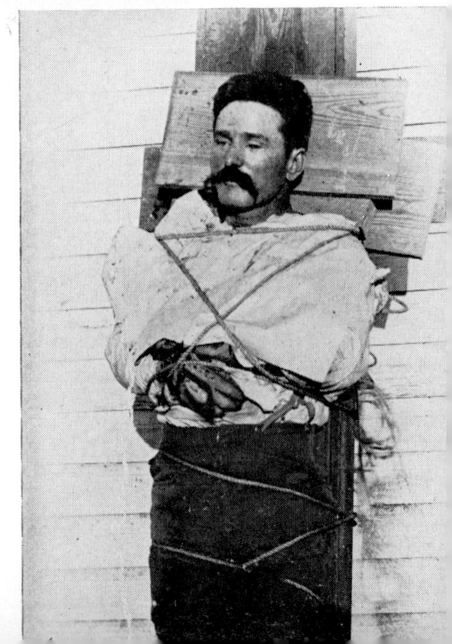

Red Buck was one of the most dangerous men who ever roamed the red hills of Oklahoma. This is what he looked like when Chris got through with him.

The United States versus Dalton, Emmett Dalton, ... Colbrook

In the Territory of Oklahoma, before United States Com'rs Court. J. J. Boles, Com'r at Guthrie, O.T.

...ge Train robbery

...nt dated November 1. 1891, and served by Deputy U. S. Marshal,

at 189

at 189

at 189

at 189

At $2 each

miles travelled to serve Writ, at 6 cents per mile, from to

...SES ACTUALLY INCURRED WHILE EMPLOYED IN ENDEAVORING TO ARREST: Not to Exceed $2.00 per Day.

		Dollars	Cents
... to Dec. 31. ... transportation of self	62	00	
Total,		62	00

...es days feeding prisoners, from ...to 189 ...ning prisoners miles, guard miles, ...and Deputy miles, in all miles, at 10 cents per mile, from place of arrest to

...f above-named Deputy during preliminary hearing before Commissioner, 189, at $2.00 per day, from place of arrest, days, at $ per day.

...arrant of commitment for further hearing and committing defendant to 189

...defendant to bail for final hearing, 189

...f guard, pending final examination before Commissioner, days, at $2.00 per day,

...e of Deputy before Commissioner at final hearing, at $2.00 per day, 189

...risoner 189

...oner on bail bond 189

...arrant of final commitment and committing defendant to Jail, at in default of bail for trial, 189

miles travelled by Deputy, guards and prisoners, to execute, at 10 cents per mile each,

... detailed to hunt these train robbers and his expense a considerable more than this ... besides losing his time

...Com.: Guard:

...NA FOR PLAINTIFF'S WITNESSES BY ABOVE-NAMED DEPUTY.—At 50 cents each.

miles to serve same, at 6 cents per mile,

...ve same,

	Dollars	Cents
	62	00
...excessive, (Expense on Dec 5th 1891 ... served Papers	2	00
...ed, on that day)	60	00

...lemnly swear that the above account is true and correct; that the services and travel charged for were actually and necessarily ...herein stated, and that the expenses charged for feeding said prisoners and endeavoring to arrest were actually and necessarily ...aid.

C. Madsen

Deputy United States Marshal.

...n to and subscribed before me, this day of 189

Clerk U. S. Court for the Territory of Oklahoma.

Chris chases the Daltons. This is his expense account for the entire month of December, 1891. He put in a claim for $62, but two dollars of this was disallowed because he served other papers while on the hunt. Chris spent much more time than this on the trail of the Daltons; this reproduction shows only one month.

Heck Thomas, with whom Chris Madsen worked in bringing in the outlaws of Oklahoma. Heck Thomas was one of the "Three Guardsmen," the first to die.

Chris in his later days. He was a great marksman; one of his sad moments was when he discovered that his eyes were clouding up and that he could no longer shoot so well.

Chris and White Buffalo at the unveiling of the monument where Buffalo Bill killed Yellow Hand. White Buffalo fought against General Custer.

"All right. You will be my chief deputy and I want you to bring along four deputies to serve under you."

"Vhy so many deputies?"

"Because of the prisoners. We're going to take with us two 'prison wagons' each filled with men to be tried. They're from the three counties and have to be tried there."

Chris blinked. Well, this was something new—taking prisoners across the state to try them. The reason for this was there were no sturdy jails in the strip—"overnight jails," they were called—this revealing how long some of the prisoners stayed. As a result some of the prisoners had been sent to Dodge City, Kansas, some to Wichita, and some to Guthrie.

They were to start from El Reno to Beaver City—one hundred and ninety-one miles. One wagon of prisoners arrived from Dodge City, another from Guthrie, the third was made up of El Reno's contribution to outlawry—a generous one, indeed. At last came the big day. The wagons assembled; the people of El Reno piled out to see the prisoners and the men who were going to get them to Beaver City, maybe. Into the wagons went the most dangerous, the most desperate men in the Indian Territory.

In one wagon were Judge Burford, Chris, and the clerk of the court—if court would ever be held. Also in this wagon was equipment for the courtroom—the judge's bench, the witness box, even books and papers which were to become court records. In the prison wagons the men were chained together so that they could not hop over the side and disappear into the brush. The drivers of the prison wagons were unarmed, and as it would be too easy for one of the prisoners to clout the driver over the head, seize his pistol, and create a situation, this was taken care of by the guards who rode horseback alongside the wagons, each with a rifle over his saddle and two pistols in his holsters, loaded for bear.

Judge Burford's driver gave a signal and down the street went as strange a cavalcade as ever turned up in America. It was spring. And Oklahoma has a special spring all its own. It throws off winter quickly and seems to rise on its elbows and look around to see what it can see, like a cowboy getting out of his bedroll. New green grass peeps out of the red ground, not quite sure whether to come out into the chilly world or stay where it is warm and comfortable. There are patches of bluebonnets, the white of the prickly poppy, the yellow of the wild mustards, and, here and there, as if on an artist's palette, are daubs of the scarlet of the Indian paintbrush. All this is beautiful, something that will never be forgotten by anyone who has seen Oklahoma's special spring.

When evening came, Burford's driver gave the signal and the wagons drew up alongside each other. The shackled prisoners began to gather firewood, hobbling along in pairs like Siamese twins, watched by the guard with his rifle in his hands. No foolishness, please.

The fires were started and the unhappy prisoners who had been elected to cook tore into it. And then, with their tin dishes, the men ate with no outstanding attention to formality. After supper, the men sat around the campfire telling stories, the guards edging in close enough to hear but not close enough to have their guns snatched. At last—sleepy time. Tents were pulled out and set up; blankets were spread on the ground, and the prisoners were chained to the wheels, the suspicious guards still nursing their rifles. What an experience! What a way to live! But this was Oklahoma then. Crude, but vigorous, dreaming of great things to come.

The cavalcade caught up with a bone-hauler with his slow, lumbering wagon and its brisk smell. As one of the wagons traveled alongside his, the bone driver cupped his hands and called, "Are you the men who're goin' to Beaver City to hold court?"

"We are," he was told.

"You ain't goin' to find yourself very welcome."

The prison wagon clucked on past the bone wagon, the old grizzled bone-hauler looking at the men curiously. Pretty soon his wagon fell behind and so, after a time, did the smell.

As they came closer to Beaver City, more people appeared. Some came up and talked to whoever would talk; sometimes they rode alongside the wagons silently; then, after a time, they would ride silently away.

Two grizzled cattlemen came up and rode alongside Judge Burford's wagon. For twenty years the men had been kings; now somebody was threatening their authority. One of the men cupped his hand to his mouth. "Are you the new judge?"

"Yes," said Judge Burford.

"We feel we've run things pretty well without interference from outsiders."

"I've been sworn in as trial judge and I mean to carry out my duties."

The men rode on for some minutes, then turned and loped away and soon were out of sight, even in this flat, treeless plain.

The wagons rolled for six days. Now and then they passed a bleached buffalo skull. Hawks hung in the air; buzzards sailed by, seemingly without a movement of their wings.

At last the men came in sight of Beaver City, the town that believed so implicitly in its future. At this time, in 1893, it was a one-street town; on this street was the post office, which was the dividing line between the north side and the south side. The north was the "tough" part. Here was the freighter camp, and the dance hall that looked so glowing to the cowboys who came in and tied their horses to the gnawed hitchracks and went in to see the beautiful girls hopping around to the music of a tinny piano. It was lovely, it was exciting, it was wonderful. The cowboys would think about it for days after they got back to the ranch. *Whoopee!*

And there, also on the north side, was the jail—a wooden affair, except for the locks and hinges. A child wanting to break out would experience no difficulty. But there it was, the famous Beaver City Jail, known from one end of the Indian Territory to the other.

As the prison wagons came clucking up, the prisoners in the jail pounded their tin cups on the bars of the windows and shouted tauntingly at the prisoners in the wagons. The prisoners in the wagons stared silently, not shouting back any insults at all, a very unusual situation.

The wagon prisoners were not put in jail, for the jail was jammed; they were chained to the wagon wheels. After the trial—if they lost—the condemned men would be taken to the federal penitentiary in Fort Leavenworth, Kansas; or to Menard, Illinois. Now and then one would be hanged.

There was no place at the hotel, as everybody had come to town to see the fun. The local people had arranged for a courtroom, which turned out to be over a saloon. To add to the insult, Judge Burford and Chris would have to sleep in the courtroom.

The wagons must be unloaded; and this Chris, with the help of his deputies, started to do, carrying the tables and chairs up the outside stairway of the building. The people stood on the ground, watching like lynxes.

Chris and Judge Burford went to the Cimarron Café to have supper. They could feel the ill will; no one spoke to them; men sat looking at them, talking in low tones. After supper the two walked up and down the streets. An unusual number of men were in town—tough, sinister characters. A group stood on the sidewalk. As Chris and Judge Burford came up, the men stopped talking and silently watched Chris and Judge Burford as they passed. After they had gone by, the men began to talk again.

When bedtime came, Chris and Judge Burford went up to the courtroom over the saloon where two cots had been placed. The two men had no more than lain down before there was pistol fire and bullets came splintering through the floor.

Chris dressed hastily, pulled on his boots, went down the stairway, and stepped into the saloon which consisted of a big room and a small room. In the big room were gambling tables; beside each table was a flat wooden box filled with sawdust—a cuspidor. The men, absorbed in gambling, did not notice Chris. The small room was the barroom proper and was entered through swinging doors. Inside was noise and confusion and the sound of many men talking at once. Chris stood outside, listening and peeping through as best he could. Three men were laughing loudly and boasting what they had done. They had another drink, then one of them said, "Let's go out and shoot some more flyspecks off the ceiling."

"All right, let's do that," said one of the others.

One of the men drew his pistol and pushed the swinging doors open. Chris seized the man's hand and twisted the pistol out of it. The astonished man yelled, but he had lost his gun.

The second man came reeling through and saw his friend without a gun, and then he saw Chris. He blinked drunkenly, then said, "I'm a son of a —— from Cripple Creek."

"I knew who you were, but I didn't know where you were from," said Chris.

Suddenly the man made a lunge and tried to strike Chris. Chris dodged, then gave the man a whack on the head with his gun, knocking the man down. Instantly the place was in an uproar; the men at the gambling tables drew their guns and watched Chris ominously. The third man, having seen part of what had happened to his friends, pulled out his pistol and started through the swinging door to avenge his friends. As he pushed open the swinging door, Chris shot the gun from the man's hand. The man stood there, shocked at the swiftness with which events had moved.

The two men were picked up from the floor and stood beside the man who had just lost his gun.

"One false move from any of you, and I'll shoot the flyspecks off of you," said Chris. And now, taking the men prisoners, he marched them to one of the prison wagons and had them shackled to the wheels.

Chris went up the stairs again and to Judge Burford who was lying on his cot. "I don't think we'll have any more trouble tonight, Judge." Chris was right. The saloon and gambling rooms had been considerably damped by Chris's fast action, and soon Chris and Judge Burford were fast asleep and all was well in Beaver City, Oklahoma Territory.

Word of what Chris had done spread over town. The next morning, while Judge Burford arranged his official papers, Chris went to the café alone. He saw that the men were silently watching him; he pretended not to see this, and went on eating. Finishing breakfast, he went outside, and, as he did so, a man stepped up to him and said, "You're the new deputy, ain't you?"

"Yah, it is so."

"I'm goin' to do something I expect I shouldn't," said the man, pretending to be doing Chris a favor, "and that is to tell you that you'd better leave town."

"Vhy is it I should go from the town?"

The man came a little closer and lowered his voice. "Last night you hurt some men. Word has got back to the ranch where they work and their friends are coming to call on you."

"I vill be here," said Chris.

It was not long until two tanned men came loping in, rode up to a gnawed hitchrack, and dropped their reins. When the men got off it was seen that each carried two six-shooters, low-slung, and that their eyes were searching the street.

"Is there somet'ing I can do for you gentlemens?" asked Chris.

"There sure as hell is. There's a new deputy marshal here and we want to see him."

"You are seein' him now," said Chris. "I know vhat it is you vant. You two get back on your horses and get out of town as fast as you can." The two men stood hesitating, studying that square block of a face. "Is it you go now, or do I have to kill you?"

That calm voice, that level look, those cold blue eyes.... It was a humiliating experience for the two men; they had come to town to run somebody out and were now being run out themselves. They went slowly to their horses and resentfully swung up into their saddles.

"Lope," said Chris. "Get out of town as fast as you can."

The men did. The incident had been seen by the men on the sidewalk and on the street. Well! this new deputy marshal had courage; maybe they had better think twice.

It was a tense moment when time came to open court. Tough, determined fanatics filled the upstairs room, all armed, all dangerous, all hating this judge who had come to rule their town.

Chris had placed a deputy in front of the saloon which even this early in the morning was doing business. The armed men were drinking and talking in low voices. In the back of the courtroom Chris had placed two deputies, and now he himself went to the front of the courtroom and took his place beside Judge Burford.

A bailiff was waiting. When the judge appeared, the bailiff

made everybody stand and called for order in the court. As soon as the judge was on the bench, the bailiff cried out in a loud voice: "Hear ye! Hear ye! The United States District Court, for the second district of Oklahoma, is now in session."

Even in this primitive court there was something that appealed to Chris so deeply—respect for the law. No one could enter the courtroom with a cigar or pipe in his mouth, either lit or unlit; and no one was allowed to read a newspaper in the courtroom. Anyone suspected of carrying firearms was searched and, if a weapon was found, he was promptly ejected. No noise or disturbance of any kind was allowed. Anyone who wanted to address the court was required to stand and face the judge before he spoke. The shackled prisoners were brought forward and tried. If a man was found guilty, he was returned either to the jail from which he had come, or to his prison wagon.

Day after day the court rolled on and, as it did so, the opposition became less and less. After all, the people found, the court was impartial and it was just. Some prisoners would have to hang; some would go free. But that was life—the good and the bad. People had always been that way; they would always be that way.

When a man was found innocent, he was set free, then and there, but he had to find his own way back home. One man, who was found innocent, started to walk home on foot, a distance of more than two hundred miles. In the clothes he had been wearing in the prison wagon, and with little or no money in his pocket, he set off across the sandhills and buffalo wallows. Little was thought about this, for life at this time was rugged, but so were the people. The people were founding a new state and making new homes for themselves, and they meant to let nothing stop them. The man got home safely.

At last all the prisoners had been tried. The ones found guilty were put back into the wagons, but this time the men would not be taken to the jails where they had been before, but to the federal penitentiaries to serve out their sentences. And so little by little, as the wagons rolled along, the prisoners became fewer and fewer. Finally the wagons got back to El Reno from which they had started. The law had come to No Man's Land.

CHAPTER 6

The Outlaw Situation Grows Worse. The Story of Peter Schneider, Who Played the Rollicking Tunes. The Fight of the Luxuriant Whiskers.

INSTEAD OF GETTING better, the outlaw situation got worse. The reason for this was that new settlers were flocking in. The Run had brought in thousands. In fact, as has been pointed out, there had been three land openings, and these had brought in outlaws. It was the old sheep-and-wolves story. If there are only a few sheep, there are only a few wolves. But if there are many sheep, then the wolves come on the run. And so it was now in what was called Oklahoma Territory—more people, more outlaws. Many of the travelers carried money, for they had come to buy land. Some came on horseback, lone riders of the buffalo grass. Others traveled in covered wagons, camping out at night, sleeping in their wagons, or in tents pitched beside their wagons. These people had a way of disappearing, especially if they had been inquiring about where they could buy a farm. Whole families disappeared; sometimes a buzzard-picked body would be found in the buckbrush.... When some ghastly murder took place, or some family disappeared, the local people were shocked and said something should be done. That, of course, ended matters. The people were too busy establishing themselves in a new land to try to solve the murder of someone they'd never heard of.

Another factor made itself felt. At first each outlaw worked by himself, robbing and murdering as he saw fit. Then the outlaws began to form bands. They fortified caves and supplied themselves with provisions.

On top of this, the railroads were pushing through; this, in turn, meant that money was traveling through. Jesse James and his stalwarts, across the line in Missouri, had had a go at train robbing and bank lifting and had done well at it—except that some of them had got themselves killed. That was bad. But, thought the Oklahoma men, they wouldn't make the mistake the James boys had made. They'd be a little smarter. Jesse James wouldn't have been killed if he hadn't harbored a snake. Well, they themselves wouldn't do anything like that.

In addition there were the Negro farmers and the Indian farmers who, for a modest sum, would hide a person who wanted rest and seclusion. As a result, an outlaw's trail would disappear like turkey tracks in buckbrush.

All these things, Chris, new at the saddle and subpoena business, had to face. He was beginning to find it far more dangerous than popping away at Indians. Indian battles were few and far between; but in the law business somebody might take a pot shot at him any time. In addition there was the problem of his family. Maggie was always depressed when he had to answer a call. When he got safely back, she was relieved. But she did not ask him to give up his position, for she knew that Chris was a family man and was doing the best he could. And it was nice to have that two hundred and fifty dollars a month in the cookie jar. Also, tremendously important, was Chris's great respect for the law. Possibly this had come from Denmark where law and order were so important. Whatever it was, this respect for the law was deep in him.

There was excitement and there was variety in a deputy's life. He did not know from one day to the next what kind of case he would be called on next, for the erring were not all outlaws, robbers, claim jumpers, or whisky peddlers. Sometimes people who were considered good citizens would cross the law line.

One day he got a telegram from Grimes's office to go at once to Fort Sill and see the commanding officer. In the telegram there was no clue and no explanation. The marshal's office used the telegraph, but it didn't use the side of a barn.

When he got there he found this to be the situation: one of the soldiers was a man named Peter Schneider. He had a good record and was considered a model, with an interest in music. His great love was his accordion. He was the company entertainer, the man who played for the soldiers when they wanted an hour of relaxation. He was well known for his rollicking music. One day he was invited to go to a country picnic near Medicine Creek, a few miles from Fort Sill.

The country people ate and danced to his music and all was well. As so often happened, some of the soldiers from the fort heard about the dance and proceeded there to have fun and entertainment. They had been drinking, especially one of them. The country people didn't like this, but the soldiers didn't care; they wanted to dance with the girls and this they proceeded to do. The soldier who had been drinking too much began to have a wonderful time—that is, he thought it was wonderful. Peter Schneider protested, but the drunken man paid no attention to the pleas. Schneider put his accordion down on the grass and went to the man and protested even more earnestly.

"Go away. Get out of here," said the drunken man.

"I have a right to be here," said Schneider.

Words flew. Suddenly the drunken man ran to the accordion and kicked it. Schneider stood almost stupefied, looking at the battered box. The dancers were shocked and demanded to know why the drunken man had done such an uncalled-for thing. But the man didn't care, merely saying he'd show Schneider he couldn't talk back to him. Peter Schneider protested, but the drunken man laughed mockingly and said, "What are you going to do about it?"

The dancers, who had been so gay a few minutes before, sat around, subdued and depressed. Peter Schneider picked up the remnants of his accordion and started off across the fields by himself. When he got to the fort, he slipped quietly into the kitchen, got a butcherknife, and started back across the fields. He secreted himself in the bushes. Dusk came; in the half-dark the drunken man padded noisily along on his way back to the fort. Suddenly Peter Schneider leaped out of the bushes.

"Peter Schneider has disappeared," said the commanding officer. "You are to find him."

Chris felt sorry for the man who had acted so impulsively, but orders were orders. A problem immediately presented itself. A deputy United States marshal was not allowed to arrest a man outside of the marshal's district. In other words, if Schneider had gone to Texas, Chris would not be allowed to arrest him unless Chris had been sworn in as a deputy in the state of Texas. There was a great deal of jealousy and rivalry between the marshals of the different states. Peter Schneider was on the run; Chris would have to move fast.

The problem was solved when the commandant of the fort listed Peter Schneider as a deserter. This meant that Chris had authority to arrest him any place he could lay his hands on him. Off went Chris. Chris found that Schneider had crossed the Red River into Texas where he had gone to the railroad yards of the M. K. & T., expecting to hide himself on an outgoing train. Schneider found that one of the firemen was sick. Schneider volunteered to shovel coal for him. Soon Oklahoma was far behind.

Chris learned this and no more—for Schneider had disappeared like a prairie chicken into a fog. Days went by and Chris found no clues at all. Then, by the merest chance, he met a soldier from Schneider's company who had just returned from Los Angeles. The soldier had seen Schneider in Los Angeles but hadn't known that Schneider was a wanted man.

Chris got as many details as possible, then went as fast as he could to Los Angeles. But Schneider had disappeared. Chris was beginning to see that these blind trails were the curse of the business of running down a wanted man. Chris finally found that Schneider had got a job on a ranch near San Francisco, and there Chris hastened. Schneider had left a few days ago. Sorry.

Chris sniffed around for a few days, finally finding a worker on a nearby ranch who knew Schneider. The man said that Schneider had told him that he was trying to save enough money to go to Australia.

Australia! Off Chris went in a lope to San Francisco, figuring that Schneider would take the boat from there. This was fine thinking, except that when Chris got to San Francisco he found that Schneider had already left for Australia. Chris walked along the water front, disheartened. He would have to go back empty-handed.

Now came an extraordinary piece of luck. He saw a policeman. Going up to him, he asked the policeman if he could recommend a hotel on the water front.

"Does it have to be on the water front?"

"Yes."

"Why?"

"I want to watch for a man who is planning on taking a steamer to Australia."

"Why do you want to watch for him?"

Chris showed him his badge and explained what he wanted to do. The policeman looked at him with more interest. "Describe your man." Chris described him. The policeman grew agitated. "There he goes now!" Chris looked but saw no one. "On that boat! Out in the harbor." A boat was pulling out. The policeman explained that the man had asked him questions about the boat and that he, the policeman, had walked with him to the boat and had put him on it. What luck! What miserable luck!

At this moment an army boat named the *McDonald* drew up at the dock and two military men got off. Chris stared, for one of them was a man he had served with in the Fifth Cavalry; the man was now a captain. Chris hesitated. Should he appeal to this man to race after Schneider, or should he say nothing and let Schneider escape? After all, Schneider was not a bad man. He had been an excellent soldier with a fine record, but his temper had got the better of him. Now, if Chris said nothing, the man would be out of the country and would never again be a problem.

But respect for the law was deep in Chris. Schneider must be captured. Chris had made his decision. Going up to the captain, he exchanged a few words of greeting. Chris hurriedly explained what had happened and pointed to the boat which was now about a quarter of a mile from the shore. The captain, when he grasped the situation, rushed to the general who was in charge of the boat (he was General Sheridan's father-in-law) and told what had happened.

The general gave orders to the military boat; signal flags were run up and the Australian steamer slowed down. Chris was put on the military boat, which hurried toward the great steamer; in a few minutes it drew up alongside. A mystified officer came down the ship's ladder. What did all this mean? The captain of the military boat indicated Chris and said, "This man is a deputy

United States marshal, and he wants to take a man off your boat charged with murder."

"Murder?"

"Yes."

"Is he a passenger?"

"Yes."

"Oh!" he said, relieved. "What's his name?"

In a few minutes the astonished Peter Schneider was brought down the ship's ladder. The captain of the army boat gave a signal to the steamer and in a few moments it was again under way, after this strange and bizarre delay.

Schneider was taken to Alcatraz Island where he was to be kept until an order could come from the Adjutant General's office in Washington. In a few days the order came—Peter Schneider was to be taken back to Oklahoma and tried by the civil court for murder. On went the handcuffs, and, alone and without help, Chris started on the long trip back. He felt sorry for Schneider who had been a good soldier but had made one mistake.

Peter Schneider was found guilty and was sentenced to the penitentiary for life. All this made Chris think about the strange destinies people weave for themselves, and he was sorry for the hot-headed, music-loving Peter Schneider, but the law was the law and it must be obeyed.

Chris got back, turned his prisoner in, and hurried home, getting there just in time to have Thanksgiving dinner, 1891, with Maggie and the children. It was a happy time.

Chris was confronted with other matters besides bringing in lawbreakers. One was his family. Maggie was always apprehensive when he got out his grip and put in the handcuffs. Would he come back? He always assured her he would, but wives are wives the world around.

One of the interesting things about his work was the variety of cases he was sent out on. The reason for the variety was that Oklahoma Territory was growing; with new people pouring in, new problems were arising. One was "The Case of the El Reno Claim Jumper."

John A. Foreman homesteaded a farm of one hundred and sixty acres in what was later to become the El Reno townsite. No sooner had he staked it than John W. Brewer said that the claim belonged to him, and to be gone with you. Foreman refused to be gone. Immediately the two were at law. By this time El Reno was a thriving town and the land was valuable. Who was to have it? That was the question, and a good-sized question it was. Foreman had reason to believe that Brewer had not even been in the Territory of Oklahoma at the time he said he had filed his claim. Brewer said that he had been, and there the two embattled gentleman stood, glaring at each other.

How to prove that Brewer was an impostor—that, too, was a question. After some inquiry, Chris found that Brewer had come from the Texas Panhandle. Well, this was a good-sized place, but off to Mobeetie Chris went. He found that the man in charge of the Texas Rangers in this section was Captain George W. Arrington, a tall, tough Texan, quick on the draw and quick on the chaw, with as many lines in his face as on a ten-dollar bill.

"Did you ever hear of a man named Brewer?" A smile broke across Arrington's face, and Chris asked, "What do you know about him?"

"I know he's got a good set of whiskers. They're long and tough."

"What do you mean?" asked Chris.

"I mean I had a whiskers fight with him." Chris asked what a "whiskers fight" was and got a glimpse into the way men settled things in the Texas Panhandle.

This is the story: Captain Arrington and Brewer had had

trouble, but instead of shooting it out after the immemorial way, they decided on a new approach to human understanding. Each had a magnificent set of whiskers—magnificent even in a day when whiskers were a man's pride and glory. The two men decided that each would grab the other's whiskers and then, bare-handed, settle the difficulty as two men should. They were men of action. A referee was chosen and the two men walked into the street, and then each wound his fingers into the other's whisker crop.

"Get ready! Go!" shouted the referee, and this the two gentlemen did. *Plop! Plop! Plop!* It sounded, according to Captain Arrington, like a mule running in the mud.

At last it was over. The two men stood ruefully, looking like roosters with their tail feathers blown away in a cyclone. "Shake hands!" said the referee. The two brushed the whiskers out of their hands and shook.

The police came along after the strange battle was over and arrested the two; there was a trial for disturbing the peace. The case, however, was dismissed. Chris examined the court records and found that the fight had taken place at the time Brewer had sworn he was in El Reno.

Chris returned to El Reno. "You've got an unusual-looking set of whiskers, Mr. Brewer."

Brewer was pleased, but only for a moment. "In what way do you mean?" he asked suspiciously.

"Some of them seem to have been pulled out. They're kind of ragged-looking."

"What do you mean?"

"I was just wondering if any of them had been pulled out in Mobeetie, Texas."

"I don't know what you mean."

"Captain Arrington, in Mobeetie, had a fine set of whiskers, too. In fact, there is mention of them in the records in the courthouse."

This was too much for Brewer. The case came to trial, but he asked to change his testimony so that he would not be sentenced for perjury. Finally the case was settled, with Foreman winning by a whisker.

CHAPTER 7

The Story of the Outlaw Who Turned Peace Officer. Prisoners Didn't Linger Long in Jails; They Escaped.

THE Jim Hughes Ranch, on the Washita River, was a hideaway for outlaws. One of the men enjoying its peace and solitude was named Lewis. He was the father of a boy named Kid Lewis, who was as tough as nature made 'em. Kid Lewis and his friend Tom Foster killed a man at Anadarko, and off went Chris and his men to tell Kid Lewis to mend his ways. Meantime, Kid Lewis and his friend took another fling and robbed the City National Bank in Wichita Falls, Texas, and, in doing so, killed the cashier, a matter frowned on in Texas. When Chris and his men got to Wichita Falls, they found that Lewis and Company were in jail.

Meantime, Chris met Captain William J. McDonald of the Texas Rangers—lots of professional talk here. The two left on the same train—Chris to go to El Reno, McDonald to Fort Worth. At Bellview, forty-eight miles from Wichita Falls, a telegram was handed Captain McDonald. It said that the town of Wichita Falls was in a dangerous mood and that a crowd might try to lynch Kid Lewis. Chris and Captain McDonald changed trains together and returned to Wichita Falls. As they were drawing into the depot, Chris was looking out the window. Nudging Captain McDonald, he motioned for him to look out the window, too, and there, hanging on a telegraph pole, were two bodies—none other than Kid Lewis and his esteemed friend Foster.

When Chris and McDonald got off the train, one of the Texas Rangers came up to Chris and said, "You can have 'em and take them back to Oklahoma."

Chris said, "You hung 'em—they're yours."

All of this was just another experience in the life of an Oklahoma deputy United States marshal. The date of the Texas double lynching was February 25, 1896.

As Chris became interested in outlaw psychology, he tried to understand why young men passed from respectable life into outlawry. He found that once a man crossed the line, he never returned; from that time on he lived an outlaw life and usually died an outlaw death. There was, however, an exception.

Big Jim Bourland was a ranch boy in Texas, sunny and good-natured. Everybody liked Big Jim, and he, in turn, liked everybody. He would exhibit his great strength by picking up a bale of cotton and tossing it around as if it were a bag of laundry. Big Jim got the idea he would go to Oklahoma, pick him up some easy money, return to Texas, and settle down—the old, old lullaby. And he did go to Oklahoma, and there helped organize a gang, with Bob Hughes, Felix Young, Nate Sylva, and Jim Fuller to play on his team. The team planned to rob the Rock Island train on the night of April 9, 1894, at Pond Creek, Oklahoma, just south of the Kansas border. Things were never planned better. Alas! things never went worse. By chance William Fossett, an express-car guard, happened to be on the train that night and with him was his faithful traveling companion, his trusty Winchester. When the train stopped at what he knew was the wrong place, he slid out into the night. It wasn't long till he saw Bob Hughes. That was unfortunate for Bob Hughes. Fossett set up such a fusillade that the rest of the gang decided to get out of there as fast as horseflesh would take them; and this they did, without having got their hands on a single dollar.

There had been enough light for the men to be recognized; Big Jim's size was a giveaway. Jim knew he must move and move fast, so he pulled for Texas, a bad piece of judgment, for he was picked up and popped into prison, which left him plenty of time to think about the uncertainties of life. This rob-and-run business wasn't all that the boys had told him it was. He decided to give it up, and this he did. As soon as he was out, he came back to Oklahoma—no foolish ideas in his head now—and settled down in Anadarko where he got a job as deputy sheriff. He was a good one; the town and county were proud of him and everything went as sweetly as a taffy pull.

He was so good as a deputy sheriff that he was appointed deputy United States marshal, April 1, 1906. He became active against Fred Hudson who had taken part in the killing of Lute Houston who was one of Chris's informers. (The story will be told later.) Hudson hated Bourland bitterly, but Bourland didn't worry too much about that—he could take care of himself, he said.

One night in Anadarko Bourland was called to a dance hall where Fred Hudson was making a nuisance of himself. Hudson was a tough article. For a time he, too, had been a deputy marshal. With this as a cloak, he had killed Bert Casey, the outlaw king, at Cleo Springs, Oklahoma. He had killed Bert Casey for the reward money. That is all we need to know about Fred Hudson.

When Bourland got to the dance hall, Hudson was there and he had with him, of all things, his lawyer—a new idea, it would seem, in dance etiquette. Bourland walked across the dance floor and said, "Hand it over, Fred," and this Fred did. Then Bourland took Hudson and his legal adviser to Bourland's office where Hudson promised to abide by the law and asked Bourland to turn him loose.

"I will, Fred, if you will promise to go home and go to bed."

"I promise, Jim"—with the easy familiarity of outlaw and officer in Oklahoma's rip-roaring days. The treacherous Hudson left, accompanied by his lawyer.

Bourland himself went to bed, but hardly had he done so when he received a telephone call asking him to come to a saloon where someone was making trouble. Bourland suspected it was a ruse. Hudson would be there, Bourland thought, and would offer Bourland a drink which Bourland, as an officer on duty, would have to decline. Hudson would pretend to be insulted, fly into a rage, and try to kill Bourland. That was a game two could play at. Bourland was a courageous officer, but handling a bad man takes more than courage—luck, among other things.

Bourland decided to go; he'd be prepared for anything that Hudson might fancy. When Bourland got to the saloon, he pushed against the swinging double doors to open them. Evidently someone was waiting for this moment, for the person pushed from the inside. Bourland then drew the doors toward himself in order to step through. Inside was Hudson with a pistol in his hand. He fired, hitting Bourland in the stomach. Bourland was at a disadvantage. He had just recently purchased a new automatic .45, and was not yet accustomed to its shape and feel. As a result, he twice fired low. He hit Hudson in the legs, one shot in each. Later Bourland said that if he had had his old gun, he would have needed only one shot. Hudson was taken to the hospital where the doctors told him he would have to have both legs amputated. Hudson said, "If I have to go to hell,

I'll go on both feet." And he did. Big Jim Bourland, the reformed outlaw, died in the same hospital three days after he was shot. The date of his death was May 25, 1906.

Meantime, things hadn't gone too well with Felix Young. He was captured and popped into jail; he didn't like jails and soon escaped and was gone like a bit of fluff from a Russian thistle. This was just another example of the cardboard jails of Oklahoma. A man who couldn't break out of jail was looked on as a softie, with no standing among real men.

Chris kept looking for Felix Young and then, one day, got his reward. On May 12, while the federal court was in session in El Reno and the town was crowded with people, someone saw Felix Young and came and told Chris. Young was on the street talking to a small-time gambler. Chris approached within forty yards before Young saw him. Away went Young on the dead run for his horse, Chris shouting to Young to stop. Getting on his horse, Young whirled and fired twice at Chris. Chris fired five times, one bullet hitting the horse above the hock. The horse ran a few yards, then fell. Young leaped from the animal and started to run. But trouble came and touched him with its cold hand—Young got hung up in a barbed-wire fence. Chris darted forward—it was his great opportunity—and started to climb the fence, but got caught, and there the two men hung, like flies in a spider web, each popping away at the other. The battle went against Chris, for Young finally freed himself and started to run again as fast as his legs would take him. Chris got free, too, and started after him. Life is full of uncertainties and one now overtook Young—a clothesline, nothing less. It caught Young under the chin and threw him on the ground as flat as a porous plaster. While he was trying to pick himself up, Chris arrived, and, pointing his pistol, told Young he would deal with him if he made a false move. Young, it seems, was a man of logic, for up went his hands and out came Chris's faithful handcuffs.

It was not long before Young was enjoying the hospitality of the county. But not for long, for he escaped. Young was captured again and returned to his jail, mad as a wet hen.

Chris took Young to the federal jail at Guthrie. Finally Young was brought to trial. After an immense amount of lawing (too detailed to go into here) Felix Young was sent to prison and passed out of public interest.

A word about Nate Sylva. He was captured the same day Felix Young was and thrust into El Reno jail. But he didn't like jail and left, going to Texas, which proved to be a mistake, for he was grabbed and again jailed. Chris Madsen's office learned about this and asked that Sylva be returned to Oklahoma and tried for the Pond Creek robbery. He was returned and put in jail. It developed that he didn't like this jail, either. One night he crept out, leaving no forwarding address. He was picked up after the usual lapse of time and returned to his native habitat. He was tried but freed.

Soon he was in mischief again—harness stealing. This time he was put in jail in Butler, Missouri, which prided itself on having a jail much better than the makeshifts across the line in Oklahoma. Now comes something new and different. His wife arrived at the jail in a covered wagon, with three children, and camped in the alley behind the jail. Sylva could look out and see them, a boon, no doubt, to the family. One day the wife told the jailer she was going to leave and asked if her husband could come and help her with the packing. The kindhearted jailer said yes, and Sylva went out to the wagon, where he worked like a Trojan. At last the wagon drove off, with the children waving to their daddy—a touching sight. Sylva started back to the jail, but, some way or other, missed it, not getting there at all. The sheriff sent a man to trail the covered wagon as it moved toward Oklahoma, and Sylva was again brought back to a rich Missouri welcome. In three weeks he was out again, this time taking the sheriff's horse with him, which must have made the sheriff smart under such crass treatment. Sylva headed for the Indian Territory where he disappeared into a prairie-dog hole. The case against Sylva was dismissed. Sylva was a free man and he settled down to a drab, law-abiding life.

CHAPTER 8

The Story of Zip Wyatt from Cowboy Flat

An example of what happened to cowboys in these changing times is Zip Wyatt. This is the brief background of the Wyatt family: In 1889 William Wyatt, his wife, and two sons left Indiana and moved to Oklahoma Territory with stars in their eyes. The family settled twelve miles northeast of Guthrie, near the Cimarron River, in a section known as Cowboy Flat. It was part of what had been the Oscar Halsell Ranch. But the ranches in this section were being broken up; plows were going into them, fences were as thick as weeds in a widow's garden.

The sons worked here and there as cowboys; finally there were no jobs at all. The two were restless and roamed over the county, carrying pistols and popping away at fence posts. Sometimes, at night, they would ride into a town and shoot it up after the established way of such things, then disappear into Cowboy Flat. The law frowned, but there was no charge serious enough to send a deputy marshal into the sand hills. The neighbors counseled with Mr. Wyatt. His sons would get themselves into trouble. Mr. Wyatt realized this, but what could a man do with two wild sons?

The neighbors were right. One brother was killed in Texline, Texas. Instead of this being a warning to Zip, he became more bold and reckless than ever. The boy who had started out as a wild one was now a tough one. He was traveling the outlaw trail, from which there was no turning back.

Other unpleasant things were brought up against Zip. He was accused of murdering E. H. Townsend in Blaine County, Oklahoma. Also of killing Fred Hoffman, treasurer of Dewey County. These indiscretions were hard to explain. People were becoming more and more anti-Zip.

One night (June 3, 1890), just for the fun of it, Zip started to shoot up Mulhall, Oklahoma. He came down the street on his horse at dead run, shooting right and left and having a good time generally. It happened that some non-fun-loving citizens were loafing in front of a saloon. They whipped out their hoglegs and had some fun of their own. Zip whipped back and wounded two men. This was too serious for him to go back to Pa's, so Zip headed for Greensburg, Kansas. It was not long until the law was eying him coldly. Zip lit out again, trailed, this time, by a deputy sheriff named Andrew Balfour who followed Zip to Pryor's Grove, Kansas, a distance of about ten miles. Walking up to him, the deputy said, "Zip, I've got a warrant for you."

Zip whirled. "I've got this for you." It was a bullet; in a moment the sheriff was dead. The fun-loving ex-cowboy hopped his horse and headed for the sand hills. The governor of Kansas offered a reward of one thousand dollars, dead or alive. Zip was in real trouble, for money was money and a thousand dollars would buy a lot of prairie hay.

It was not long until Zip was in jail. It was not long till he escaped. Again the boring business of catching him.

On May 9, 1890, the Santa Fe train was held up at Whorton, Oklahoma, sixty miles south of the Kansas line. The station agent was at his telegraph key sending a call to Guthrie for help. Zip saw him and shot and killed him. This was going too far.

Chris happened that day to be on the train following the one that had been robbed. The conductor said that he had had orders to stop at Whorton to see if he could find any clues, and asked Chris to go with him. The body had been taken away but the bloodstains were still there, silent tribute to Zip. The outlaws escaped. At this time, no one knew that Zip was one of them. Later, however, the sheriff noticed that Zip was no longer at his old haunts. Off to Indiana went the sheriff and there he found Zip; in no time Zip was enjoying Oklahoma's hospitality.

On the last day of December 1892 the Salvation Army came to the jail in Guthrie to tell the inmates the exciting news that a man can be down but not out. In this they were slightly mistaken, for, in no time, Zip was definitely out. The way it happened was simple: the town authorities were putting a sewer pipe in the basement. When time came for the services, the workmen hastily nailed up the entrance to the excavation and went upstairs to hear the singing. Zip, having no real interest in music, slipped downstairs, ripped up the boards, crawled through the opening, and was soon out where the skies were blue and the air pure and exhilarating. At the end of the inspiring services it was found that Zip was not there. In a few minutes it was discovered why he was not there. Everybody was mad at the ingrate.

That evening Chris was sitting at home with his family when a colored deputy sheriff from the jail came panting to the door and gasped out what the scoundrelly Zip had done. Chris told the deputy to get his own horse and be prepared to go; then Chris ordered two other deputies to join him, and away the four went, hot on Zip's trail. But not too hot, for Zip had disappeared like a black cat into the night. Chris and his men searched the roads and the river crossing, but no Zip and no word of him. Finally Chris headed for Zip's father's. When he arrived, it was nearly midnight.

It was customary in the Territory for travelers to shout from the road, and when the owner of the house came to the door to identify themselves. But officers of the law observed no such nicety. They usually went to the door and gave it a whang, and this is what Chris did, rapping at the door with his pistol butt. There was a creaking of floor boards, then a light went on. A girl about eighteen, dressed in a nightgown, came to the door, carrying a coal-oil lamp.

"Are you Zip's sister?"

Shading her eyes with her free hand, the girl peered into the night. "Who's askin'?"

"I'm Deputy United States Marshal Madsen."

"Yes, since you want to know, I'm Zip's sister."

"Where is he?"

"I don't know."

He told her what had happened, then said, "I'm going to ask you again—is Zip here?"

The girl gave a laugh, which startled Chris. "If Zip was here, you'd be dead. Get out of here." And with that the girl slammed the door in Chris's face. It wasn't often that anyone slammed a door in an officer's face, but the girl had done this, and with a lusty bang.

Chris decided that Zip wasn't there, or the girl wouldn't have been so defiant, and, leaving two deputies to watch the place, he and the other deputy mounted their horses and again started on a manhunt. They rode to the Guthrie-Stillwater crossing of the Cimarron River to see if anybody had passed that night. They struck matches, but there were no traces of any kind. (Later, there was some evidence that his sister had been waiting for him with a wagon.)

Chris and his weary men returned to the main road and there, some distance ahead, they saw a light. It was by now two o'clock in the morning—a shocking hour for a light to be seen in a farmhouse. This time Chris did not rap at the door, for the man heard them coming.

"Why are you up so late?" asked Chris, coming directly to the point.

"We've been to a New Year's party and we've just got back."

"We're looking for Zip Wyatt," said Chris. "Have you seen him?"

"No," said the man. "I heard he was in jail in Guthrie."

"He was, but he's not now," said Chris bitterly. There were a few moments of conversation, then Chris said, "Could your wife cook us up some supper while we feed and water our horses?"

"Sure my woman could. I'll help you with your horses, while she gets supper started. We'll enjoy talking to you. We don't often get to visit with strangers."

It was not long before Chris and his men were in the house and busy upon the fine—or so it seemed—meal the wife had prepared. "Now you just tell us the news," said the hospitable man. "How did Zip get away? I'll be interested to know, won't you, Mary?" Mary said she would. Chris told the story.

"Zip was always a slick one," said the man when Chris finished the sad tale. "He's a no-good. I hope you ketch him and put him back in jail. Did you meet his sister?" Chris said they had. "She's a nice girl, not worthless like Zip."

Chris noticed that a room was being added to the house and that the ceiling joists had been put in. On top of them were some boards. Chris saw a man lying on a pallet on the boards; evidently he had been sleeping until Chris and his men arrived.

"Who's that?" asked Chris.

"That's our carpenter." This was believable, for carpenters often lived with a family while working on a house. In this case, however, the genial host was mistaken, for the man was Zip Wyatt. "I sure hope you ketch Zip," continued the affable gentleman. "If I can find out anything about him, I'll let you know.

Zip ain't no asset to our community." He was distressed about the condition Zip had put the community in.

At last supper was over. Deputies always paid for their meals, for later this sum could be put down on their expense accounts. "How much do I owe?" asked Chris.

The man was insulted. "Not a penny, Mr. Madsen, not a penny. It's been a pleasure for the woman and I to entertain you."

Chris and his well-fed men rode off into the night, leaving Zip softly slumbering.

Zip became more and more troublesome. More and more post-office and small-store robberies. The summer of 1895 came. Zip overextended himself—again Chris was on his trail. If Chris found anybody asleep now he'd pull down on him.

One day Chris got a telegram from the depot agent at Waukomis that Zip had passed through there at noon, and was in hiding near there. Chris got together a posse of three men, and hopped a train. It was like old times. Before dark Chris was in Waukomis, his trigger finger twitching. He was told that the elusive Zip was hiding four miles east of Waukomis. Chris knew a man who lived near Waukomis, and he took his posse and asked his friend if they could stay overnight. The friend said yes, and Chris and the possemen went to the barn to sleep. Chris was up early the next morning and with his men gobbled breakfast and set off for a creek crossing. There he learned that a man answering Zip's description had stopped during the night and had got for himself some corn bread and buttermilk. Then he had ridden on down along Skeleton Creek on the northeast side.

After a time Zip's horse was sighted. Now for Zip himself—Zip, who had been a terror so long—Zip, the good boy who had become the most dangerous man in Oklahoma.

He was discovered by Bill Fossett's posse lying in a cornfield, asleep. The men crept forward as silently as wind in cornsilk.

They did not call out to him to surrender but silently made a signal to each other, then shot.

"Don't shoot any more," Zip called. "I'm bad hit." Two of the men held their rifles on him; a third man advanced and got possession of Zip's Winchester and two holstered pistols. The wounded man was placed in a wagon that jolted off toward Enid. But he did not complain. It was the code of the outlaw to die game, and this Zip intended to do.

One of the officers said, "Zip, don't you wish you'd lived a different life?"

His old spirit flared up. "No, I don't," he said defiantly.

Chris went to Enid to see him. Zip was in jail, suffering horribly but uncomplainingly. "It took you a long time to get me, didn't it?" he said boastfully. "Damn your soul for shooting at me when I was asleep."

"It wasn't my posse who shot at you," said Chris.

"All posses are the same. I hate them all."

As Chris had been talking, he had come to the cell and was standing with one hand on a bar. Suddenly Zip's hand leaped out and snatched at Chris's pistol. Chris jumped back out of reach.

"I guess that'll be my last chance," said Zip wearily.

Gangrene set in and in a few days he was dead. No one claimed the body and it was buried in the pauper's field in Enid. And thus came to an end the story of a boy from Cowboy Flat who could not take up a different kind of life.

There is an aftermath to the story which is worth setting down, for it shows the mixed-up conditions in the Territory during this time. One day Chris, in another part of the county, stopped at a nice-looking home to ask a question. The woman looked at him closely and said, "Aren't you the marshal who tried to capture Zip Wyatt?" He told her he was. The woman then identified herself—she was the girl who had slammed the door in Chris's face. She was now married to a man named Ike

Prickett. She then said that she had been raised as a young girl among outlaws and had known no other life than outlawry. "I've got a good husband now and I want to live differently."

Chris was sorry for her, for evidently she was sincere and in earnest. Whenever he was in that section he stopped to see her and the two became such good friends that Chris had Christmas dinner with her and her husband. They talked, he said, about the old days in Cowboy Flat where nearly everyone was, more or less, an outlaw. This was owing, in the main, to the changed life the men had had to lead.

Despite many triumphs of law and order, the battle between the outlaws and the marshals was still going against the latter. So many crimes were being committed that some were not investigated. These were usually in remote sections, but they were crimes, and they led other felons to dark deeds. A wave of economy was sweeping through the United States Department of Justice, in Washington, and the department would not authorize any more marshals. On top of this, the Justice Department treated its deputies badly. There was the old trouble that had been going on so long—the way Washington delayed in paying the expenses of the deputies. The deputies really had to advance money out of their own pockets to pursue criminals. They had to pay train travel, livery-rig hire, meals for prisoners, meals for themselves, and other expenses in the matter of bringing law to the border. This now seems incredible, but this was the situation at this time in Oklahoma, and in Washington. Some of the deputies became discouraged and went into business; some ran for sheriff in the counties where they lived and thankfully moved to a local office instead of working for the great United States Government.

Something had to be done.

Judge Frank Dale's court was in Guthrie. He sent word that

he wanted his deputies to appear before him. That was all they knew. He was known as a fearless judge. He had been born in Leland, Illinois, and was a year older than Chris.

Chris and Heck Thomas had returned from Stillwater, Minnesota, where they had delivered prisoners, when word was brought for them to come to chambers. The other guardsman could not come, as he was ill. Chris and Heck went to Judge Dale's office and took their seats. In a moment Judge Dale came in. Although it was only the office and not the courtroom, the two men arose out of respect for the judge.

Judge Dale was in an unusually sober mood and sat for some moments, silently. He then reviewed the law-enforcement situation, pointing out that the law was losing. Leaning forward, he dropped his voice. "The situation has become so grave that I am instructing my deputies to bring them in dead." Never before in America had such an order been issued by a judge. There was silence, then Chris said, "Do you mean it exactly that way, Judge?"

"I do," said Judge Dale in a choked voice.

Chris and Heck left. A new kind of warfare had begun. Was this the way law should be enforced? When the outlaws heard the order, would it make them more ruthless? Or would it drive them out of Oklahoma?

CHAPTER 9

Chris and Some Indians— White Buffalo and Chief Whirlwind

One of the strange experiences Chris had at about this time concerned White Buffalo, a full-blooded Arapahoe. White Buffalo came to Oklahoma and he and Chris became acquainted. In so doing they discovered they had fought against each other at the Battle of Slim Butte in North Dakota. They took this lightly. White Buffalo even laughed in speaking of it, and said that the Indians had outwitted the whites.

Chris discovered that White Buffalo had been in the Battle of the Little Big Horn. This was an entirely different matter. So deep, so bitter was the feeling that White Buffalo would not speak of the battle. He and Chris would talk of other things, but not of this.

White Buffalo began to steal horses. To the Indians to be a good horse thief is something to be proud of. Alas! the laws of Oklahoma Territory did not look on this the same way and soon Chris was hot on the trail of White Buffalo. Chris had with him as guard Yellow Man, a Pawnee. Chris was on White Buffalo's trail eight days and nights, and ran up an expense account of seventy-eight dollars and fifty-five cents. At last, July 31, 1891, Chris caught up with White Buffalo near Canadian City, Oklahoma, and put him under arrest. White Buffalo glared at Chris. "It not horses," White Buffalo said bitterly. "You arrest me because Big Horn. Me know."

"Me arrest you for horse stealing," said Chris.

"Me know," said White Buffalo.

Chris, White Buffalo, and Yellow Man had to ride together in the spring wagon that Chris had hired. Chris and White Buffalo talked easily and naturally, the way marshal and prisoner did in Oklahoma, until the subject of the Battle of the Little Big Horn came up; then all naturalness was gone. Although Yellow Man was working for Chris, his Indian loyalty was so deep that he took sides with White Buffalo. The two Indians belonged to different tribes but they were still Indians. Yellow Man had not been in the Battle of the Little Big Horn, but he felt deeply about it. Conditions became so strained that the three had to drop the subject. Finally White Buffalo arrived at the prison and the bitterness was over.

He received a light sentence and was soon out of jail. No more horse stealing.

In his army days Chris had had his share of problems with the Indians who lived near Fort Reno. Not too long before they had been fighting Custer; all their lives they had been warriors, and now the government put them on farms and told them to become farmers.

They knew nothing about any kind of farming more complicated than hoeing, and soon were in distress. The government told them to come to Fort Reno where they could get rations and supplies from the regimental quartermaster sergeant—and that person was none other than Chris himself.

Chris dealt in what was called the Beef Issue—that is, he was the one who passed out the meat to the Indians. The Cheyennes were quartered on the reservation next to Fort Reno, and so came to Chris for their supplies. One of these was Chief Whirlwind who had fought against Custer. But when the subject was mentioned, he always became quiet, for none of the Indians wanted anyone to know they had campaigned against Custer—this for fear they would be punished. Since Chris gave out the supplies, Chief Whirlwind looked on Chris as great as a general and treated him with extreme deference.

Chief Whirlwind was a sincere man and quite religious. But the white man's ways he could not understand. The Reverend J. J. Methvin, a Methodist minister, began a revival meeting at Darlington. He spoke in Cheyenne. Chief Whirlwind sat entranced. The white man's religion was wonderful. In the group who listened night after night was Woman's Heart. One night the minister, rising to a climax in his sermon, said that most men were sinners and that they needed a savior. Chief Whirlwind sat drinking this in, tremendously impressed. Abruptly he rose, his blanket over his shoulders, moccasins on his feet, and went down the aisle to Woman's Heart and said in tones loud enough for everybody to hear, "He means you," then went back and sat down.

Chief Whirlwind had a daughter named Wolf Belly Woman of whom he was extremely proud. In fact, he was a devoted father who would do anything in the world for his wife and children. He had a wife named Anna whom he loved. It was a nice Indian family.

In the meantime, Chris and his family moved to El Reno, but Chief Whirlwind was still his devoted follower. Anything that Chris did was exactly right.

One day word was brought to Chief Whirlwind that his grandson was so seriously ill that he was not expected to live. Chief Whirlwind was shocked; he must see his grandson, so he hurried to the pasture to catch a horse. But the horse kept moving away from him. The day was hot and Chief Whirlwind was eager to catch the horse, and kept running after it, holding out a nubbin of corn and calling to it in order to get close enough to seize the halter. The heat and exertion were too much. In a few moments he was dead of a heart attack.

Shortly after this Chris and his family, in El Reno, were surprised to see an old dilapidated covered wagon draw up in front of the house. Children began to pour out, and then a procession started up the front walk led by Chief Whirlwind's widow. Chris let them in, glad to see them, but wondering what had brought about this strange visit.

The widow took a pipe from her blanket and handed it to Chris. "This is Chief Whirlwind's pipe. I am now giving it to you. You are now head of our family." She looked at him proudly.

"What do you mean?" asked the flabbergasted Chris.

"Chief Whirlwind love you like a brother. There must be the head of a family and he always said you must be our chief if he die." And then, with Indian stoicism, she told how Chief Whirlwind had died; she spoke slowly and calmly but with deep feeling. "But now we are with you," she finished, in the manner of one who knows everything will be taken care of, "you are now our chief."

The widow spoke to Wolf Belly Woman and to the other children, all of whom got up and went to the wagon and proceeded to bring in the things—pallets, dresses, skins, cooking pots. "The children are good children," she said proudly. "They will help."

Before Chris and Maggie knew it the family had moved in, in the manner of people who knew they would be welcome.

When dinnertime came, the widow went into the kitchen—she was going to do her part of the work. Maggie tried to show her how to cook the food the white way. Anna didn't think much of the white way, but if white chief's squaw want it that way, then she do um. The children ate with their fingers, talking hardly at all, their faces, however, beaming, so pleased were they to be with their new white father. When bedtime came, there were not enough beds, but the children didn't expect beds and lay on pallets on the floor, delighted with the new life they were entering.

The next morning the children were up at dawn, in Indian fashion. They tried to tiptoe about the house and to whisper among themselves, but they discovered so many new wonders that Chris and Maggie were awakened. They remained in bed, dreading to get up to face a new day. However, they must not hurt the feelings of their friends who loved them so deeply.

They had breakfast, the children sitting silently and eating with their fingers. The day began. Would it never end?

Two days dragged by. Chris and Maggie took their own children, Reno and Marion, and escaped in their spring wagon for a drive. It was wonderful. When they had to come back, they found Whirlwind's squaw in the garden, working. She beckoned for them to come and proudly showed them what she had done. And there she stood, barefooted, with the hoe in her brown hands, waiting for their praise. She had chopped down a bed of parsley which she had thought was weeds.

"You like?" she asked eagerly.

Chris gazed at the dying plants. "Me like," he said faintly. They went into the house and the process of cooking supper began, Anna standing in the kitchen in her brown bare feet watching the silly way the white people went about it.

Another weary day dragged by. Finally the strain became too much. "Anna," he said, painful as this was, "you will have to go back to your old home."

She looked at him in blank amazement. "Why?"

"Because . . . well, for one thing, the house is small."

Anna looked at the rooms. "House big," she said. "Children make noise morning?"

"Yes," said Chris, seeing his chance. "Me no sleep."

"Oh." Disappointment was in that broad, brown face. But she did not offer to punish the children, for Indians never whip and rarely punish their children. "They sleep in wagon."

Chris and Maggie could hardly ask this. "I'm afraid you'll have to go, Anna," he said.

She looked at him intently, studying every expression on his face. "Me go," she said finally.

The wagon was hitched up again. Chris and Maggie stood beside it, suffering almost as much as Anna. The wagon was ready to move, but something troubled Anna. Reaching behind her, she brought forth the treasured pipe she had presented to Chris. "You keep um," she said.

The wagon rolled off down the street. The children poked their heads around the canvas sides to have a last look at their wonderful home.

CHAPTER 10

The Story of the Fascinating Three-Finger Roberts. How Chris Trailed Outlaws.

THE CONTEST BETWEEN law and disorder went on. Sometimes the outlaws would score; sometimes the deputies would win.

A band of horse thieves was operating in a wild section between Navajo and Rush Springs. They did not steal from local people, but from ranchers who lived some distance away. When the outlaws came back from a foray, they had friends to protect them. The leader of the outlaws was a tough character known as Three-Finger Roberts, the name coming from the fact that two fingers of one hand had been shot away.

Chris and Heck Thomas received orders to make a call on Three-Finger, and got into Chris's faithful spring wagon. They did not know Three-Finger by sight, so went to a man named Estes who had a blacksmith shop—a blacksmith shop was always a source of news. They identified themselves and asked the blacksmith if he would point out Roberts to them. The blacksmith said that it would be too evident if he did it, then suggested his son do so.

The boy sauntered down the street and paused in front of a hotel where a tough-looking group of men was idling. Chris and Heck followed, pretending not to be aware of the boy.

One of the men in the group rolled a cigarette. The boy nodded. Chris and Heck drew their pistols and ordered all the men in the group to throw up their hands. Not one man obeyed. Instead, they all looked coldly at Chris and Heck. The two men realized they were in a situation and could not back out.

Then someone in the crowd said, "It's Chris Madsen and Heck Thomas." Up went every hand.

"We want only Three-Finger Roberts," said Chris. "Roberts, step forward and drop your holster." Chris and Heck put a pair of handcuffs on him, and soon the spring wagon was creaking off in the direction of Chickasha. The two men had been pulled out of a ticklish situation by the great respect their names carried. (The boy later, as an adult, was the respected V. G. Estes who lived near Altus, Oklahoma.)

It wasn't easy to trail outlaws; in fact, nothing was easy about man hunting. There were two ways Chris went about it. One was before the land was fenced. When word came that outlaws were trying to escape, Chris would assemble his posse, rush to the place where the outlaws had raided or robbed, and try to "pick up the trail."

It was a harder trick than it would seem. Chris would try to find somebody who had seen the ruffians, get a description of them, find in which direction they had ridden, and how many of them there were—this latter very important, for sometimes the outlaws outnumbered the officers. This was bad.

He would examine the prints left by the horses to see what kind of shoes they were wearing, or if any of the horses were unshod. Then he would determine which way the outlaws had started, and then off on the trail Madsen and his men would clatter.

Stories were written and stories were told that outlaws sometimes turned their horses' shoes around backward, so that a posse would be riding like mad in the wrong direction. An intriguing story—a favorite of fiction writers—but not true. Horseshoes cannot be turned around.

In summer the grass was high, and by watching closely Chris would see where it was trampled. The first thing was to determine in which direction the bad boys were traveling. But keep an eye open—sometimes the outlaws changed direction just for the heck of it; sometimes they would double back and try to come up behind the officers.

In winter there would be drifts of snow, and the frozen ground would hold hoofprints longer.

After a time the country was fenced and the outlaws could not ride in any old direction. They had to keep, for the most part, to the roads. But this wasn't always true, for often the outlaws carried pliers, as part of their professional equipment, cut the barbed-wire fences and rode off in any direction they pleased. This practice, however, did not always favor the outlaws, for it left a trail as easy to follow as an elephant walking on plowed ground.

The outlaws had other tricks, too. Sometimes they would stop and mend a fence so that a posse, riding along the road at a hasty clip, would not see what fresh devilment the outlaws had been up to.

Chris would try to find a camp where the outlaws had stayed overnight; plenty of footprints here. Maybe one of the horses had thrown a shoe. And the condition of the outlaws' horses could be judged. Were the horses spent? Had one gone lame?

Watch close at "hay crossings." A hay crossing was a place where the river was low and where the bottom was firm; here wagons loaded with hay could get across. These crossings were vastly different from a ford, which was used by many people and which usually was crisscrossed by wagons and buggies and specked with hoofprints. Outlaws didn't leave their names and addresses at a ford as plainly as they did at a hay crossing.

A great help was the information passed along by people. Chris would ask if they had seen horseback riders; and they would tell him. Where were the men going? How fast were they riding? Usually the people were eager to give the information, for the ranchmen wanted the outlaws rooted out. On the other hand, it wasn't always this way; sometimes a person would not give information at all, for fear of what might happen to him or to his family. And sometimes a cattleman was in league with the outlaws, working secretly and under cover. Sometimes the people who gave the information did not know that the riders they had seen were outlaws. Sometimes these people had talked to the outlaws and were able to tell where the outlaws were headed. But it wasn't always so easy; sometimes the outlaws purposely gave wrong information.

Chris had "informers"—people who passed along information as to what mischief the outlaws were up to. But Chris could not openly call on them. The information had to be relayed secretly. Sometimes these people carried water on both shoulders; they pretended to help the outlaws and they pretended to be on the side of the law. This was walking Niagara Falls on a tightwire with an armload of eels. If a man made a misstep...

Country stores were a great help. When Chris and his men got to a small town, they would go to the local general store and ask the proprietor if anyone had stopped there. Had the travelers bought ammunition? Had they bought food? What condition were the horses in? Which direction did the men go when they left? And so the game would go on—law versus outlaw.

Sometimes Chris and his lads would get on a "cold trail." This meant that the outlaws were so far ahead that Chris and his men had lost the trail—no tracks, no information, no ranchers who had seen the outlaws. Back home Chris and his men would have to go, defeated. But they would not be low in the mouth long. Another call would come to chase outlaws and away Chris and his men would go, hell for leather. What a world! But that is the way things were in Oklahoma and the Territory in those wild days.

When outlaws vanished like frost on a sunny morning, and Chris and his men had to go back empty-handed and low in spirits, this didn't always mean that the lawbreakers had won. Sometimes, later in a different section, Chris would catch up with the outlaws, face to face. Time for action now. Out, gun. Up, hands. Chris would hear that such and such an outlaw was in that section; then Chris would post himself in the town and watch the streets. Sometimes Chris would hear that the wanted man was staying at the home of a rancher. Chris would then form a posse and would go to call on the ranchman and his guest. But Chris had to look sharp—ambush! The battle between law and outlaw was a bitter one, grave take the loser.

The outlaws usually had the fastest of horses; as a result the marshals had to do a bit of thinking. The marshals would put their horses into a boxcar, have it attached to a train and rushed to the depot nearest where the robbery had taken place. The freight car would be backed up to an embankment and the horses made to jump out onto the bank. The marshals would mount and away they would go, *cloppety clop*.

Finally, with luck, came what Chris called "the close in." This was the capture, or attempted capture. Often the bandits hid in canyons; they had lookouts and guards who liked nothing better than to bring down a deputy marshal. Usually, when the outlaws were tucked away in a canyon, Chris and his cohorts came at night and hid themselves. In the morning one of the outlaws would leave the camp or cave and come out to water and feed the horses. Grab him. After a while another of the men would come out to see what was the matter. Give him, when he stepped toward the horses, the pistol-in-the-ribs treatment. It wasn't always pie. Sometimes the outlaws holed up in what amounted to a fort, and then Chris and his men would have to take it, come what may.

At times the outlaws hid themselves in the timber. Chris and his men would then have to work their way through the trees, with the outlaws popping away like Roman candles. The game of life or death went on, devil take the unwary.

CHAPTER 11

Chris Teaches Respect for the Law. Could Frontier Marshals Outshoot Today's Police Officers?

CHRIS AND THE other deputy marshals had not only to arrest and bring to court the unruly, but also had to teach them respect for the law. Respect for the law! That was deeply ingrained in Chris. One day he taught this respect in an impressive way to a group of young toughs.

Reports had been coming in to Chickasha that four boys near Walnut Creek were becoming unruly and that the people in the neighborhood were afraid of them. They were outlaws in the making.

Chris decided to try an experiment. By inquiry he found they had old-fashioned rifles; he knew enough about human nature to understand that the boys believed in their guns. He made it a point to drive out there in his famous spring wagon. On arriving, he found that the four were in the timber practicing shooting. He drove up as close as he could and spoke pleasantly. They looked at him sullenly, for he represented the law. Then he inquired about someone who he knew did not live in the neighborhood but whom the young men had probably heard of. He was given a civil answer, then, as soon as he could, he brought the conversation around to shooting. Taking his Krag-Jörgensen out of the spring wagon, he showed it to them. He remarked that it could outshoot any other kind of rifle. The boys were skeptical, for they thought well of their own rifles.

"It'll shoot through a tree," said Chris.

This was too much. "What kind of tree?"

"It will shoot through that one." Chris pointed to a fair-sized tree. Then he showed them the bullet, which was a steel-jacketed 30-caliber 220-grain bullet, and was one and one-fourth inches long.

"It shore never'll do it," said one.

"Ve vill try."

Chris took a position, fired, and then all five walked to the tree. On the far side was a puffed-out place in the bark.

"That don't look like no bullet hole to me," one of them said.

Chris selected a bigger tree and had the boys examine the bark on the far side. He fired. When they walked behind the tree to look, the bark was puffed out. The boys fingered the bark, only half convinced.

"Let me try my rifle," one of the boys said. He fired. There was no puffed-out place.

Chris talked a while longer, trying to make the occasion seem casual, then got into his spring wagon and drove away. There was no further trouble from the Walnut Creek Boys.

Chris was an expert shot. I asked his son his opinion of his father's shooting skill. He answered about as follows:

"His ability as a crack shot was the pride of his life. He was always showing me what he could do. When we were out together in the spring wagon, he would ask me to whip up the horses to a lively clip and then, with his pistol, would shoot the fence posts, one after another, as we whizzed by.

"He was a better shot than most of our police officers of today. The old prairie six-shooter was a cumbersome thing, that is, compared to today's marvelously smooth action, smokeless-powder, hand-fitting lead-slingers. However, I believe that any one of the Three Guardsmen could have outshot, in combat, most of the police officers of today. What the peace officer of my father's day had that many of the peace officers of today haven't got was that he understood the psychology of killing. They had all been in difficult positions and had learned, when the crisis came, not to become flustered. In such a situation the average man wants to be the first to fire. The men of my father's day knew this. They knew that the outlaw was so eager to get in the first pop that he usually missed. If an outlaw showed signs that he was going to shoot from the hip, my father and his fellow deputies knew they had him. Some of the bad men even fired from an open-ended swivel holster. My father said he had never seen a man wounded—let alone killed—from firing through an open-ended holster. Also some of the outlaws prided themselves on 'fanning.' When the close in came, they felt they had to live up to their reputations and 'fan.' They didn't seem to know it, but they were busy making a form-fitting coffin for themselves. My father said that in all his days in the law-enforcing service he had never seen an outlaw, or police officer, bring down a man by fanning. The man who shot only once was much more dangerous than a man who blazed away like a shooting gallery.

"One of the stories they used to tell concerned Billy the Kid's great shooting ability. It dealt with what a wonderful shot Billy was from the saddle. The story said that Billy could take a six-gun in each hand, ride down the road at a gallop, and shoot every fence post he passed; the ones on the right he would nail with his right hand; the ones on the left he would get with his left hand. My father said this was utterly impossible. He said that no one could be that accurate with a pistol from a running horse.

"He always said that many of the outlaws of Oklahoma were not good shots. He was rowing upstream here, for legend always has them as dead shots. My father said that most of them were ex-cowboys and were much better horsemen than pistolmen. He said the deputies could far outshoot most of them. One reason for this was that the officers practiced more. Many of the lawmen had been in the army, or in the Indian service, and had been firing pistols and rifles for years. On top of this, he said that many of the bad men had been drinking before they got into a gun contest, and, as a result, were not always—thank goodness! —deadly. But the tradition has always been that they were the finest shots in America and I suppose the tradition will continue as long as there is an interest in the Old West.

"My father said that he never saw a 'Buntline Special' in Oklahoma. It had a twelve-inch barrel and only twelve were ever made. But the stories of peace officers using Buntline Specials will go on forever.

"The usual method used by the marshals was to walk in close and then if the man made a suspicious move, hit him with his Colt rather than shoot or kill him. The close-in method had its perils, but it kept the marshal from killing the man he was arresting, and he still had a loaded gun in his hand.

"Some of today's officers are fine marksmen, but many are mediocre. Their firearms, mostly 38 caliber, with a snub-nosed, two-inch barrel, are not nearly so effective at long range as the old Frontier .45. The old Colt Frontier six-shooter was hand-fitted and was a masterpiece of the gunmaker's craft. My father purchased a German Luger automatic pistol when they first came to the United States, which was about 1902 or 1903. That gun was as expertly made and as accurate as any gun made today, but it was not so rugged as the old Colt. A small amount of dust would cause its mechanism to stick and the gun would misfire, or quit firing at a critical moment. My father carried the thing for a while with a handkerchief over it to keep the dust out, but felt that someday it would jam at exactly the wrong moment, so he discarded it and went back to the faithful old Colt. Another item that entered into his thinking was that an automatic pistol is no good to hit a man with—there's nothing better for that job than the old Colt.

"Most of the early officers carried a pistol with a barrel from four and a half to six inches long, according to individual preference. If an officer got too close to a bad man who wanted to fight, the officer would hit the man on the head with the barrel of his gun—never with the butt as is so often done in the movies and in television. An officer knew that if he whacked a man with the butt of the gun, the man might snatch it, or fire it while both men had hold of it. An officer would hit a drunken man, or a man whom he knew was not armed, with his fist. But if he was close enough, he would hit a bad man with his gun first rather than shoot him—shooting a man was always a last resort.

"My father was a great admirer of the K-J. It was adopted by the United States armed forces in 1893, displacing the old single-shot Springfield. In 1903 the Springfield rifle displaced the Krag. The Springfield cartridge was used in our Garrand eight-shot automatic rifle, and, so far as I know, is still our standard rifle. The Springfield 1903 cartridge used a pointed 180-grain bullet which was propelled by a heavier powder charge than the Krag used. It had a higher muzzle velocity, and its range was slightly longer, but the Krag's long, heavy, round-nosed bullet had a greater penetrating power in such material as wood, and its action was more like a punch drill. The pointed Springfield bullet, with its higher velocity and wedge action, would shock a wider area of tissue but was easily deflected, and if it struck steel it would disintegrate—that is unless an armor-piercing bullet was used, and this latter was not standard.

"My father knew Wild Bill Hickok slightly, for he saw him when my father's company was in camp in Kansas. My father said he was chiefly a gambler and a miserable failure as a peace officer in Hays, Kansas, and later in Abilene. My father was surprised, in his later years, when he heard the stories that grew up about Wild Bill. He said there were men in his military company who could outshoot Bill and who had more raw courage than Wild Bill ever displayed. But enough of that; people don't want their idols destroyed.

"My father himself did not know Pat Garrett, but he knew many men who did; and they all seemed to agree that Pat Garrett was an egotistical, hard-to-get-along-with man, and was always pining to pull down on an outlaw and gather to himself the honor of having killed him. But there again we're up against a million people. And can a million people be wrong?"

CHAPTER 12

How Chris Used Informers

So ELUSIVE were the outlaws that Chris had to employ the ancient device of informers. He must find people he could trust—who also were on friendly terms with the outlaws. Chris had to move with extreme caution, for this was tricky business.

Some informed for money, some to get themselves out of trouble, some because they feared the outlaws, some because they thought it was their duty as citizens. All who engaged in this slept on uneasy pillows.

Chris wanted to find out about the Bert Casey Gang, just then the roughest boys in Oklahoma Territory. They had killed several sheriffs and deputy sheriffs, and were aching to kill more. Chris had reason to believe that the band was in hiding at the Jim Hughes Ranch which was the most dangerous, the most notorious of all the harboring places. The Hughes Ranch was on the Washita River, near Fort Cobb, west of Anadarko—a particularly inaccessible section.

Near Chickasha lived Lute Houston whose sister had been married to Jim Hughes. They had been divorced, but Chris believed that Lute Houston was still on good terms with his tough brother-in-law and with Bert Casey.

Lute Houston was a rather nice boy, but suffered, as did so many of the boys of this period, from being thrown at an impressionable age into bad company. He got a job working on the ranch of his brother-in-law Jim Hughes where he became acquainted with the outlaws hiding there. To him they seemed glamorous and dashing, and they did not have to work. The result was inevitable.

Chris approached Houston, who was about twenty-one. "How would you like to work with me?"

"What do you mean, Marshal?" the boy asked cautiously.

"I need information."

"How much does it pay?"

"A posseman's fee and a share in the reward."

"I think I might be interested. Who is it you want information on?"

"Bert Casey."

"Oh!" said Lute Houston.

Houston, however, started in to get his "information." One night he came to Chickasha to report to Chris. He was not known in the town, and the problem of reporting seemed an easy one. However, as he was walking down the street, the night marshal stopped him and asked who he was. Houston was evasive. By reason of his delicate work, he did not have credentials, but Chris had given him the right to carry a pistol. This was quite all right, as Houston was playing the part of an outlaw.

"Take me to Marshal Madsen," said Houston.

Chris ordered the night marshal to turn Houston loose and not, by any means, to let the information get out. Houston was freed. Bert Casey, however, learned that Houston had been arrested for carrying a pistol and had been released immediately. In a few days Houston went out to the Hughes Ranch. Bert Casey, who was there, studied him, saying nothing.

"Lute," said Casey in a friendly tone, "we're going to rob a bank in Cleo Springs and we want you to come along." Cleo Springs was twenty-six miles west of Enid.

"All right, Bert. I sure want to."

"We'll start tomorrow."

"I'll be ready, Bert."

In some way that is not now known, Houston crept out and sent a message from Mountain View (the nearest railroad point to the Hughes Ranch) to Chris in Chickasha. A hack driver named Smith Brown was lounging outside the telegraph window. He could not understand the telegraph code. The operator, however, stepped away for a moment. The hack driver, peering through the window, saw the name signed to the message and noted that the message was to be delivered to Chris.

Chris immediately notified the other officers who were to participate in the capture plan, and they started to close in from several directions—Chris, from Chickasha, with his posse. In addition, an ambush was set at Cleo Springs in case the outlaws eluded the officers.

Casey and his men discovered that Lute Houston had been to Mountain View. They said nothing. That morning the men mounted and rode in the direction of Cleo Springs. When they got to Cobb Creek, Casey made a sign and the armed men drew up in a group, surrounding the boy.

"Lute," said Casey, "we've got a little business to attend to before we call on the bank. The business concerns you. Drop your holster."

The boy saw the evil, hard faces. "What is it, Bert?" asked the terrified boy. "I ain't done anything."

"I said drop your holster."

The men put a rope around his neck, threw the end over the limb of a tree, then put Houston back on his horse. As the body swung by the rope, the men filled it with lead. Then Casey wrote a note addressed to Chris and pinned it to the riddled body. "Here is one of your men." That was all the note said. It was enough.

Chris, meantime, had formed a posse, put them on a train, and started for Mountain View, fifty-three miles away. The train was delayed by high water and the posse had to get off and try to locate horses to continue the pursuit. When Chris and his men reached the Hughes Ranch, the outlaws were gone. Then Chris heard that the bank hadn't been robbed, after all, and returned to Chickasha. The next day a man rode up in front of Chris's office, dropped his reins, and came in.

"I have a note for you, Marshal," the man said.

He handed the note to Chris. It was the one that had been pinned to the dead boy. Chris sat holding the note, shocked by what had happened to his young informer.

However, before this tragic slaying Chris had had a "talk" with two outlaws in jail in Guthrie—Fred Hudson and Jim Lockwood. They had been with the Casey Gang, and now, following Chris's suggestion, prepared to rejoin it.

The two men went to the Hughes Ranch, and there were Bert Casey and another member of the club in good standing—Simms, by name. Hudson and Lockwood, in order to carry out their deception, had to take part in the boy's murder. And now, this unpleasantness over, the two men waited for their grisly opportunity.

Four days after the murder of the boy, the gang got ready to go to Cleo Springs to take care of that tempting matter. Hudson and Lockwood, not being known there, rode into the town to read the situation. They were caught in a rainstorm and finally came dripping into the Casey-Simms camp. After some casual conversation, the two moved up close to the campfire and took out their guns on the pretext of cleaning them. The other men, sitting around discussing the proposed robbery, did not notice the suspicious actions. Suddenly, on a prearranged signal, Hudson and Lockwood opened fire. The other outlaws tried to get to their own guns. Casey did succeed, but was able to fire only one shot. Both Bert Casey and Simms were killed, then and there, in the dripping camp. Fred Hudson said later, "We emptied our guns on them."

CHAPTER 13

How Chris Moved Prisoners

RENO TELLS THIS STORY:

"In 1901 my father and I were given three prisoners to take to Ardmore, Oklahoma, where they were to be tried in the federal court. We started from Chickasha, Oklahoma, where my father was stationed at this time. We went on the Rock Island Railroad to El Reno where we changed to the Choctaw Railroad, finally arriving in Oklahoma City. We got on the Santa Fe and rode to Ardmore, a distance of ninety miles, traveling south.

"It was about five when we arrived in Ardmore and as the train pulled into the station and stopped, we were surprised to hear the sounds of an angry crowd. We looked out the window and there was a large crowd waiting, the men armed. The crowd began to shout threats. Thinking this could not possibly have anything to do with us, we started to take our three prisoners outside.

"A big, burly man appeared in the door. 'You can't get off here!' he shouted. 'If you do we will kill you.'

" 'We are officers of the law and we have federal prisoners,' my father said.

" 'We don't care who you are or who you have with you. Don't you get off this train.'

" 'Why not?'

" 'Because you are from Chickasha.'

" 'What difference does that make?'

" 'They have smallpox and we don't want it here.'

"My father had to act, and act fast. He put the prisoners back in their seats and in a few minutes the train moved out, and after a time reached Gainesville, Texas. This was out of my father's district but he was allowed to take the prisoners to the jail, where they were kept overnight. The next day we brought the prisoners back to Ardmore. There was nobody at the depot to object to our bringing the prisoners back, as the people were not expecting anyone from Chickasha to arrive from the South. If the people had recognized us as the men from Chickasha we would have been set upon. This was just one of the incidents that came up when marshals had to transport prisoners."

In 1901 Chris was given warrants to "pick up" two horse thieves who were making nuisances of themselves near Marlow. Chris took with him, as deputy, a man named Metcalf, and the two got into the spring wagon and went rolling across the flatlands of Oklahoma. They found that the two were in a house on Bear Creek, and Chris and Metcalf went there to arrest them. When the thieves heard Chris and Metcalf, they darted out the door and into the night. Chris succeeded in grabbing one and in holding him, but the other thief was racing away as fast as he could. Metcalf hesitated not a second; he was going to capture that horse thief. Metcalf pulled off his boots and took out after the horse thief, come *hi-de-ho*. Metcalf was famous in that section as a fast runner, and now he pursued the thief by sound. He began to gain on the thief and soon was almost up to him, but ran off the high bank of a ravine and broke his leg.

Chris waited for some time, leg-shackled his prisoner, then went to the home of a man named Hiram Lee Guthrie and roused him. The man was willing to help, for farmers hated horse thieves as a mongoose hates a snake. Chris and the man walked through the night, shouting the deputy's name, but there was no response. Finally they went back to the ranchman's house, had breakfast and, in the light of day, started off again, looking for the deputy who had so mysteriously disappeared.

After a time they heard a shot, and directed themselves toward it. They heard groans and finally located them. There, at the bottom of a ravine, lay Metcalf, in great pain. From time to time, during the night, he had fired his pistol until his ammunition was exhausted except one load, this he had kept for himself. He was carried to the ranch house where he was given breakfast; blankets were put in the wagon and again the spring wagon was on the move—this time to Marlow where there was a doctor.

The thief who darted into the night was never heard of again. He had escaped, though Chris hadn't really captured him or put handcuffs on him. In all his career Chris had only one man escape after he had fitted him to handcuffs.

Once Chris was given the assignment to take twenty-three men from Oklahoma City to the federal prison at Leavenworth, Kansas. They were as tough men as you could scare up, every one panting to escape or to knock Chris over the head with handcuffs. This is the way he went about delivering his wares:

The men were in the county jail; they would have to be taken a mile to the depot where they could be put on a train that would take them on their sight-seeing tour to Leavenworth. Chris decided to march them through the street. He had five men to manage them: himself, his son Reno, and three other men—five against twenty-three. Before opening the prison gates he handcuffed eleven pairs together—the right wrist of one, the left of another. The whites were handcuffed together, the blacks separately. And now a guard was placed to trail behind.

The gates were opened. "March!" said Chris, and the men clanked out. Down the street went the strange procession with

Chris and his son on one side of the line, two guards on the other, the fifth man in the rear to see that none of the prisoners got silly ideas. When they got to the depot, Chris made the men stand in line in this Oklahoma daisy chain. People edged up to talk to the prisoners.

"Nobody talks to t'e prisoners. Keep avay!" ordered Chris.

So curious were the people that even then he had to tell the guards to eject anybody who came near the silent, watchful prisoners. If the men were to escape, they must do so before the walls of Leavenworth closed around them. The men began making excuses. One said he must go to the men's room, one was desperately hungry, another became ill and wanted to be unchained before he fainted.

"You vill stay where you are."

Chris had the passengers removed from the front half of the smoking car so that no unknown person could sit near the men. Immediately the convicts wanted something. The first was that their handcuffs be removed and leg irons put on. The law was that a prisoner could not be shackled to any part of a train—this in case of a wreck. Leg irons were put on, and now each man's hands were free. There was a rush of men to the toilet room. In it was a window without bars. The problem was solved by leaving the door open, with a guard near. The men began to talk among themselves in low tones; this was forbidden. Hunger struck, for they had not eaten in two hours. So Chris wired ahead for coffee and sandwiches. This presented a problem. The coffee and sandwiches were passed through the windows; outside, on the depot platform, a guard watched the men as they received the lifesaving liquid and sandwiches.

Next morning the men were again facing starvation. And now Chris marched them into the lunchroom in the Kansas City Union Station. They were made to sit with their arms folded.

When the food was on the table, Chris called, "It is now you can eat," and the starving men did.

After a time the prisoners reached Fort Leavenworth. It was the custom never to admit prisoners at night, and so these men arrived during the day. The doors opened; the convicts walked in—not a man missing.

The men were marched into the "reception room," where the prison guards took over. The first thing was for the men to have their heads shaved; then they were put under a shower, where guards armed with clubs ordered them to scrub themselves with coarse brushes. The convicts had been treated gingerly in Oklahoma and in the Indian Territory, but here the guards showed the men they would have to obey. It was called "breaking their spirit"—something that is not done in modern prisons.

Chris and his men were free and, to celebrate, "took in" Kansas City. After a lapse of time they got back to Oklahoma City—not a man missing.

Sometimes transporting even one prisoner presented a problem. Chris once received a warrant to arrest a Negro named Jo-Jo. This was the way his name appeared on the warrant; no other name was ever known for him. Jo-Jo lived in the Arbuckle Mountains, west of Ardmore. These mountains sheltered some of the toughest characters in Oklahoma Territory, but Chris didn't dream how tough a man he would have to deal with. By chance he took young Reno along, more for companionship than because he thought he would need the boy.

Chris's regular driving team was hitched to the spring wagon, a saddle horse was tied behind, and all left Marlow, Indian Territory, at four in the afternoon. They drove all night; the next morning they stopped at the home of Alex Robinson, a full-blooded Indian who could talk a little English.

"Who you want?" the Indian asked, recognizing the silver

star. Chris told him. "Jo-Jo bad man. He say he expect the law to come for him, but he say no lawman can take him alive."

"I expect we can take care of him," said Chris, and drove on. Later he stopped at a mountain home for a drink of well water. A tall, thin, sallow mountain woman came to the door and stood leaning against the jamb like a man. Chris explained what he wanted.

"The gourd's hangin' agin the well curb. He'p yoreself." She eyed Chris more closely. "Who you goin' to fotch?"

Chris told her. She shook her head. "He rides past here often. Always has his Winchester with him."

This was not too unusual in the wild mountains. And so, dismissing this, Chris rode on. Finally he found the place where Jo-Jo lived, and drove up to a crude mountain cabin. A man was operating a well windlass. As he turned the handle, the rope coiled itself around a wooden roller.

"Where's Jo-Jo?"

"He's gone," said the man, turning the handle.

"Where did he go?"

"Huntin'. Be gone two or three days, he said."

Chris saw a Winchester leaning against a tree. "Whose is that?"

"Jo-Jo's. He's got two."

Chris looked down the well. There stood a tall, evil-looking black man. "Come up, Jo-Jo. I have a warrant for you."

"I'm not comin' up for nobody."

Picking up a spade, Chris began to throw dirt down.

"Lower the bucket."

The bucket was sent down. Jo-Jo put one foot into the bucket and his helper began to reel. A tremendously tall, fierce-looking Negro stepped out of the bucket. He wore huge brass earrings which made him look even more fierce.

"Put the cuffs on him, Reno," Chris said.

Jo-Jo balked; then Chris put his hand on his pistol. The handcuffs were put on. Jo-Jo silently studied the two men.

How to get him to Chickasha, that was the problem. After some deliberation, Chris put him in the spring wagon, on Chris's left side. Chris's pistol was on his right hip; if Jo-Jo made a grab he would have to reach around Chris to get the gun. Reno was placed behind the spring wagon, on horseback, with a rifle in his saddle scabbard and a pistol in his holster. Chris shook the lines; the wagon moved off.

This was at ten in the morning. From time to time Jo-Jo talked to Chris; now and then he glanced back to see what the boy was doing. When evening came Jo-Jo complained he was worn out and asked Chris to camp for the night. Chris was wise enough to continue as they were doing. They arrived at Chickasha at two in the morning. The jailer was awakened and Jo-Jo was told he could now sleep all he wanted to.

He was tried, and sentenced to three years. Later, word came out that Jo-Jo wore his big brass earrings all the time he was in prison. Afterward he returned to the Arbuckle Mountains and made no more trouble.

A twist came in the matter of moving a prisoner. Chris was given a warrant of arrest for a Negro living on Walnut Creek, east of Chickasha. (Note: Readers may like to know that it's pronounced Chick-a-shay.) Chris made inquiries and found that the man had a good reputation, so Chris decided to go alone. Hitching up the spring wagon that had brought in so many arrested persons, he set out along a lonely road for Walnut Creek.

At last he arrived at the cabin where the man was supposed to be living. Drawing up in front, he called for the man to come out.

There was a wait. Then the door was cautiously opened; the man stood half in the door, one arm out of sight. It was the old device of having a rifle handy, so often used when strangers rode up in front.

"Come out." The man stepped outside. "I have a warrant for your arrest and I'm going to take you back with me to Chickasha."

The man moved uneasily, then said, "Boss, I'd like to get an extension. I don't want to come just yet."

"Why don't you want to come?"

The man opened his shirt. "It's this way, boss. I've got smallpox. I thought maybe you could give me an extension."

Chris thought so, too. "You come to Chickasha as soon as you get well, and report to me," said Chris, driving off as fast as he could without seeming to rush matters.

The man did. And that ends the story of one prisoner who was not moved at all.

Wong Lee ran a laundry in Ada, Oklahoma. One day a man, a gun in his hand, appeared in the laundry, ordered Wong Lee into a back room, and proceeded to pull at the cash drawer. Wong Lee went into the back room but came back with a long, savage-looking knife with which he made a slash at the intruder. The man, thoroughly frightened, darted outside and ran like a jackrabbit, with Wong Lee at his heels screeching at the top of his considerable voice.

The police had been aroused, but it was too late. The man had got away. The police started to question Wong Lee and soon found that he had got into the country illegally. He was tried at Guthrie and an order of deportation was issued against him. Chris was commanded by the Department of Immigration, in Washington, to escort Wong Lee to San Antonio so that Wong could be returned to his honorable ancestors.

Chris put Wong on the train, his wrists chained, and then Chris and Wong, side by side in the daycoach, started for Texas where anything can happen. It did. And at once. A telegram awaited Chris from the Attorney General, in Washington, ordering him to take Wong Lee and other Chinese prisoners who had been concentrated in San Antonio to San Francisco. The message said further that the prisoners were not to be treated roughly, as they were "subjects of a foreign power friendly to the United States."

Chris found that there was a "prison car" which was used by the United States Government for that very purpose. He found also that he would have almost fifty Chinese to chaperon. The prison car had barred windows. There were no bunks, only wooden seats. He was warned by the immigration man in San Antonio not to let any of the Lotus boys escape.

Chris was given four guards, and the prisoners were ushered into the car, chattering like jungle birds. Chris and guards took one end of the car; two guards were stationed at the other end, and the prisoners told they were not to come near. The engine whistled and away went the train brimming with Chinese.

The prisoners sat or squatted—mostly the latter—for some time, then began to grow restless. When told they could not do something, they pretended they didn't understand and went blithely ahead. Soon they became hungry, uttering the pitiful groans that precede starvation. Chris wired ahead to Del Rio, Texas, telling them to be prepared to feed forty prisoners. By that time the prisoners were so hard to control that Chris decided not to march them into the station restaurant, but to have the food put through the barred windows—no knives or forks, please. When the train arrived, these subjects of a foreign power friendly to the United States began to snatch at the food and shriek at the top of their voices. The guards tried to quiet them, but the prisoners no savvy, and continued to screech. What a meal!

When the meal was over, the prisoners began to gamble. Soon they seemed to be accusing each other of cheating, for all were shrieking at once. The guards tried to sleep turnabout, but some of the Chinese were always talking or quarreling—it was hard to tell which. At last the traveling prison reached San Francisco. The haggard Chris staggered off and turned the prisoners over to the immigration authorities; the happiest man on the Gold Coast was our Chris. He started back to Guthrie. The train couldn't go too fast.

The most colorful means of all was the "prison wagon." It rolled across Oklahoma, picking up a man here, adding another there until it was filled, then off to prison it bumped. The wagon had a driver and a garnish of guards. The driver sat in the spring seat, unarmed; the deputies on horseback rode near the wagon, armed to the teeth. Sometimes the wagon carried a colored cook. If he rode in the wagon he, too, was unarmed. Sometimes he rode on horseback beside the wagon, doubling as a guard. When time came to start the fire, he passed his pistol to one of the guards so that none of the prisoners would rush him when he was at grips with the flapjacks.

At night the prisoners slept in the wagon, or under it, or beside it. Leg irons were put on, or the men were chained to the wagon wheels. And there on blankets, on the ground, the prisoners spread themselves out. A guard was posted so that none of the prisoners would bang a guard over the head with handcuffs. The next morning the prisoners were taken to the creek to wash. Then they were put to work—peeling potatoes, washing dishes, and making themselves generally useful. No complaints, please.

When a farmer saw a prison wagon rolling along, he would get on his horse and ride beside the wagon, visiting with the prisoners. They would tell him their news, and he would tell them his. When the wagon rolled into a small town, its arrival was a social event. People came out as if it were a circus. Sometimes they knew some of the prisoners; sometimes their kinfolks would be in the wagon—a little family awkwardness now.

This, in main, was how Chris moved his prisoners.

CHAPTER 14

The Picturesque Courts of Oklahoma

OKLAHOMA handled cases quite different from those in the early-day courts in the West—in states such as Texas, Wyoming, Montana, and Colorado. In these latter courts the cases that came before them had to do with Vigilantes and Regulators, fence cutting, wars between cattlemen and sheepmen, cattle rustling, cattle branding, and feuds between landowners. There was little or none of this in the Oklahoma courts. Here it was, so far as Chris was concerned, mostly the matter of outlaws—the robbing of banks and railroads, with now and then a store thrown in for good measure, or the holdup or murder of some hapless traveler wandering across the wastelands.

The courts were picturesque, and the ways of some of the judges were picturesque, too. The courtrooms were filled with as odd an assortment of human beings as one could well come upon: outlaws, cowboys, Negroes, Freedmen, ranchers, horse thieves, Indians. Some of the latter were "blanket" Indians who would sit silently, moving hardly at all; if the courtroom was crowded, they would stand against the wall, seemingly paying little attention, but really seeing everything, hearing everything. Some of the Indians had been away to school and had fair educations, but, back among their own people, and in the presence of whites, they would not show it. They often came as witnesses; sometimes they demanded an interpreter when, as a matter of fact, they could understand everything except some of the law terms; they liked to use an interpreter, as this gave them time to think. As witnesses they got two dollars a day. When they were through they would go to the deputy's office where they had to sign a voucher. When asked if he could sign his name, the Indian would usually shake his head and grunt a no. Someone else then would write the name and the Indian would put an X after it.

If an educated Indian was asked, he would usually say, "Maybe, a little, I'll try," and then would sign his name in beautiful copperplate. The Indians who had learned to write employed a hand that was smooth and even and beautiful to see. Chris himself was a fine penman and admired the writing of some of the Indians. Once he got a pen and he and an Indian sat down in a deputy's office and took turn about displaying their handwriting.

Chris had an impassioned desire to uphold the law. If it was the law, nothing else mattered; it must be observed.

Judge Edgar S. Vaught remembered: "One time I sent Chris out with a jury. He sat immediately outside the jury room. The day dragged on. Eleven o'clock at night came. The foreman came to the door and said, 'We want you to tell the judge we cannot agree.'

" 'How do you know you can't?' asked Chris. 'Go back.' They went back and they agreed."

Another from Judge Vaught: Duke Stallings was an understudy to Chris. He was a capable man, but had ideas of his own. One day Judge Vaught gave him an order to serve. Stallings read it, then said he would not serve it because it was not legal. Chris overheard this statement and was filled with indignation.

"Since when have you become the law?" he demanded. "It ees none of your business whether it's legal or not. Dot is for the judge's business. Serve the order like the judge say." And the man did.

One time Judge Abraham J. Seay was to hold court in Arapaho, which, at that time, was a primitive place. There was no building in which to hold court. Chris had had army experience and suggested army tents, and this was done. Chris had to buy provisions for the officials. But before he could pay for the articles contracted for, the judge had to approve the bill. One day the bill read: Bread $2, Whisky $26. The judge studied the bill a moment, then said, "Why do they want so much bread?"

Bizarre as were the courts, even more bizarre were some of the decisions handed down by the learned judges. A suit was tried before Judge Franklin who was a justice of the peace of El Reno. A man sued the Rock Island Railroad. The man lost. Judge Franklin deposed that the man would have to pay the expenses of the case. The man got to his feet and asked to speak to the judge, and this was granted. The man said that he did not have enough money to pay the cost of the case. The judge grew thoughtful, then said, "I have reconsidered and will charge the cost to the railroad, which can afford to pay." And it was so ordered.

This same justice of the peace had a long-drawn-out case come before him. It was spring; the judge kept looking out the window into the inviting outdoors. But the case dragged on. The day was Saturday and the middle of the afternoon came. Finally the judge said, "We will now adjourn court until Monday morning when we will again resume the trial and when I will render a decision in favor of the defendant."

Even the great Judge Frank Dale met practical situations in a practical way. There was a loan shark who was battening on the money he loaned to railroad employees, and was charging the hard-pressed men as much as 20 per cent a month. Judge

Dale listened until the testimony was in, then said, "The plaintiff cannot collect, as the interest he wants is plain usury."

The attorney for the moneylender leaped to his feet and said, "So far as I know there is no law on the books in Oklahoma against usury."

This set Judge Dale back, but only for a moment. "There may not be a law in Oklahoma against usury, but there is one against robbery, and that settles the case." And it did.

Another story of the direct ways of the courts concerns Judge McCarver, who was a Negro justice of the peace. A traveling quack doctor had come to town and was curing people right and left. Many people believed in the wonders these "doctors" could work; and so, it would seem, did Judge McCarver. One of the patients, however, refused to pay, contending that the medicine the traveling doctor had given him had not helped him. The doctor brought suit.

The patient's lawyer argued that since the medical man was not a duly-licensed physician, he could not collect for his services as a doctor. This troubled the judge only briefly. "The court agrees, but the evidence shows that the plaintiff went to Crescent, out in the country, and collected roots and herbs for preparing medicine for the defendant. A laborer is worthy of his hire, so the court renders a decision in favor of the doctor."

Another story of the same judge: Some cowboys who had been making merry in the town were brought before the judge in the early part of the night. The cowboys had been disarmed but were feeling good and were creating an undue amount of noise and confusion. Finally the judge could stand it no longer. "Silence in the court!" he ordered. "You men are making so much noise that I've sentenced one man without having heard more than half of his testimony. From now on have respect for the court and remain quiet."

Even the subpoena servers were a colorful crew. One was

Fatty Hopkins. One day Chris sent him to No-Man's Land to serve subpoenas. In due course of time Fatty got back to Guthrie where his returns showed that he had served subpoenas on all the men he had been sent to pin down. Later, when the name of one of the men was called in court, there was no response. The clerk shouted the name even louder. No answer.

Chris hustled over to Fatty. "Your papers show that you served this man. Where is he?"

"He's dead."

"You mean you served a subpoena on a dead man?" demanded Chris indignantly.

Evidently Fatty had been preparing for this moment. "The law says if a witness can't be found, then the officer can leave the subpoena at the party's last known residence, so I went to his grave, put the papers on it, and laid a stone on them."

Chris reported to the judge, who gave Fatty a lecture. Fatty's defense was pretty substantial. He said he couldn't afford to travel all over Oklahoma without pay. This was too true, so the judge dropped the matter.

Crude as these courts were, the judges and the juries did have common sense, and usually arrived at fair decisions.

As time moved along, the Three Guardsmen were helping to bring about a greater respect for the law.

CHAPTER 15

The Beanblossom Murder

Out of a clear sky, August 5, 1901, came the Beanblossom murder. On this date, or rather the day after, the Caddo, Comanche, and Kiowa reservations were to be opened to white settlement. The occasion was in a small way like the Cherokee Strip run, except this was a drawing of numbers. The settlers came flocking, eager for free land, as everybody was in Oklahoma.

The outlaws had learned a great deal about what happened on an opening day, and now three of them prepared to take advantage of this occasion. The men were George Moran, Bert Casey, and Mort Perkins.

Moran, half Chickasaw, was the most skillful and dangerous horse thief in Oklahoma and had the reputation of having stolen more horses than any other man in the state. He had killed one man who had tried to interfere; he was ready to kill others. That was Moran.

He knew there would be a tremendous influx into the opening and that the people would have money. He began to make his plans and got the two men mentioned above—and they prepared to relieve the pilgrims of their money—as fine a triumvirate of horse thieves, murderers, and outlaws as you could find in a day's ride.

On the morning of the opening the three appeared on the road which the land-hungry would have to travel from the railhead at Rush Springs, Indian Territory, to what is now Lawton, Oklahoma. They hid themselves, peeping out of the brush from time to time to see how things were going. As soon as a group came up, the men would pounce out and rob them. If a member resisted, one of the three would tap him over the head with a pistol. They would warn the people who had been robbed to stay where they were; then the crafty three would ride on down the road and overtake the party ahead, rob them, and tell them to stay where they were, a nice how-dy-do. Thus no one got ahead to tell the officials about the mischief going on in the rear. It was a perfectly planned system of robbery. There was only one thing wrong: it didn't work.

The robbing went on till sunset; twenty-six robberies were performed. The money was piling up, and so was the jewelry. The three men congratulated themselves. This was certainly better than stealing horses. A few curses, a whack or two over the head, and all went well. So far everything had been dandy.

It happened that Dr. Z. E. Beanblossom from Oklahoma City was driving from Rush Springs to Lawton to try for free land. He was a much-loved doctor, with a thousand friends. He was in a surrey and with him he had his son Jay, who was eleven years old. In addition, Dr. Beanblossom had a driver and two other men, friends of his; in all, five people in the surrey.

Suddenly the three outlaws rushed from the brush. "Hands up!" The driver stopped the surrey; in the front seat with him was the boy. The driver made a motion that Moran interpreted as reaching for a pistol. But the driver was unarmed. Instantly Moran shot but missed; instead, he hit the boy. Moran was a bit set back by this, but business was business, and he ordered the men to take the boy out of the surrey and lay him on the ground.

Moran and his men went about the business of robbery, paying no attention to the boy, who was moaning pitifully. When the three had finished their work, Moran said to Dr. Beanblossom, "Stay here!" and then the three men galloped down the road. Dr. Beanblossom opened his bag and gave what aid he could to his son.

Soon a family was seen coming along the road. They were asked to stop at the first place where there was a telephone and get a message through to Fort Sill. "God speed you!" said the doctor. In due time an ambulance came bouncing down the road, drawn by four mules. It was a military ambulance from Fort Sill about fifteen miles away. At this time in Oklahoma all military ambulances were drawn by mules.

"Handle him as gently as you can," said the doctor. The boy was put inside and the doctor moved in with him. On the way the boy died. The surrey that, shortly before, had had such a lighthearted group now went along the road carrying the doctor's driver and two friends.

That night Chris was in the sitting room of his little house on the wood reserve, near Marlow, when a horseman came galloping down the road and shouted from horseback, as was usually done. Taking up his Winchester, Chris opened the door and peered into the night. "Vhat iss it?"

"Dr. Beanblossom's boy has been killed," the rider shouted.

Chris came out and stood beside the man on horseback and was told the shocking news. "Can you give me a description of the men?"

"No. I did not see them. I am only the messenger."

The next morning Chris hurried to Rush Springs. Immediately the word was spread and the people who had been robbed came in with descriptions of the men. But which direction had the outlaws gone? While Chris was deliberating, a man came running up; in a moment he was identified as a camper on the wood reserve. During the night three of his horses had been stolen. Instantly Chris was alert: three horses, three outlaws.

Chris hurried back to the wood reserve where he found that the fence on the north side and the fence on the east side had been cut. This was valuable information: the outlaws were traveling southeast. On top of this, three spent horses were found. The robbers had exchanged their worn horses for fresh ones belonging to the camper. And now the solution hit Chris: the men were going to the John Holt Ranch on Bear Creek. The Holt Ranch was a harboring place. Well, this required a bit of thinking, for it was almost impossible to take men at a harboring place. A harboring place had neighbors who rushed word to the owner that officers were in the neighborhood, and an ambush was arranged. In addition, a harboring place was heavily armed; indeed it was a small fort.

Chris told his son where he was going. Reno—aged eleven—was agog with excitement. "Pa, can I go?"

"No."

"But, Pa, you'll be outnumbered three to one. You know I can shoot straight and I'm not afraid."

"You'd better put that off for a while," said Chris, amused by the boy's eagerness to bring justice to Oklahoma, "but you can go with me as far as Marlow."

The two went to Marlow, a town as tough as mulehide. There Chris learned that the men were going to Holt's Ranch and from there to Moran's farm on the Washita River, near Durant. Moran's farm was near Robbers' Roost—a place correctly named.

Chris wired Heck Thomas and Bill Tilghman to meet him in Durant, bad business on hand. Chris, however, did not wait for a reply.

"Now eet iss time for you to go back home, son," said Chris. The boy was bitterly disappointed but knew his father must be obeyed. Then, astonishing at it seems, Chris got in his buggy and started for the Holt Ranch alone. Nice work if you can get it.

On the way he found that the outlaws had stayed overnight

at the Holt Ranch but early the next morning had saddled and left. Chris learned from a sharecropper on Holt's Ranch that the outlaws had departed in the direction of Moran's place. And now Chris himself rolled on toward Durant.

At Ardmore, Chris left his team and buggy and took a train to Durant in the hope of getting there ahead of the outlaws. But things didn't go quite as he expected, for when he got to Durant he received a message saying that Thomas and Tilghman could not come. Well, that was something to think about. He'd have to do the trick alone.

He found that Moran was tucked away in his arsenal near Robbers' Roost. How was he to take him? The thing was to get near Moran's place without shouting it from the housetops. He learned that the neighbor next to Moran raised cotton, and that this was cotton-picking time. A brilliant idea came to Chris. He would hire out at the neighbor's as a cotton picker, although in all his life he'd never picked anything bigger than a piece of lint off his clothes. Going to a general store, he bought a pair of overalls and a jumper, took them down the road and dragged them in the dirt until they looked as if they had performed many a day's honest work. He hid his store suit; then he wrapped up his rifle in some field rags, hid it, and started down the road trying to look like a hard-working cotton picker.

The neighbor next to Moran's enjoyed the name of Mrs. Dollar White. She was a tall, thin, high-voiced crackerneck, as such people were called in this section. She looked him over carefully, chewing snuff as she studied him. "I need more he'p an' I'm glad to talk to you. How much cotton kin you pick in a day?"

"I kin pick a hundred pounds."

" 'A hundred pounds!' " she repeated, delighted.

"I kin, ma'am. I'se a good cotton picker."

"I'll git a bag for you an' you kin start right in."

"That's what I was a-hopin' you'd say, ma'am," said the new cotton picker respectfully. Dollar White gave orders for one of the men to bring Chris a bag, then went to the house.

There, in plain sight, was Moran's house, with two or three hound dogs scratching and stretching—the whole thing the very picture of laziness. Well, Chris would change that. If Moran came out, Chris would uncover his rifle and make Moran a prisoner then and there.

At the end of the day Dollar White came shuffling across the cotton field and looked at the bag. "Why, you ain't got enough cotton there to darn a sock."

"I done the best I could, ma'am."

Chris left the bag between the rows and followed Dollar White to her cabin. She unwrapped an old cloth bag in which evidently she kept her money. "I oughtn't to pay anything to a lazybones like you."

"You needn't pay me anything," said Chris in his natural voice. "I'm not a real cotton picker at all. I'm a deputy United States marshal." He told her why he was there.

Her eyes got as big as duck eggs, and her manner changed. It then developed that Moran owned the farm where she was living, and that the two had had trouble over money and that he had threatened to eject her. She said, delightedly, she would help watch for Moran. Chris went back to cotton picking, conditions now completely changed. He slept in a cabin nearby and she cooked him the finest and best meals she could.

Dollar White had a grandson; she told him to help watch for Moran, and to this the boy gladly assented. Toward the end of the second day the boy came hurrying across the cotton patch. "Gran'ma says to come to the cabin." She had big news for Chris.

Moran and two men were coming along the bottom road in a wagon on their way to the hay crossing on the Washita River where they were going to inspect their pen of stolen horses. The two men, Chris knew, must be the other two outlaws. And now all that Chris had to do was to capture them, alone and unaided —quite a task for a simple, everyday cotton picker.

Chris got his Winchester, hurried down the road the boy had said the three would take, and hid himself behind a log. The wagon came clacking along, but the three men were not all in it. Moran himself was on horseback, following the wagon.

Chris decided to wait till the two men were in line opposite him and then kill them both with one bullet. He felt justified in doing this, since the men had so brutally treated the Beanblossom boy. With the two men dead, or at least wounded, Chris would then leap to his feet and have it out with Moran. Chris felt that he would be better placed than Moran, for he would have his rifle ready and would not have a nervous horse under him. The wagon clacked on, and so did Chris's heart.

Always the unexpected must happen! And so it was now. Just before the wagon got opposite Chris it turned off the main road and started down a lane toward the horse pen.

Chris waited until the wagon was out of sight, then followed with his faithful Winchester. Again the unexpected happened. Moran turned around and started back along the same road on horseback.

Chris darted into the brush and threw himself on the ground, his heart again clacking, and lay there as Moran came clopping toward him. Suddenly Chris leaped to his feet. "Hands up!"

Moran was startled, but not so startled that his hands didn't go up. "Who are you?"

"I'm a deputy United States marshal and I'm arresting you for murder."

"Who of?"

"The Beanblossom boy."

Moran stood watching craftily. "I don't know what you mean."

"Turn around, start down the road," said Chris. Chris marched him a short distance to where a cotton picker was working. "Come over here," Chris called, and when the man came, Chris said, "Put these cuffs on him," and this the man did. Chris let the cotton picker go back to work, then said to Moran, "I want to go to your house and take a look around."

Moran marched ahead of him, resentful and alert, caught but not conquered. Moran's wife—also half-Indian—met them at the door and eyed the two without speaking. The two entered.

"I want to put on my other clothes," said Moran to his wife. The cabin had only one room. The man's wife went to some pegs on the wall where clothes were hanging and came back with some old ragged garments. The woman had comprehended what he meant; it was a clever maneuver, for in the suit was a six-shooter.

For once Chris didn't think fast enough. His idea was to get evidence against Moran. Chris saw a large trunk in a corner of the room and, going to it, lifted the lid. On a tray were several watches which Chris knew must have been taken from the people on the road to the opening of the Indian lands. Chris had started to dig down into the trunk when he heard a noise that he did not understand. He looked around; in the room was a small table and on the table was a newspaper. The wife was trying to put a six-shooter under the paper when the gun clinked against the table top. Moran, a few feet away, was watching with the same hatred he had had from the moment Chris had jumped out from the brush.

"Drop that!" The woman moved back. "I'll take that," said Chris, and, going to the table, pocketed the pistol.

Chris found twenty watches and some jewelry in the trunk and an arsenal of guns and ammunition. These he gathered for evidence. While he was doing this, he heard a noise outside. Going to the door, he saw the wagon the three outlaws had been riding in; it was being driven by a boy alone; no one else was in the wagon. The boy was bringing back the wagon from the pen where the stolen horses were being kept. Chris popped out. "Who are you, son?"

The boy was so startled he could hardly answer. Finally it came out that he was Moran's wife's brother. "In that case I am arresting you and your sister on the charge that you have been harboring outlaws." The boy did not blubber, for he had courage. Nor, for that matter, did Moran's wife. They were tough, early-day Oklahoma characters who could take anything that Fate handed them.

"We're going to use that wagon again," said Chris. "I'm going to take the three of you to Tishomingo."

Moran's wife looked at Chris a moment, then said, "Can I change my dress?"

"Yah."

In a few minutes she came out of the cabin in what passed as a good dress and carrying a shoe box. "I made up some lunch for us," she said in the same casual, indifferent tone.

Chris put Moran and his wife and the boy in the spring seat and took his place in the back of the wagon, with his Winchester. The woman looked back over her shoulder. "I reckon you'll need something to set on. I'll get you something." She climbed down over the wheel, entered the unlocked cabin, and in a moment came out with an upright chair with a corded seat and handed it up to Chris. "It's the best we got." Then she climbed over the wheel and back into the wagon. Chris ordered Moran to drive fast. What if the word got out and the outlaws came?

It was a strange, long trip—thirty miles; the three in the spring seat, Chris in the upright chair with the Winchester in his lap. The trip went fairly well until the wagon came to the Cumberland Hills, near old Fort Washita. The Cumberland Hills were the hiding place of many wanted characters; here they had friends; sometimes the outlaws lived in caves in a kind of wild savagery. When travelers came by, the outlaws suddenly appeared....

Moran, who had been silent and surly most of the trip, began to whistle. Chris punched him in the back with his Winchester. "Dot is enough moosic."

Three mounted men were seen coming down the road. One of the men had a spyglass, as so many of the outlaws had, and put it to his eyes. Moran took off his hat and scratched his head.

"Stop! We will let them pass," said Chris, for he wanted the wagon to be standing still.

The men came on, the horses making blowing noises, indicating they had been ridden hard. The men silently passed the wagon, speaking to no one. After they were out of hearing, the men drew in together and began to talk.

"Go on now," said Chris. The wagon rolled on.

Chris had been up two nights and began to nod. Now and then Moran turned and looked back over his shoulder.

They came to a small crossroads hotel near Tishomingo where Chris ordered the horses fed and supper for the three prisoners. The three sat at a table in the corner of the room; Chris sat some distance away, his Winchester leaning against the wall. The prisoners ate silently; the woman spoke only once. "It's nice to eat away from home," she said.

Chris rented a room for the three, taking precaution to drive a nail so the window could not be raised. Then he took his place in a chair in the hall, his Winchester at his side. Half an hour passed. The proprietor came to Chris and said, "Someone outside wants to see you."

"Send him in," said Chris.

A man wearing a double holster came in. The man turned out to be a deputy United States marshal from Madill, Indian Territory. He had been trailing an outlaw, but the man had escaped and the deputy was on his way back, empty-handed, as so often happened in Oklahoma.

Chris explained the situation. The deputy volunteered to guard the prisoners, and Chris went thankfully to bed. The next morning he woke nervously, but the prisoners were still there and all was well, at least so far.

They had breakfast. Chris paid for the meals, as was customary for deputies to do, and the little one-wagon cavalcade started on again—two men behind now, but only one chair. The two agreed to take turn about enjoying its hospitality. The wagon rolled on, Moran sullen and silent in the front seat. His wife looked at the changing scenery, seeming to enjoy the ride. Chris thought again of the pathetic words she had uttered at the table.

They came to Honest Tom Tillery's. He was the biggest horse thief in the county. A team, attached to a light spring wagon, was tied to a gnawed hitchrack. From inside the house came the sound of music—very rare in Oklahoma. Leaving the new man to guard the prisoners, Chris started toward the house. Abruptly the music stopped and a man came out the back door and started to run. Chris commanded him to stop, but the man kept on, even faster, if possible. He was going toward a strawstack. Cattle had eaten holes in it, and now the man dived into one of them.

"Come oudt."

The man did not stir. Chris fired two shots near where the man had gone in. The man came out, sputtering straw, his hands up. Chris stared in surprise. He had thought it was one of the outlaws he was trying to capture, but he had never seen the man.

"Who are you?"

"Willie Starr."

The shots brought two people out of the house—Honest Tom Tillery's wife and an organ salesman. At this time in Oklahoma it was the practice for an organ salesman to go to a home, take the organ into the house, and play a few tunes to captivate a possible buyer. This was what was happening when Chris's wagon came up.

Chris ordered the prisoner to go around in front of the house. As soon as the deputy saw him, he called out excitedly, "Why, that's the man I'm hunting! He's wanted on a murder charge."

"I'm innocent," said the man.

"You don't run like it," said Chris.

Chris had the two men shackled together.

"Where's your husband?" he asked Honest Tom's wife.

"He went to Gainesville. He ought to be back soon."

Almost as she spoke, a horseman appeared. When he came up and saw Chris and the deputy, he turned pale. "I haven't done anything," he said, and began to protest at great length as to his honesty and as to how law-abiding he was. In fact, he was so profuse that Chris became suspicious.

"Honest Tom, let's go out and look at your horses."

The pasture was filled with stolen horses.

"I didn't know they were stolen," said Honest Tom, almost weeping over the way the stolen horses had strayed into his pasture.

Chris wrote down the brands and told Honest Tom he would leave the horses in his custody and would hold him responsible for their safekeeping until the deputy marshal of that district could take charge of the matter. "I just can't account for it," said Honest Tom, wiping away a tear.

The two prisoners were put into the wagon, the boy moved back, and sat himself on the floor. Moran's wife picked up the lines and released the brake. Chris and the deputy got into the back part and once more the wagon rolled on. The salesman put the organ into his spring wagon and followed Chris down the road, meditating, no doubt, on the strangeness of life.

Chris decided to take Moran to Ardmore, as it had a jail much stronger than Tishomingo's. That was thirty miles more. At last the wagon rolled up in front of the Ardmore jail. Moran and the other prisoner got down and stood beside the wagon, under guard. Moran's wife sat in the wagon, holding the lines. "Come back when you can, George," she said.

"I will," said Moran. Moran started inside. Moran's wife clucked to the horses and the wagon rolled on again.

There was considerable pother about what was to be done to Moran. The Beanblossom boy had been killed on the Oklahoma Territory side of the line, so Moran was tried in Lawton, the county seat. He was found guilty, and was sentenced to life imprisonment.

Perkins, one of the other outlaws, was finally found, arrested, and sentenced to life imprisonment just as Moran had been. In October, 1902, as we have seen, Bert Casey was shot down near Cleo Springs, Oklahoma Territory, thus ending the story which started the morning of the land opening.

CHAPTER 16

The Story of the Bad Poe Brothers

It is almost unbelievable how cruel, how heartless, how depraved were some of the outlaws. Human suffering meant nothing to them; nor human life. A good example of this was the Poe brothers: Bose and John. Along with them was Oscar Smith who was just as inhuman as were the brothers.

The three worked out a fine idea. It was to wreck the westbound Santa Fe train at the bridge over the South Canadian River, near Canadian City (now Canadian), Texas. The bridge was a high one; it was fifty feet above the river bed. Their idea was to place logs on the bridge; this would pile the train up on the dry river bed below. Then the three would help themselves to the money in the express car, go through the pockets of the dead passengers, mount their horses, and ride blithely away.

One small matter went wrong. When the engineer saw the logs he put on a burst of speed and hit them with such force that he knocked them completely off the track, thus preventing the derailment of the train. When the three saw the train get safely across the bridge, they began firing into the rear car. The horses were tied nearby and now the men mounted and rode away, mad as hops.

A Texas posse started out after them as fast as horseflesh would take them. The posse followed the outlaws' trail to the Oklahoma border, a distance of about thirty miles. There the men had to stop, for Texas posses were not allowed to ride into Oklahoma. The Texas leader telegraphed to the United States marshal's office in Guthrie, telling what had happened and the direction the men were traveling.

The men from the marshal's office launched themselves on the trail as it crossed into Oklahoma. The trail became thinner; the county was so sparsely settled that the deputies could not ask anyone if they had seen suspicious characters. Nightfall came and the deputies had to give up. This left the three outlaws riding high, wide, and triumphantly.

It happened that William Grimes (Chris's chief) was at Kingfisher, Oklahoma, and with him was Fred Dodge, the chief special agent for the Wells Fargo Express Company. The two rode out to a small Negro settlement and learned that three men, answering the description of the wanted men, had robbed a store and post office in Wanamaker, Oklahoma, a distance of about sixty miles.

Grimes and Dodge hired a rig and went whooping across the prairie to Wanamaker (it no longer exists) where they found that the robbers had taken not only money, but had got a coil of rope in the store and had cut off three lariats—one, presumably, for each man.

The two men examined the severed rope and found that the job had been done with a knife that had a piece broken out of the blade, and which left a rough, jagged cut. Grimes took a sample of the rope, about a foot long, and then the two men climbed into the livery rig and set off on the outlaw trail which was leading toward the Cherokee Outlet. To their dismay they found that a large herd of cattle had trampled up the ground and that the trail disappeared completely.

Back to Kingfisher where they had started. At about midnight Chris received a telegram from Grimes ordering him to round up the outlaws. Chris could find only one man he could deputize,

Frank Cockran, and the two started out. They caught a freight train and had the engineer let them off near the Witherspoon Ranch, then walked to the ranch house, arriving at four in the morning. Mrs. Witherspoon, all excited at having officers suddenly burst into her life, buzzed about and produced a fine breakfast. Neighbors and cowboys were called in, but no one had seen the outlaws, so the trigger marshal and his men went back to Guthrie empty-handed.

About eleven o'clock that morning a rough-looking man walked into the marshal's office.

"You wouldn't be looking for some outlaws, would you?"

"Ve vould."

The man turned out to be an itinerant carpenter. He said that three men had stayed overnight with George Richards, a well-known harborer of outlaws. After breakfast the men had ridden off at a fast clip. This was getting somewhere.

It was the old routine of hiring a livery rig and chasing off after the outlaws. While Grimes was arranging for the livery team, Chris went to the jail to see what he could learn. Inquiry revealed that there was a prisoner who knew everybody who was anybody in the outlaw world—one Jack Boone, better known as Three-Fingered Jack. Jack was waiting a pistol-packing charge —not a very serious matter in Oklahoma. Chris found that Three-Fingered Jack knew all about the wanted men and that he would help chase them if the law would go easy on the pistol business. Chris talked to the prosecuting attorney and was able to tell Jack that he would get every consideration if he helped to bring in the Poe boys and their friend. Jack said he'd be delighted.

In no time at all the three were at the Richards Ranch. Richards said he didn't approve of men willing to wreck a whole train just to get into the express car when the car might not have any money at all, and said he would start the law out right. He said the men were trying to get to the Indian Territory and were planning to cross the South Canadian at a place called Silver City, which was not a town at all but merely a hay crossing. The exact location was six miles down the river from Minco, Indian Territory. The river itself was a trouble-maker and was full of quicksands.

Off the three went. When they got to the hay crossing they found that the trail led up the river, so upriver they went. So fast were they moving that they had to exchange horses twice. Most ranchmen were glad to cooperate; it helped thin down the number of outlaws; in addition, the ranchmen knew their horses would be brought back. If a horse was killed, it would be paid for; this might take a year, but, some time or other, the money would wander in.

As they were dashing along they were surprised to see a horseman coming toward them; he did not see them until he was almost up to them and could not turn back. The man did not speak, a suspicious bit of business in itself, in this land where everybody stopped to pass the time of day. He passed on Chris's side and there, in the scabbard, Chris saw a Winchester. He ordered the man to halt. Getting out of the rig, Grimes came around and searched the man, the man not speaking. The Winchester was taken, also a revolver from the man's belt. A lariat was hanging from the man's saddle; when Grimes examined it, he saw that the lariat had been hacked off a longer piece, and when he compared the end of the rope he had brought, he found that the two ends matched, both having marks of a knicked blade.

"Who are you?" asked Grimes. The man refused to answer. Grimes asked other questions. The man still refused to answer.

Three-Fingered Jack had been listening intently and at the same time studying the sullen man. Making a motion, Three-Fingered Jack led Grimes to one side and said in a low voice,

"I think maybe he'd tell me. Will you let me take him off a distance and be with him alone?"

Grimes did not wholly approve of the idea of turning a captured man over to another prisoner, but Three-Fingered Jack seemed so sincere and earnest that Grimes, upon being urged by Chris, decided to do this.

"I'd like to take him off alone in that patch of timber," said Jack.

"Can't you go off to one side and talk to him here?"

"Not so good. Stay here until you hear a shot." Jack tied the man's hands, then placed the loop of the lariat around the neck of the man. "Come on." Jack and the man walked off, the man ahead, Jack holding the rope. The two disappeared into the timber.

There was silence for a while, then someone began to shout at the top of his voice for help. "He's got Jack's revolver," said Chris, and ran as fast as he could toward the timber.

When he got there he was astonished to see that Jack still had the lariat around the man's neck, but now had the rope over the limb of a tree. Suddenly Jack swung his weight on the rope and pulled the man off the ground; then, after a moment, he lowered him and shouted, "Are you goin' to talk?"

The prisoner shouted for help. Jack swung his weight on the rope again, and up went the man. In a moment the man was lowered.

"Are you goin' to talk?" demanded the earnest Jack.

Just as Chris arrived, the man was lowered again. "I'll talk," he said. And he did. He said his name was Oscar Smith and that the Poe brothers were the other men and that they were going to George Isaac's harboring place on the Washita River, near Chickasha, Indian Territory.

The new prisoner was handcuffed and put in the spring wagon on the seat beside Three-Fingered Jack who had tried so hard to hang him. Grimes got in and picked up the lines. Chris mounted Oscar Smith's horse, and off went the jolly men, hot on the trail of the Brothers Poe.

Chris and his men exchanged horses with ranchmen twice more. The strange procession rode on, Three-Fingered Jack and Oscar Smith now chatting in a friendly way. Late that afternoon, ten miles south of Minco, Chris and Grimes saw two men ahead of them on horseback. Chris and Grimes exchanged places, Chris now in the spring wagon. Chris turned the lines over to Three-Fingered Jack and got his Winchester ready. The ground was soft, as it had been tramped up by cattle, and the two men did not hear Chris and Grimes until they were within fifty yards of them. Grimes, with his six-shooter in his hand, rode up alongside them. "We know who you are. Hands up!"

The man nearest Grimes put up his hands. The other—unseen by Grimes—secretly drew his pistol to kill Grimes. Chris saw what was happening. Although he was thick and pudgy, he could move with astonishing quickness. Bringing his Winchester to his shoulder, he fired—not at the outlaw, but at the horse. The bullet went through the horse and struck the rider in the leg; the horse fell on the man's other leg and there the man was, pinned down. He still had his pistol in his hand but wasn't foolish enough to try to use it. Grimes took the pistol, then helped pull the horse off the man. The other man was made to dismount, his pistol was taken from him, and a pair of handcuffs put on him.

"Who are you?" Grimes asked.

"Bose and John Poe."

The wounded man was put into the wagon—three outlaws now—and with Three-Fingered Jack driving, the spring wagon began rolling toward Chickasha. Chris and Grimes came behind on horseback—no foolishness from the prisoners.

When they arrived in Chickasha, the wounded man was taken to the doctor; the other Poe and Oscar Smith were tucked away in jail. The helpful Three-Fingered Jack slept in jail, but not as a prisoner. The next day Grimes and a guard took the two prisoners to Kingfisher.

Chris and Three-Fingered Jack went back over the trail, paying the farmers for the use of their horses and the wives for the meals. The story ends pleasantly—the fascinating Three-Fingered Jack was given a light sentence for helping to bring in the three tough ones, and the Poe brothers were sent to the penitentiary to think over what they had done. The story is also enlightening in that this is the first time that a head marshal ever went into the field after outlaws and the only time a deputy ever saved the life of his superior. The duty of a head marshal was to attend the courts when they were in session. There were from three to six districts, and, as the country opened to settlement, there were seven judges to hold court, so the head marshal had to keep hopping.

CHAPTER 17

Chris Goes Alone to Arrest Red Odem, Who Has Killed Fifteen Men

LAW FLOUTERS would stop at nothing. An example of this law flouting was Red Odem. He was a deputy sheriff in Oklahoma, but Odem wasn't his real name. He was on the dodge from Texas and thought the best place to hide was behind a silver star, so he landed a job as deputy sheriff and wore the silver star.

At this time, in Oklahoma, it was not uncommon for an outlaw to try to get himself a job as peace officer. Sometimes a man would be an outlaw a while, then move over to the side of the law. Often there was no sharp line between law and anti-law.

By chance, in the spring of 1891, Red Odem discovered there was an old federal statute on the books which made it unlawful to graze cattle on Indian lands. The law was out of date; hardly anyone even knew there was such a law. But Red Odem did, and he went into action. The law provided a fine of one dollar for each head of stock found grazing on Indian land—half the fine going to anyone who would make the complaint and furnish the proof. It was his pie.

He engaged Al Jennings and set about the matter in a businesslike way. He knew many of the cowboys who were working for cattlemen in the Indian country, so he went to them and made secret arrangements. It was not long before he had a list of cattle owners on unopened Indian reservations. Red and Al succeeded in filing their complaint, and the United States marshal was ordered to take charge of the cattle—quite a little chore.

Chris was told to help round up the men who were disobeying the ancient law. It was not a job to his liking, but his respect for the law was deep, and he meant to do exactly as it specified. So off on horseback he went, two pistols in his belt, his Winchester in his saddle scabbard. He rode straight to Al Jennings' camp on Deep Red River, a branch of the famous Red River of the South.

His arrangements with Marshal Grimes was that he would stop at certain towns to see if a telegram had come in. Sure enough, one had. It ordered him to return to Guthrie for instructions. Chris returned, wondering what it was all about. Grimes said: "I have learned that Red Odem is a fugitive from justice. He is charged with having killed fifteen people. You are to arrest him and bring him back."

It seems that Red Odem had killed most of these people during the feuds between cattlemen. One of the cattlemen announced that he was going to fight the law. One day the cattleman's little daughter was sitting on the steps in front of their house, playing. Red Odem rode up, killed her, and calmly rode away.

Red Odem was ahead of his time. He told the cattlemen he would "protect" them, and this they agreed to. But from time to time he raised the amount they would have to pay for protection. The cattlemen complained, but he kept demanding more money. At last the cattlemen sent word to the Texas law authorities that Red Odem from their state was in Oklahoma.

In no time at all a sheriff from Texas arrived in Oklahoma with a requisition for Red. He was on his way to Governor Steele to present his requisition when Red Odem heard about it. A man called on the visiting sheriff and said that if the sheriff presented the requisition he would be killed. The sheriff's enthusiasm waned noticeably. In fact, he did not present the requisition at all—he mailed it to him and started for Texas as fast as he could clop. When the governor got the requisition he sent it to Marshal Grimes who called in Chris and said, "Red Odem is wanted. Bring him in."

Red Odem, learning this, gave out word that he would kill anybody who tried to arrest him. Chris found that Odem had taken up a claim and was hiding on it with his wife. Chris went alone to bring Odem in. Leaving his horse some distance away, he approached the cabin at night. A light was shining in the window—a signal light, he decided. A dog came charging out, barking fiercely. Chris whispered to the dog and finally got it to quiet down. Then Chris found that Odem was not there.

Chris returned the next night. The dog was more friendly now. While Chris was watching the house, he heard the sound of a horse approaching. The man put the horse in the stable, then started to the house. The dog ran to meet him, barking joyously. The woman, hearing the barking, came to the door, then, picking up the baby, stepped outside where she greeted her man. Chris was close enough to hear the conversation. Odem told his wife where he was going to hide the next night, and for her to come there to meet him.

The next night Chris was in hiding near the ranch house where they were to meet—no dog. As the two stood talking, Chris darted forward from behind and shoved his rifle against Odem's back. "Hands up!" The instinct of most outlaws, caught in such a situation, was to whirl to "shoot it out," but Odem seemed to realize that one false move would be his end, and so his hands went up.

Odem's wife, seeing that Chris was an officer of the law, began to cry and moan. Chris made her put the handcuffs on her husband, and as she put them on she sobbed deeply. Odem patted her as best he could and said in a kind of rough tenderness, "Don't get worked up. I'll soon be back."

Odem asked for five minutes alone with his wife, but Chris could not grant this. He told Odem to get on the horse, Chris mounted his own, and the two men rode off into the night, leaving the woman alone in the doorway with the baby. It was a hazardous trip, if ever a marshal made one, but finally Chris got Odem to El Reno and placed him in jail. The next day he wired the Texas sheriff to come to Oklahoma City where he could have the pleasure of meeting Red Odem.

At that time the Choctaw Railroad from El Reno was finished only as far as Yukon. Chris took Odem to the end of the road; all safe so far. Al Jennings was there to meet Odem. Chris waited for them to exchange a few words, then ordered Odem to get into the horse-drawn hack that was to convey them to Oklahoma City.

Al said, "Can I sit with him alone? I have legal business to talk over with him."

"You can, after I search you."

"You don't have to search me. Here it is." He handed his pistol to Chris.

There were three seats in the hack. Chris put the two men in the middle seat and took his place behind them. The driver shook the lines and called to the horses; the hack started down the lonely road to Oklahoma City. On the way it had to pass through Council Grove, a particularly wild and desolate spot. Jennings and Odem had been talking, but now grew silent, and the two kept looking into the trees. Chris sat alert, watching every move the two made.

Chris called for the driver to go a little faster. At last the hack moved out of the timbered strip. Al Jennings kept looking back, but finally gave up and settled down. Finally the hack arrived in Oklahoma City where Chris marched Odem off to jail.

The next day the sheriff from Texas arrived and took command. Odem died in jail in Texas before he was tried. And that was the end of a heartless bad man typical of the outlaws Chris had to deal with.

Chris had trouble from a source that one would not ordinarily expect—the very bankers whose banks he was trying to protect. Example: Henry Starr was three-quarters Cherokee, and as tough as a stay chain. He robbed banks, having no interest in trains. He, with his fellow craftsmen, accomplished something that no other robber band in the United States had ever successfully brought about—the robbing of two banks at once. This was at Stroud, Oklahoma, March 27, 1915. However, Starr had a bit of bad luck. He was shot in the hip and captured; his men dashed away with the faithful grain sack and escaped.

Starr had been so successful that the governor of Oklahoma became suspicious, and told Chris to go to Stroud and have a talk with Henry Starr, whom Chris had known most of Starr's life. Chris asked to be alone with the wounded man who was being nursed in the Stroud jail. After talking a few minutes, Chris came to the point. "Henry, I want you to be honest with me. I have a list here of the bank robberies in the state and I think you have been in several of them. I will read them and you tell me if you were in them."

He started to read the list. When Chris came to one of the banks, Starr made a gesture of satisfaction. "That was an easy job. The president of the bank paid me five hundred dollars to rob it." And this was true. The banks were insured; sometimes they were in delicate financial condition.

CHAPTER 18

Chris Meets the Daltons

THE UNEQUAL BATTLE in the Territory between officers and outlaws went on—the outlaws winning. There were reasons for this. The counties had no money to pay the local officers; in fact, some of the counties hadn't enough money to buy blanks for the officers to make out their reports, so the local officers bought school scratch-pads and turned in their reports on these. The sheriffs had to take their pay in "scrip," which they sold usually at seventy-five cents on the dollar. So the matter of combating the outlaws fell to the deputy United States marshals. It wasn't pie. As a result it was hard to get marshals. Meantime, crime was growing like germs in a test tube. Sometimes there would be a murder, and no officer at all bothered to investigate it. Outlaws from other states—especially Arkansas and Texas—heard of this and came on the run.

The Daltons were the big boys. They organized themselves into a gang and started out with brotherly cooperation to get some of the gravy. They were well fitted for their new undertaking. Their father was James Lewis Dalton, Junior, usually known as Lewis Dalton. A contract for marriage was signed by him and Adline Younger, March 12, 1851; this can be seen in the courthouse in Independence, Missouri, page 214. She was Cole Younger's aunt, and thus Lewis Dalton became Cole's uncle by marriage. Dalton had little influence on Cole, for Lewis

Dalton moved to Oklahoma and Cole saw little or nothing of him—a blessing.

There were seven Dalton boys, but only four showed promise as outlaws. The other three were just plain, ordinary farmers—no glamour. William Marion Dalton, usually called "Bill," Grattan, whittled down to "Grat," Bob, and Emmett were the stars; they put the family in the headlines. The three farmers added nothing at all to family glory.

The following story gives a telling insight into the ways and methods of the Daltons. It was told by Frank Shufeldt, of Lenapah, Oklahoma: "When Bob and Grat were deputy United States marshals they would ride across the country until they caught up with a covered wagon. Bob would ride up close enough to engage the driver in conversation. He would explain that he and his brother were deputy marshals, and would ask where the man had come from, where he was going, and so on. While Bob was doing this, Grat would slip a bottle of whisky into the wagon. Then the two would ride on ahead. When the wagon came up, they would say that they'd decided the wagon and driver looked suspicious and that they would have to search the wagon. This they would do, discovering, of course, the bottle of whisky. Then they would say, 'Do you know what this means in Indian Territory?' Then and there they would fine the man, tell him how lucky he was not to have to go to jail, and then ride away."

Two of the "boys"—Bill and Grat—went to California where they were busy robbing trains and making nuisances of themselves. The heavy hand of the law finally tapped Grat on the shoulder and flung him into the Tulare County jail. The law now wanted to tap Bill; and this it did, but Bill proved that he was as innocent as Peter Pan and was freed from jail. In the meantime, inconsiderate Grat escaped from jail. The law—annoyed no end—set a trap for him. The officers decided to watch Bill; sooner or later he would go to see Grat. Then they would grab Grat and tell him to come home. A fine, watertight scheme. The only thing that could be said against it was that it didn't work.

In October 1891 Chris was asked to go to California to help to apprehend Grat. In no time Chris was in San Francisco where he reported to the attorney for the railroad.

"We're shadowing Grat. When he goes to see his brother Bill we'll nab him," said the attorney.

"Bill Dalton is not in California."

The railroad attorney looked at Chris pityingly. "Our detectives are watching every step he takes."

"There's a mistake somewhere. He's not here."

"If he's not here, where is he?" said the attorney witheringly.

"In Kingfisher, Oklahoma."

"What makes you think so?"

"Because I talked to him there on my way here."

"Do you know him?"

"I do."

"I'll wire my chief of detectives. I think that will settle that. Come back in an hour."

When the time came, the lawyer looked at Chris triumphantly. "I've heard from my chief. He shadowed Bill Dalton last night. Maybe you'll want to revise your Kingfisher statement."

"I'll stand on my statement."

Another detective was put on the job and turned up what had really happened: Bill knew the detectives were following him, so he went to a store and bought an unusually "loud" suit of clothes. He hired a horse and buggy, and, each evening, drove with his wife through a timbered section, the detectives creeping along behind ready to pounce on Grat. This went on night after night—no Grat, no pounce. Bill Dalton got a man to put on the loud suit and drive out of an evening with Bill's wife. The detectives followed the suit—and found the wrong man in it. Bill, meantime, was on his way to Oklahoma in a suit that fitted his modest nature.

All hands turned out to bring Grat to his knees. Chris went to the sheriff's office in Visalia, California. The sheriff had everything fixed up, he said. Grat had a hideaway in the woods where he was this very moment; all they had to do was to go grab him. Chris was dubious; the Daltons were clever and they were courageous, also dead shots.

A reformed outlaw called Doc Middleton had set the trap; he would take them to it and there Grat would be, surprised no end. The sheriff, the reformed outlaw, and Chris got into the spring wagon and started off to grab Grat.

The reformed outlaw stopped the team and pointed to a dugout across a ravine. "He's in the dugout. I'll hold the horses while you go and get him," he said helpfully. Chris and the sheriff advanced through the timber and brush and there, sure enough, was a dugout, half in the ground, half out, the top covered with canvas, the logs thick enough to defend Geronimo. Chris crept up to one end of the dugout and the sheriff crept up to the other. The sheriff thrust his rifle through a notch in one of the logs and shouted, "Hands up, Grat! If you move, you're a dead man."

Nobody moved and there was no sound. The sheriff again shouted his warning. Then a voice peeped, "Don't shoot! Don't shoot!"

"Come out, Grat," the sheriff ordered, "with your hands up."

The man came out—a friend of Grat's. There was no charge against him and he was turned loose. What had happened was this: Grat had a dog which had barked and away had gone Grat like a greyhound himself.

Chris and the sheriff walked back to where the reformed outlaw was supposed to be holding the horses. But the man wasn't there. Chris and the sheriff set out on foot and finally caught up with him. The man said the horses had been nervous and he'd taken them where there would not be any shooting. He was a man who was kind and thoughtful to animals.

Grat and a friend of his named Bill McElhanie got on horses and started for Dover, Oklahoma. The trip took one hundred and seven days. Now for some fun.

The Dalton boys got busy organizing themselves into a band. They got together the finest outlaw band that had ever roamed the red hills of Oklahoma. Their roster: Bob Dalton, Grat Dalton, Emmett Dalton, Charlie Pierce, Bill McElhanie, Bitter Creek, Bill Doolin, Charlie Bryant, Bill Powers, Dick Broadwell.

Pitted against them were Chris and other trigger marshals. The teams would soon be on the playing field.

The first day of June 1892 found Chris in Kingfisher attending United States court. On this evening he and Judge Burford and the United States attorney were sitting in the lobby of the hotel, smoking and talking, when in sauntered Bill Dalton, at peace with the world and himself. Coming over to the three men, he told them who he was and began to talk with them. He kept the three amused with his stories which centered mostly around himself.

The big clock in the lobby struck. "Oh! It's ten o'clock," said Bill. "I'll have to hit the hay." The fascinating man told the three good night and left.

Arrangements were made for the three to have breakfast together. As they were sitting at the table, Bill Dalton breezed in and asked if he could join them. He talked as entertainingly as before. As they were talking a messenger arrived from the telegraph office in the depot in Kingfisher. The telegram was addressed to Chris. He opened it and read it. Handing it to Judge Burford, he said, "Read it aloud, Judge. I think it will interest all of us."

The telegram was from the chief of detectives for Wells Fargo, and said that the Santa Fe train had been held up at Red Rock at ten o'clock at night and robbed. "That's shocking," declared Bill. "I hope they're caught and punished." He was quite upset over this flouting of the law.

As a matter of fact, Bill was the lookout for the gang and wanted to know where Chris was so that he could warn the others. The men who committed the robbery were: Bob Dalton, Grat Dalton, Emmett Dalton, Dick Broadwell, Bill Doolin, Bitter Creek, Charlie Pierce, Bill Powers.

They were as tough men as you could scare up. The meanest, orneriest of all, however, wasn't there—Red Buck. Compared to him the others were choirboys with sweet, appealing faces and lovely haunting voices.

The telegram asked Chris if he would get on the trail. Chris decided that the outlaws would probably head for the hospitality of Riley's Ranch where wayfarers (if known) were treated so tenderly; and so Chris hopped a Rock Island train to Wichita; there he caught a Santa Fe train to Woodward Station, the nearest place to Papa Riley's. When he got there he learned that a posse had been sent by the Santa Fe direct to Woodward Station. The outlaws, however, escaped, and that was that. Chris found that he was two days behind the outlaws. He knew the case was hopeless and took the train for home. The train connections were such that it would be best for him to stay overnight in Winfield, Kansas, and so Chris climbed wearily into bed. Hardly was he in bed before there was a knock on the door.

It was a clerk with a telegram asking Chris to come to Guthrie to identify Bob Dalton. That was good news—the brains of the Daltons languishing behind the bars. Then an extraordinary story came forth, only such a story as Oklahoma Territory could produce in those wild days.

It centered around a woman spy for the Daltons using the

name Tom King. She was believed to be married to a man named Munday. The two cooked up a fascinating idea. There was a reward of one thousand dollars on Bob Dalton's head, dead or alive. She would lure some man to her home and so fascinate him with her charms that he would stay until she could get word to the officers that Bob Dalton was at her house; they knew that she was on friendly terms with Bob Dalton and would come on the run. She would instruct the man she was entertaining in her simple way to resist the officers. They, she told herself, would shoot him and she would get the reward for tipping off the law. On top of this, the clever woman arranged with the none-too-bright railroad agent to have a certified check ready the moment the man was identified as Bob Dalton.

She displayed her charms and got a man from Kansas to come to her house to get better acquainted. The man was all smiles, thinking of the fine conquest he'd made. As the two were enjoying each other's society there was a dreadful pounding on the door and in rushed two men under command of the city marshal.

"Defend yourself!" she said to her shocked admirer.

He had taken off his pistol, as the evening was warm, and he could not get his hands on it. When he saw the guns, all pointing at him, he began to blubber. "I haven't done anything wrong," he said. This had reference to pistol work.

The officers took him to jail, and there he was when Chris arrived, behind the bars, looking no more like Bob Dalton than he did like Grover Cleveland. "Please wire my father in Kansas to come and get me out," begged the poor man.

"I'll get you out," said Chris. "You're not Bob Dalton, so the officers will let you go free." The man got out—glad, no doubt, to get back to quiet, peaceful Kansas.

Nothing was done to Tom King. In fact, she continued to spy for the Daltons; they divided with her and she was considered a regular part of the band. She was adept at getting out of jails: she escaped from Oklahoma City, Guthrie, and El Reno. Chris arrested her three times. Once, as he arrested her, she said, "What's the name of the jailer where you're taking me?"

"Why do you want to know?" asked Chris.

"Every jailer in Oklahoma has his price. If I know which one this is, I'll know his price."

Later, Tom King reformed, gave up her wild days, got truly married, and settled down to a humdrum life.

In his ghost-written book, *When the Daltons Rode*, Emmett Dalton says that the Daltons got the following sums:

Whorton, January 1891	$14,000
Lelietta, September 15, 1891	$19,000
Red Rock, June 1, 1892	$11,000
Adair, July 14, 1892	$17,000

This is not to be believed; outlaws liked to tell what tremendous hauls they made; on the other hand, the railroads liked to play down the money. As an example, the Santa Fe said that at the Whorton affair the robbers got only fifteen hundred dollars—and so it goes. The truth was probably somewhere in between.

A further example of Emmett Dalton's romantic approach to writing is the beautiful love story he tells about himself and Julia Johnson. She was sixteen, he says, when he met and lost his heart to her. She waited faithfully fourteen years while he was in the penitentiary; as soon as he was out they were married and lived happily ever after. But she was hardly a white dove. The facts are these: she had had two husbands (both of whom were shot to death) before her ecstatic marriage to Emmett Dalton. One of her husbands was Ernest Lewis, a murderer. Once a newspaperman wrote something that reflected on Ernest Lewis. This so enraged her that she horsewhipped the newspaperman on the street. Otherwise she seems to have been a charming lass. Emmett wrote that she was his "first and last and only love." Julia seems not to have been quite so single-minded.

And so the days moved along for Chris, relieved only now and then by murder or a train robbery. When such a matter happened, off he would go, sometimes coming back victorious, other times with his leg irons in his satchel. And then came the astounding raid on two banks at the same time in Coffeyville, Kansas.

It has been told a thousand times that Bill Doolin did not go on the raid because his horse went lame. This is not quite accurate. After the unpleasant matter was over, Bill Doolin told Chris that he had had trouble with Bob Dalton over how the money had been divided after previous robberies. And so Bill did not even start; he remained at the Fitzgerald harboring place in Cowboy Flat, fifteen miles northeast of Guthrie. If he had gone, would the decision have changed things? Would he have fallen? Would the outlaws—with cool, clear-headed Bill Doolin to lead them—have triumphed? Nice speculations for the boys in the back room.

At noon on that sorry day Chris was sitting alone in his office in Guthrie. The other marshals had gone to dinner. A messenger from the depot dashed in and handed Chris a telegram from the mayor of Coffeyville: "An attempt has been made by the Daltons to rob two banks. Our citizens are fighting them in the streets. Three of the robbers have been killed, one has been captured but is so badly wounded he may die before night. One escaped and started, on a fast horse, toward the Oklahoma state line. Please try to capture him, if he reaches Oklahoma."

Chris took up a blank and wrote out a message to all the deputies in Oklahoma to be on the watch. Before he finished, the messenger was back with another telegram from the mayor. This one said that the outlaw who had escaped had been found dead.

Then the message added: "The one we captured is Emmett Dalton."

Chris called the two newspapers in Guthrie and told them that if they would send reporters he would have news for them. The papers did not wait for the regular editions; soon newsboys were going down the streets whooping out the news. Hardly were the extras on the street before Bill Dalton walked into Chris's office. But now he was not his jaunty, talkative, confident self. "Is it true what the papers say?"

"Yes."

"I wish you would find out if I can go to Coffeyville and take my mother with me," said the very much subdued Bill Dalton.

Chris wired the mayor. In a few minutes the answer was back. If the two would report to him as soon as they arrived in town, he would give them protection.

Here is the harvest of those five minutes on the streets of Coffeyville:

KILLED

Outlaws	Officers and citizens
Bob Dalton	Lucius Baldwin
Grat Dalton	George Cubbins
Dick Broadwell	Charles F. Brown
Bill Powers	Charles T. Connelly

WOUNDED

Emmett Dalton	Charlie Gump

Emmett Dalton's strange point of view about the whole matter should be set down. When he came out of the penitentiary he gave an interview in which he blamed the cashier of the bank for the death of the eight men. Logician Dalton said that if the cashier had not lied about the safe being time-locked, the bandits would have taken the money and quietly departed. This was Emmett Dalton's mind at work.

Coffeyville, in effect, was the end of the Dalton Gang. But not quite. Three of its most lethal members were still roaming—Bill Doolin, Charlie Pierce, and Bitter Creek. Soon they got together and organized the Doolin Gang which made the Dalton Gang look like a group of kindhearted deacons.

CHAPTER 19

Chris Tries to Capture the Doolin Gang, a Man-Sized Job

It was a contest between Bill Doolin and Bill Dalton as to which would be the leader of the new band that was being organized. Glib-talking Bill Dalton had never been much more than a spy for the Dalton Gang; he was never in where the lead was singing. So the boys voted to make Bill Doolin the leader. He had been born in Arkansas, the son of a poverty-stricken farmer. He was tall and rangy, with boyish freckles and huge, knobby knuckles. He had little education, but he had courage and was a natural leader of men. He had worked for Oscar D. Halsell on the H-X-Bar Ranch in Cowboy Flat in the Cimarron Valley. When this section was opened to settlement, his job was gone. Some of the deposed cowboys peddled whisky to the Indians; some picked up mavericks; some became wood haulers. But their legs were shaped to the saddle. The cowboys began drifting about the country like tumbleweeds. They would meet and "talk"—the usual conversation was about how much money the banks and railroads had. The end was inevitable.

The following sprightly gentlemen made up the new gang: Bill Doolin, Bill Dalton, Tulsa Jack, Charlie Pierce, Little Bill Raidler, Little Dick West, Bob Grounds, Dynamite Dick, Arkansas Tom, Alf Sohn, Red Buck, Ol Yantis, Bitter Creek.

It will be seen that four of them had taken prep-school work at the Dalton Academy; now they were going off to the Doolin School for Specialized Study. They immediately settled down to business, performing brilliantly at Whorton, Spearville, and Cimarron, Kansas. Everything was going just fine.

The Cimarron robbery was May 28, 1893. Marshal Grimes was to be removed from office June 30 of this year. He had become discouraged and gone to his farm at Kingfisher, leaving Chris in charge of the office. And so, all of a sudden, the Cimarron affair came down on top of Chris. He must act and act quickly. Word came in from his informers that the outlaws were headed for Oklahoma and seemingly were going to cross the Cimarron River at Deep Hole, not far from Ashland, Kansas, and would probably enter Oklahoma about where Buffalo is now located. There was no time to organize a reception committee. What was he to do? He managed it rather nicely. He wired the commanding officer at Fort Supply, Oklahoma, to get him a posse of Indian scouts and to send them to Woodward Station as fast as horseflesh could take them. And then Chris mounted the train and was soon at Woodward. When he looked out of the window he saw a lovely sight—a posse of Indian scouts and some soldiers from the fort. On inquiry, however, he found that the soldiers could be used only on the Indian reservation and that the Indian scouts were not too eager to come face to face with the outlaws.

Beggars are not choosers and so with his haphazard posse Chris started for the place where the outlaws would probably cross into Oklahoma. The soldiers had fine, well-groomed mounts; the Indians had rough-looking ponies that no one would give a second glance. But when the two groups got to the place, the soldiers' fine horses were pooped, while the Indian ponies were going great guns.

The Indian scouts took a turn around and came back with the information that four mounted men were traveling south. Chris got his men going, and, by keeping to swales and low places, managed to get ahead of the outlaws. The outlaws looked startled when they saw the posse, but not so startled they couldn't shoot. The two groups exchanged amenities. The outlaws didn't take the matter too seriously, for the Indians and soldiers had fowling pieces last used by Robinson Crusoe. But it was different with Chris; he had a new 30-30 Winchester that shot a steel-jacketed bullet. This was one of the first guns to employ a steel bullet and had a longer range than the rifles using the lead ball. Chris began zipping away. He had a piece of luck: he whanged Bill Doolin in the foot. As soon as their leader was wounded, the outlaws got out of there at once and forthwith. (Chris didn't know it then, but Bill Doolin went to Jim Riley's harboring place where he was nursed by Arkansas Tom.)

The outlaws divided and rode in separate directions. Soon the Indian trackers were no longer able to follow the trail, and so Chris called his men off and let them go back to Fort Supply. The bandits had escaped but it had shown them that the law was becoming a formidable factor.

Where had the outlaws gone? They were like fireflies which put on a brilliant display for a moment, then disappear. The men had gone to the Dunn Ranch near Ingalls, Oklahoma. The dugout itself was in the upper end of a ravine and was fortified with rock walls. The top of the dugout was level with the ground and was covered with dirt. It was so adroitly constructed that coming up to the ravine from the open country, one could walk over it without knowing it was there. Holes had been cut in the door so that men inside could shoot down anybody who got nosy. Inside, there was a fireplace and a cookstove; and there was a storeroom that would hold enough provisions for a siege. On two walls were tiers of beds—six beds in all—and on the wall of each bed were straps for holding a rifle. If, during the night, the occupant of the bed was disturbed, he could reach over and make his presence felt.

The situation, in Oklahoma Territory, had become so intolerable that the United States Attorney General, operating through Marshal E. D. Nix, sent for Chris and told him to drive the bandits out of the Territory, and please be quick about it. Two men were chosen—Heck Thomas and Bill Tilghman. The Attorney General placed money to Chris's credit in the bank at Chandler, Oklahoma. This town was chosen because it was in the heart of banditland and the officers could get their money quick. No sending to Washington now. Chris and his men were ready to talk business with the bandits.

A team and a covered wagon were engaged; covered wagons were constantly moving through the Territory; this one would attract no more attention than a rabbit in a briar patch. Tucked away in the wagon were five men, all supposed to be dead shots and brave as lions. Surveying instruments were also placed in the wagons. The men were supposed to be surveyors busily going about their business of locating a new railroad.

Chris had heard from one of his spotters that the bandits were at Ingalls, living on the fat of the land. Well, their diet would be changed. To avert suspicion, the Three Guardsmen left at different times—Bill first, Heck second, then Chris himself, Chris on horseback earnestly looking for the railroad surveyors. The men were to meet near Jennings, Oklahoma, where the spotter lived. As Chris got near the appointed place he saw a boy plowing in the field.

"Did you see a wagon go by here yesterday?" he called.

"Yes. I couldn't figger out who they were."

"They were surveyors laying out a new railroad." After talking a few moments, Chris asked if there were any outlaws in this section.

"There sure is. They're thick as beans in a hill."

Chris talked about the surveying party, not interested at all in the outlaws, then rode on. Information was given to Chris that the Doolin outlaws were living at the Dunn Ranch. Chris and his men would call on them. Chris caught up with the wagon. To avert suspicion, Chris had his men take out a transit compass and a theodolite and set them up. The men peeped and squinted and looked, anxious to locate the railroad in exactly the right spot. Then they drove some pegs, thus nailing the railroad down. They knew a thousand eyes would be watching them, so that evening they built a roaring fire and sat around it, discussing the baffling details of railroad construction.

That night, at midnight, the men got up, mounted their horses, and set out for the Dunn Ranch, a distance of ten miles. When they got within a mile of the ranch they tied their horses and went on foot, moving as silently as Indians, guns at hair trigger. There, in the night, loomed the sleeping ranch house. Chris divided his men so they could attack the dugout from two directions. Heck had four sticks of dynamite; his simple task was to blow off the roof. Chris and Bill Tilghman, as leaders of the posse, went to the front door.

Chris fired his pistol and shouted at the top of his sergeant's voice. "Come mit your hands oop or ve vill blow you oudt." It was soon evident that none of them wanted to be "blown oudt," for there was a great shouting and the sound of men banging about in the dugout. "Hurry oop!" shouted Chris. "Ve are officers of the law." Then he sent a shot through the door to indicate they were not there socially.

The door was flung open and five men came tumbling out, their drawers down, their hands up. One of the possemen lit a lantern. Never did peace officers get a bigger shock. The five were merely low-down horse thieves—not one was a member of the Doolin Gang. The Doolin men had not been in the dugout at all and had completely escaped.

Chris was downright mad. "Which one of you is the cook?" he asked.

"I am," replied one of the men.

"Well, you're going to get a chance to cook right now. Fix breakfast for us." The cook kindly complied.

The reason the Doolin outlaws were so hard to bring in shows how matters were at this time in the Territory. The outlaws had friends who watched the marshals and told the outlaws what was happening. These friends were so clever that they were able to find out when the deputy marshals were going to make a raid, then would rush the word to the outlaws. Sometimes such a spy would ride until his horse was ready to drop. Sometimes the word would be brought by a woman—sometimes a sweetheart, or the wife of one of the outlaws. And thus the game between marshals and outlaws went on.

After breakfast the posse discovered that the trail left by the outlaws led toward Tulsa, and off went the deputies, eager to catch up with the tricky Doolins. Heck and Bill Tilghman went on one side of the Cimarron River; Chris, with some of his men, took the other side.

The bandits had separated. Part of the posse followed one of the trails; others of the posse rode another trail. Each of the trails grew thin; finally the officers gave up and went home. No outlaw had been killed, none captured, but it showed the outlaws that the deputies meant business. In fact, the outlaws hid away for a year, committing no deviltry at all. And when they did get ready for work they went outside the state—to Southwest City, Missouri. Even their next job was outside the state—this one at Longview, Texas. When they opened their grain sack, their hearts fluttered like daffodils, for in the bag was fifty thousand dollars in bills. When they looked more closely, they saw that the bills had not been signed by the president of the bank and were just so much wallpaper. Their hearts dropped back to normal.

This fitted into their next move in an unexpected way. Chris was in Anadarko, Oklahoma, and was talking with the Indian agent in his house late one night. Suddenly there was a pounding on the door. When the agent opened it, six Indians were outside. Usually Indians show no sense of alarm, but these did. They said that one of the Indians had not returned home. His name was Inkanish, and he was an Indian policeman. The reason the Indians were so concerned was that outlaws had been seen in the neighborhood.

The Indians asked Chris if he would go with them to help find Inkanish. Chris said he had no horse. This was no problem, for Indians always have horses. It was not long until Chris was on a horse and riding into the night. The guide was Inkanish's son, a boy fourteen years old. The boy led the group to the place where his father had last been seen. It was now daylight. In a few minutes the Indians found the tracks of horses—the outlaws' —and there, among them, were the tracks of an unshod horse—Inkanish's. And with the horse were the tracks of a colt.

Off went Chris and the Indians as fast as they could go. The boy soon began to weep silently, after the way of Indians.

"What's the matter, son?" asked Chris.

It was a moment before the boy could speak. "Look!" he said, pointing at the ground. Chris could see only the mare's tracks. The boy continued to weep. Finally he said, "My father's horse has a dead weight on it."

"How can you tell?"

"Horse no walk straight." They rode on, the boy weeping. About a mile farther on they came upon the mare; she had been shot. The colt was standing beside the body. The boy wept louder.

The men rode on again, soon coming upon the body of Inkanish. He had been wearing a uniform with a row of buttons down the front of the coat. The bandits had placed the muzzles of their guns near the buttons and fired. There was a series of holes in his body from the neck down, following the line made by the buttons. The outlaws had killed him, placed his body on the mare, which had made the animal walk a bit out of line, and this the sharp eyes of the Indian boy had detected. The bandits had been taking the body to a canyon, there to drop it, but had become pressed by the posse. They solved this by abandoning the body, killing the mare, and riding on. Inkanish had not been looking for them. To them he represented the law. Kill him. It was that simple, and the outlaws were that inhuman.

The posse put the body on a horse ridden by one of the men, and took it home to the Indian wife. She looked at it stolidly for some moments, then began to weep silently, just as the boy had done.

Chris left the posse, took the train to Hennessey, picked up another posse, and rode for a hay crossing above Dover on the Cimarron. The outlaws did not come, but soon a man arrived driving a spring wagon. To Chris he had every appearance of a man expecting to pick up a wounded man. The man was Rattlesnake Bill, rightly named. Chris knew there was a warrant of arrest out for him and took him into custody. Rattlesnake Bill was tried and sent to the penitentiary where he rattled for six years, then died. There were no mourners.

Chris had lost the Doolin Gang trail, but he had thrown fear of the law into them. The Doolins hid for twelve months with never a peep, then—

CHAPTER 20

The Dover Train Robbery. The End Comes to Bitter Creek.

In April 1895 Chris was living in El Reno and all was well. Life was going on about as usual: now and then the arrest of a whisky peddler, or a wood stealer, or a post-office thief. Now and then somebody broke into a store; now and then a couple of citizens whanged away at each other. That was the way it was until—

There was the sound of running feet, then a knock at the door. When Chris opened the door, there was one of the men from the depot with a telegram. The telegram got right down to business. "The Rock Island train at Dover is being held up."

In about two jumps Chris was at the depot in El Reno, pistoled and carbined, ready to go after his old friend Bill Doolin. Among the men in the Doolin Gang was Red Buck, who got the first part of his name from the color of his hair; Buck had been taken over from the Indians. He had killed four men; that is, that number had been counted. His real name was George Weightman. Everything considered, he was the meanest, the most heartless of all Doolin's boys.

Another gay blade was Bitter Creek. He was from Texas. He had come to the Cherokee Strip in the days when all the land was leased by cattlemen. His name was George Newcomb. He was a big boisterous boy who liked to sing; his favorite was a song that went:

I'm a wild wolf from Bitter Creek
And it's my night to howl.

He sang it so much that the other men began to call him Bitter Creek. And Bitter Creek he lived and died. And what a death it was!

Another trait of his was that he liked to play Indian poker. When there was a roundup and the men were together, they would spread a horse blanket on the ground and proceed to deal 'em. Bitter Creek, especially, liked these wild, noisy games; he was a harum-scarum and "the life of the party."

He met Rose E. Dunn at a country dance and he named her The Rose of Cimarron. She had been born near Winfield, Kansas, September 5, 1878, and had gone to a convent for two years. The family was not Catholic, but the best schools were Catholic, and so Rose Dunn had gone to one of them. She returned to her father's house, a few miles from Ingalls, Oklahoma. Her father died and her mother married Dr. Stephen Call, who lived in Ingalls. Some of the time Rose was at her stepfather's, some of the time at the home of her brothers. Now, very briefly, the Ingalls Fight:

September 1, 1893, thirteen deputies closed in on the Doolin-Dalton Gang in Ingalls. Rose Dunn was at the City Hotel visiting Mrs. Mary Pierce, the owner, when the battle between the officers and the outlaws began.

Bitter Creek was on his horse, riding along the street, when Deputy United States Marshal Lute Houston fired—fired so successfully that he knocked Bitter Creek off his horse. And as

Rose looked out of the window she saw him lying in the street. She saw, too, that he had only his pistol.

"I'm going to take him his rifle and ammunition belt," said Rose.

"You'll do no such thing," said Mary Pierce sharply. "You would be shot down instantly. The town is full of deputies."

"He must have help."

Grabbing his rifle and belt, Rose started out, but Mary Pierce seized her and struggled with the half-crazed girl. Shots were coming from her own hotel—Arkansas Tom, in an upper room, was firing at the officers. While Mary's attention was distracted, Rose darted up the stairs and looked out of the window. Bitter Creek was still lying in the street.

Snatching two sheets off the bed, she knotted them together, let them hang outside the window, and then, holding the rifle and ammunition, she started to slide down the white, treacherous length.

She ran, as soon as she was on the ground, toward the stricken man, bobbing along as best she could with the rifle and belt. The officers, seeing such courage, stopped firing.

She gave Bitter Creek his rifle. He struggled feebly, but was too weak to fire. Bill Dalton, who had been firing from the stable, came running out, leading Bitter Creek's horse. He handed the reins to Rose, who tried to hold the frightened, pitching horse. While she was doing this, Bill Dalton helped Bitter Creek into the saddle. Rose, still holding the reins, ran into the stable, leading the horse. Bill Dalton seized Bitter Creek's rifle and began to fire at the officers. Once more the battle was on.

When the rifle was exhausted, Dalton ran into the stable where Rose was holding the trembling horse, mounted a horse himself, and the two men rode out the back door, Dalton half supporting Bitter Creek. They rode toward the swale till they came to the road. To their dismay they saw a wire fence. Outlaws were usually equipped with cutters, and so now Bill Dalton whipped out his pair and started to cut the wires. At this moment Lafe Shadley, one of the officers, came running up to get a close shot. Dalton stopped, raised his rifle . . . it was the end of a heroic officer. Four died that day in the streets of that little town. It was a more deadly fight than the one at the O. K. Corral in Tombstone.

Another member of the gang was Charlie Pierce, who was a scowling, thick-chested man who looked like a stand-in for a gorilla. He wore his hair long and always seemed to be chewing tobacco. Now and then he would blow the chewed-up mess from his mouth, then haul out a batch of fresh tobacco and begin on that. He looked more like an outlaw than any other member of the Doolin-Dalton Gang. And he lived up to his looks.

Another standard bearer was Tulsa Jack, who had ambitions but hadn't got to the top in outlawry. Still, Jack was on his way up. Two murders could be laid at his door. There might have been more, but Tulsa Jack was always shifting his door. Indeed, a great deal of the time he didn't have a door at all, for he was hiding in caves and accepting other simple accommodations. His real name was Jack Blake, but to the trade he was Tulsa Jack. Perhaps it should be pointed out that there is no monument to him in Tulsa.

These were the kind friends and gentle hearts that Chris was going to bring in—seven in all. Chris got eleven possemen lined up. Stories of the rugged West sometimes tell how impressively a posseman was sworn in; such stories are not true, at least in Chris's case. He didn't pin a star on a man and tell him he was now a deputy marshal; in fact, Chris did not carry any silver stars. He merely said, "Come with me," and that was the end of the graduation exercises. Chris knew who could be used as possemen; the man must have a horse, revolver, and a rifle.

Some of the men did not take their duties too seriously; they liked the excitement—and they liked those two dollars a day.

The twelve men, counting Chris, gathered at the depot in El Reno, ready for what the night might bring forth. The regular passenger train from the South arrived at four in the morning; a boxcar was attached to the end of the train and the men got their horses into the car. The possemen went into the smoker and visited, talking and exchanging news, for in a way an outlaw chase was a kind of floating party. Who was sick? Who had traded horses? Who'd been born?

It was thirty-five miles to Dover; at dawn the passenger train arrived, with the boxcar bobbing along behind. The car was backed up to an embankment, the door was opened, and the horses made to jump. In a few moments the train was chugging off. In a few moments the posse would have to go chugging off, too.

Two things must be done at once: the horses must be fed and information gathered as to which direction the outlaws had taken. People told Chris and his henchmen that the outlaws had ridden west. Chris also found what had happened when the train had been held up. It had been a carefully planned affair, manned by experts, but it hadn't worked. Its failure had made the bandits as mad as yellow-legged hornets.

When the train pulled into Dover, two men had silently climbed into the tender; as soon as the train pulled out, the two men—Winchesters in hand—displayed themselves to the engineer and fireman and told them to stop the train a mile south of town, which would be a lonely, deserted spot surrounded by scrubby blackjack timber. The engineer and fireman said they would oblige.

When the train stopped, the passengers poked their heads out of the windows to see what was the matter; whereupon there was a terrific discharge of artillery. The passengers got their heads back in quicker than snapping turtles. The door to the express car was standing open. As the robbers approached, the messenger closed the door—a mistake, for the bandits began firing through it and through the sides of the car, wounding the messenger twice. Only then did he open the door. Three men crawled in. They were after a rich shipment of gold on the way to Fort Worth to pay off army troops.

"Open that safe," one of the robbers said to the wounded man.

"I can't. It's a through safe. It was locked in Kansas City and can't be opened till we get to Fort Worth when a key is brought."

"I tell you to open it," bellowed the bandit, firing a shot near the messenger's feet.

"I tell you I can't. It's an impossibility."

"Then open the other safe."

The messenger opened it. It was a way safe and had no money in it.

"Bring the engineer and fireman and tell them to open the through safe," said the leader.

The two men were helped up and set to work on the ponderous affair. They immediately broke a drill bit. They replaced it and set to work again. The second drill bit broke. The robbers watched, growing more and more nervous. Another drill bit broke. At the end of thirty minutes the hole was less than half an inch deep.

"I think we'd better get out," said one of the robbers thoughtfully. The men jumped down and ordered the engineer and fireman to get down, too. Then one of the men conducted the two to the cab where he held them prisoners.

The bandits must get money. Out came the trusty grain sack. They called the colored porter. "Take this and we'll see what's in the passenger cars," one said. "I hope to God we do better," he added with understandable fervor.

One robber walked close behind the porter; the other robber

walked in front of the porter but walked backward so he could see that no one behind the first man got ugly. "You people throw in your money and jewelry," ordered one of the robbers, and down the aisle the three went to collect the free-will offerings.

The passengers began to secrete their wallets and watches, hiding them between seats; those nearest the stove pushed them under it. The bandits could not watch every movement and so did not see what the people were up to. One of the passengers was William Grimes, the man who had hired Chris away from the army. He put his gold watch on the floor and edged it under the stove with his foot, where it ticked cheerily. When the grain sack came, Grimes held up one dollar and forty cents in small coins and said, "I'm just getting back from a trip and this is all I have."

"Put it in," said the heartless robber. Former Marshal Grimes put it in. The robber looked more closely at Grimes. "Don't Chris Madsen work for you?"

"He was my chief deputy."

"Tell him we're goin' to get him."

The grain-sack procession proceeded down the aisle, the people contributing according to their means. Later, when the free contributions were counted up, they were found to amount to four hundred dollars and a peck of watches and jewelry, Grimes's watch not included.

The robbers, mad as hungry buzzards, had to give up their idea of a better tomorrow, and told the engineer and fireman to get out of there and take the train with them. In a few minutes the train was rumbling down the track; inside the coaches the passengers were telling each other about the huge sums they'd lost.

The trail led northwest, and soon Chris and his crowd were pounding down it. They followed it twenty miles, then saw where it turned off the road and into a farmer's lane and to his house, which was set back from the highway. Chris turned in, too, and was told, as he expected, that the robbers had been there. Not only that, but they had had breakfast. This gave Chris an idea.

"Can you fix us up with lunch?" The obliging farmer said he could. It wasn't long before the men were chomping away out of the plates that the farmer's wife had supplied. When the meal was over, Chris asked how much he owed.

"Fifty cents a head." Chris paid. The farmer stood expectantly. "The men who were here for breakfast said they were a posse chasing train robbers and that another posse would be along pretty soon and would come here for lunch. They said your posse would pay for both. There were five of them, which would run it up two dollars and a half more."

Chris was flabbergasted by the effrontery of the bandits who not only knew that he and his men were coming but were having fun out of it. Chris decided that maybe at some future time he could get information from the farmer, so he let him continue to believe the first were possemen, paid the bill, and clopped down the road.

Chris found that the outlaw gang had inquired about a Russian settlement near the Cimarron River, and had ridden off in that direction. After them Chris and his men went. Darkness came and the men went into camp for the night. At daylight they were off again on the trail. And then they discovered, from certain signs, something that made them blink: the night before the outlaws had secreted themselves behind high banks where a hay crossing had been cut through, and had lain in wait. If Chris and his men had come along, they would have been shot down. On such small decisions depended the life of a marshal in those wild days.

Later, Doolin was being tried in Guthrie, and, as deputy marshal, it was Chris's duty to take him to dinner at a restaurant, which Chris did with a leg iron on Doolin. "I thank you for this meal," said Doolin. "I'm glad I didn't shoot you down at the hay crossing."

Chris divided his men. He led his own squad along the Cimarron River, eyes alert for crossings, in case the outlaws had doubled back. A group under Deputy William Banks set off on the trail. They had gone only a few miles when they came to the top of a knoll; nearby was a patch of timber and there, tied at its edge, were the outlaws' horses; the men themselves were lying on the ground asleep. Over them was a guard—Tulsa Jack himself. Deputy Banks, who was in the lead, sighted Tulsa Jack at the same moment as Tulsa Jack saw him. Tulsa Jack fired a shot as a warning to the sleeping men. Instantly the men were on their feet, but when they saw the deputies they flung themselves on the ground, and so did the deputies. A pitched battle began, one of the hottest ever fought in Oklahoma. The battle raged for three hours among the sand hills, from behind clumps of bushes, and in gullies and draws—both bandits and officers dodging from one protection to another. The outlaws were fearless and fought as bravely as any law-enforcement officer.

Tulsa Jack, who had fired the warning shot, had a bit of bad luck—a bullet hit and exploded a cartridge in his belt, ending his career then and there. It's not carved in stone who killed Tulsa Jack, but this much is known: Wells Fargo Express Company presented Chris with two .45 Colt pearl-handled, nickel-plated revolvers with his name engraved on the top of the handles and a washtubful of ammunition. To be accurate, the gifts may have been because Chris was in command of the posse.

The battle over, the outlaws got on their horses, worked their way through the timber, and escaped. The peace officers now had time to examine the crumpled body on the ground. They did not know who it was. Deputy Banks decided to take it to Hennessey for identification. A spring wagon was engaged from a farmer and the body put into it; the farmer was told to drive, and off across the flatlands of Oklahoma moved the strange procession, the men talking in low voices in the presence of death, the horses clearing their nostrils, the spring wagon creaking. The procession arrived at Hennessey at eleven at night. The body was left in the spring wagon in the street. Early the next morning the word spread, and a crowd came. They lifted the blanket and peered at the body but could not identify it. Banks again started the spring wagon, taking the body to El Reno where it was placed in the Ferris Undertaking Parlor. But none could identify it. The following morning the spring wagon again started on the move; this time the body was taken to Oklahoma City. The exciting news of an unidentified outlaw had spread, and hundreds of people came to view the body. About noon that day a ranchman, H. R. Whitset, viewed the body. "I know him," he said. "He was one of the cowboys on my ranch near Sterling, Kansas. He disappeared four years ago. I never knew what happened to him. He is Tulsa Jack. His real name is Blake."

This was exciting news, indeed, for there was a reward of nine thousand dollars on the man's head. No one was able to collect it, for a posse, receiving wages for pursuing an outlaw, was not allowed to collect reward money.

Meanwhile, Chris was pursuing the rest of the gang like a hornet. There was a hopeful sign: the number of horses, as shown by the hoofprints, had gone down from five to four; then a horse was discovered dead. The bandits were having to double up. Good news.

The next morning, April 6, Chris saw that the bandits had turned from the main road into a lane that led to a house. As Chris came up he heard a woman weeping. On seeing that Chris was an officer, she wept more copiously than ever, saying, "The outlaws have killed my husband. He is in there dead." She pointed to a room in the house. "We brought him in from the horse lot."

The man who had been killed was a Swedish preacher named Godfrey. The author of the tragedy was the cruel and inhuman Red Buck. His horse had been killed and he had been forced to ride double. Desperately in need of a horse and saddle, he walked to the horse lot where he saw the preacher. "I want that horse."

"It is not mine to give," said the minister. "It belongs to my son who is not present."

"I need a horse and I'm goin' to take it whether you like it or not."

"I will not let you take my son's horse."

"I'll see whether you will or not," said Red Buck, and shot the preacher dead. Going to the barn, Red Buck calmly got a saddle and rode up to the other outlaws who had heard and seen all that had happened.

Bill Doolin, plenty tough himself, was so enraged by what Red Buck had done that Doolin motioned for the men to ride out of sight of the house. When this was done, he equally divided the train money. "You could have taken that horse without harming anyone, yet you killed that fine old man. You are no longer riding with us. We're going to leave and don't you try to come with us. If you do, we'll kill you."

They rode off, leaving Red Buck on his stolen horse. Red Buck's cruelty depressed the men. In their code it was all right to kill a man in a robbery, or a man who was threatening them, but it was wrong to kill an innocent, unarmed man. The men rode silently. Bitter Creek and Charlie Pierce let the others go ahead, then talked to each other in low tones. Spurring their horses, they caught up with the other men. "We're pullin' out, Bill," said one of them.

"Why?"

"It's too much for us."

After a few more words the two men rode off together. The other outlaws divided. Some headed for Riley's snug harbor, some to Cowboy Flat, and some to Ingalls, Oklahoma, where outlaws were thicker than dandelions on a widow's lawn.

For Chris, the trail was becoming more and more difficult, for the outlaws were reaching the Gloss Mountains. These rugged hills—not really mountains—were covered with a form of gypsum which gave them a glossy appearance. The sand and dust were deep, and the wind was brisk. In a few hours a horse's trail was lost to sight. Knowing that he was now playing a losing game, Chris abandoned the trail and started back to El Reno. It was a bitter defeat, but one, it should be said, that might happen to any deputy under similar circumstances.

He rode up in front of his house, and, as he did so, the door was thrown open and out came Maggie, weeping for joy; with her were the two children, Marion and Reno, the latter now quite a husky lad. Maggie had a reason to be weeping for joy, for word had just been brought to her that Chris had been killed. But here he was, alive and kicking. It was a fine, a wonderful, rewarding moment.

The problem now was to bring the outlaws to their knees. Heck Thomas and Bill Tilghman were given the job. The two constantly worked together. Often Chris Madsen joined them—to form the Three Guardsmen, indeed the three greatest man hunters Oklahoma had ever known. All dead shots—Chris had four marksmanship medals. Neither Heck nor Bill had won a medal, for at that time no official medals were given in Oklahoma for marksmanship. It will be remembered that Chris walked off with his in army contests.

Off the two rode, their heads high, their pistols low. Meanwhile, Bitter Creek and Charlie Pierce—the two most deadly men in Oklahoma—rode along together. There was a reward on their heads and there was glory for anyone who would bring them in. Few, it must be said, wanted to try. But Heck Thomas and Bill Tilghman did.

A new element enters: the Dunn Ranch—the most notorious harboring place in the timbered section near the Cimarron River. Sometimes travelers stayed overnight. If they seemed to have money, they never got back to the road again, so said the people. There were four of the Dunn brothers, each one tougher than his brother.

Bitter Creek and Charlie Pierce headed for the Dunn Ranch. The Dunn brothers owed Bitter Creek nine hundred dollars. There was a reward on Bitter Creek's head of five thousand dollars. The two men jogged along, eager to get to their friends. They stopped at farmhouses for meals, paying liberally, passing themselves off as cattle buyers. Sometimes they slept in a farmer's house, sometimes in the barn. But always they were moving toward the Dunn Ranch. Bitter Creek was especially eager to get there, for Rose would be there, he thought.

Also jogging in the direction of the Dunn Ranch were Heck Thomas and Bill Tilghman. The two arrived there and waited for two days, then hired the Dunn brothers to watch for Pierce and Bitter Creek, and to report. Then Heck and Bill Tilghman rode off to another ranch where they were staying.

This was the night it happened, the night that Pierce and Bitter Creek came riding up to the Dunn house. They arrived at midnight. Before them were the faint outlines of the Dunn house. The two unsaddled, put their horses in the stable, and started for the gate that led to the house of their friends. The guns of the two brothers flashed and Bitter Creek and Charlie Pierce fell. The Dunns were still not satisfied; one of them fired again, the buckshot hitting Charlie Pierce in the soles of his feet as he lay groaning on the ground. The Dunn brothers inspected the two lying on the ground, then went calmly to bed.

According to Frank Canton, who was a deputy sheriff at Pawnee, Oklahoma, this is what happened next. The next morning the Dunn brothers hitched up the spring wagon, dumped the bodies into it, covered them with a tarpaulin, and two of them, John and Dal, started for Guthrie. They were moving briskly along when they thought they heard a noise under the tarpaulin. But that was impossible. Then they looked again. The tarpaulin was moving. Leaning back, one of them lifted it and there, under it, was Bitter Creek coming to life.

The brothers were flabbergasted. How could it be? But Bitter Creek was alive and begging for water. So they shot him again. Satisfied that he was dead, they spread the tarpaulin back in place and moved swiftly down the road toward Guthrie.

Meanwhile, Heck Thomas and Bill Tilghman returned with a posse, expecting by this time that Bitter Creek and Charlie Pierce would be at the Dunns'. They were surprised to find that the men had been killed. The Dunns claimed the reward money. There was so much hard feeling that Chris withdrew from the sorry mess. He might have claimed some of the money, for he had furnished the information that led to the killing of Pierce and Bitter Creek.

When they were examined it was found that Charlie Pierce wore blue overalls, a calico shirt, a string tie, and the spurs and high-heeled boots that all cowboys wore. Around his waist was a cartridge belt, half empty; in his pockets, twenty-six shells. Also in his pockets were a folding knife, a dirk, some loose coins —and a rabbit's foot.

Bitter Creek also wore blue overalls, a calico shirt, boots and spurs—no rabbit's foot. His pockets contained a deck of playing cards, a hand mirror, a comb, smoking tobacco, and sixteen packets of papers for rolling cigarettes, and enough cartridges— both pistol and rifle—to fight a pitched battle. In his saddlebag holster was a Winchester that had been shattered in the stock—evidently the work of the Dunn brothers.

After the coroner's examination there were no claimants for the bodies, so off they went to potter's field which was proving to be the last home of so many ex-cowboys.

The dream of easy money that the Dunn brothers had been engaging in did not quite work out. There was such indignation against them a mob formed and there was talk of hanging them on the streets of Guthrie. The two men skittled back to their happy home, but even here the angry citizens followed. The two were watched so carefully that they couldn't steal cattle, a sad situation. Finally Bill Dunn, who had taken up the highland cross, went to Pawnee to kill Frank Canton whom he blamed for the whole mess. He started to kill him, but was a trifle slow on the draw and fell in the street, the trigger finger of his right hand still working.

CHAPTER 21

One by One They Are "Brought in." The Dugout of Death.

CHRIS WAS IN over-all command of the forces trying to bring in Bill Doolin. Would he succeed? Would the elusive Bill come to heel?

The loss of those stalwarts—Tulsa Jack, Bitter Creek, and Charlie Pierce—was a severe one. Other men wanted to join, but they were untried. They might even be traitors. There was the reward money that rested on every Doolin head.

Little Bill was one of the remaining stalwarts. His last name was Raidler and he had been born in Pennsylvania of a good family. His small size had made him sensitive; to get away from taunts, he had come to Oklahoma where he could be a cowboy and carry a pistol. It was not long before he joined the Doolin Gang—now he could give orders. People had to hop when he gave the word. But hop makers have to pay a price for their position, and that price was adding up against Little Bill.

One Bill Tilghman was on his trail—bad news for a bad man. In January 1895 Bill Tilghman got out the faithful spring wagon and his traveling mules; they were small but fast and they were tough. He used a spring wagon because if he got an outlaw, either alive or dead, it would hold him. And he took a camp outfit, this for roadside meals. He had friends all over the Territory, and usually could manage it so he could spend the night with one of them. Sometimes he also was able to pick up news of men on the dodge.

This day he took with him Neal Brown to drive. The spring wagon bumped over the frozen ground. Then, at a distance, they saw something that made their hearts leap with joy—a dugout near the present town of Yale, Oklahoma. It was partly timbered with post oak, shading off to blackjack. Bill decided to go to the dugout to see if he could get news of Bill Dunn who might be able to give him information as to the outlaws. The outlaws had not been seen for some time; where they were no one knew. (As a matter of fact, they had just got back from a trip to Texas where they had done pretty well by themselves.)

Having no need for his Winchester on such a call, he left it behind. As Bill came walking toward the dugout, he saw a man outside gathering firewood. When the man discovered Bill, he dashed back inside. This seemed a bit queer, Bill thought as he walked on. Lonely settlers always wanted company.

The dugout was built on a hillside, with a sloping door outside, like an old-fashioned cellar. Half-a-dozen steps led down from the ground level to the floor of the dugout. Here was a second door, one that went up and down instead of sloping. The outer or sloping door was open. Bill went down the steps and knocked. There was no answer. He knocked again. "Come in," called a sullen voice. Bill pushed open the door and stepped inside. It took a moment for his eyes to get accustomed to the poor light and when they did he saw a man sitting near the fireplace with a rifle in his lap, silently studying him. What Bill didn't know was that the dugout was filled with outlaws and that they had hastily hung quilts before their berths, like curtains in a Pullman car. This was a temporary concealment, for the dugout did not have a back door and there was no way for the men to get out. And now, as Bill could see better, he saw that there was a rifle peeking out of each berth. Walking over to the fire, with the great pretense of having seen nothing unusual, he warmed his hands a moment, then said, "How does a man get out of here?"

"The same way he got in," said the individual in the chair.

There was a silence. "It's cold outside," said Bill. The man in the chair made no reply to the startling news. Bill had to think fast. "You tell Bill Dunn I was here and that I wanted to see him."

"Yeah."

"He said he had a bulldog that could whip mine, so while I was in this part of the country I thought I would drop by and see if we could work up a match." The man in the chair made no reply. "Well, I'll be moving along," said Bill, as one does who has finished his business, and started toward the door, with his back to the men. He heard a movement in one of the berths. His time had come. He slowly opened the door with a steady hand, trying to show no evidence of haste, then slowly closed it. Springing up the steps, he closed the sloping door and tried to pull his six-shooter out of his pocket, but was hampered by his overcoat. Holding his pistol pointed at the door, he walked backward, expecting at any moment that the outlaws would come pouring out with their rifles.

Inside the dugout a little drama was taking place. The moment the door closed, Red Buck leaped out of his berth and started after Tilghman. Bill Doolin and the man in the chair seized him. "Let loose of me. I'm goin' to kill him," said Red Buck with an oath.

"Bill Tilghman is too good a man to kill," said Bill Doolin.

"He'll be back with a posse," said Red Buck.

"We'll be gone," said Bill Doolin. So fierce, so bloodthirsty was Red Buck that the two men had to threaten to shoot him to keep him from throwing open the door and rushing out with his rifle.

Meantime, Bill Tilghman was walking backward toward the spring wagon, his pistol in his hand. When he got there, he leaped in and said to Neal Brown, "Drive as fast as you can. That dugout is filled with outlaws." Taking up his Winchester, he sat facing the dugout while Neal Brown lashed the traveling mules. Away went the spring wagon, swaying and careening but every second getting farther away from the Dugout of Death.

Tilghman wanted to raise a posse at Pawnee, but this was easier said than done. Possemen had to have fast horses and they themselves had to have courage. Mostly, posses were organized and sent out from Guthrie, or from Chickasha, where Chris knew men who could qualify. Bill Tilghman did not ride back to the dugout with the sloping door, for he knew the men would be gone.

And this was exactly what happened. The outlaws had had a long ride that day to get to the dugout and the weather was cold, but they must ride again, and this they did, dividing into groups and heading for their hideouts and harboring places—these men, the most dangerous, the most deadly in America.

A short time later Bill Tilghman stayed overnight at Bill Dunn's home and after the family went to bed the two had a long, confidential, midnight talk. Tilghman reminded Dunn that Dunn had a nice family growing up and that he ought to give up outlawry, for it was certain to end in disaster. Dunn was silent, impressed by what the law officer had said.

Finally Dunn said, "I believe I'll do 'er, Bill."

"I don't want to see anything happen to you for your family's sake."

"I don't, either," said Dunn.

"I'll help you."

When Tilghman got back to Guthrie, he went to the district

attorney and asked him to drop the cattle-stealing charge against Dunn and to give Dunn a deputy commission. The district attorney was shocked at such a wild request, but finally gave in. E. D. Nix did give Dunn a commission, but this was kept secret.

Tilghman soon picked up the trail of Little Bill and found that he was hiding in the timber on the Sam Moore Ranch in the hilly Osage country, on Mission Creek. Moore's wife had Osage blood, so the two had a right to be there. Moore farmed, after a fashion, and ran a couple of hundred cattle. At this time the Osage country was leased in big pastures to the cattlemen; the "natives" could graze their stock on the same land, for that was their privilege. This semi-wild section was an ideal place for an outlaw to be tucked away. Little Bill Raidler slept in the Moore house at night and had his meals there, but during the day he hid out in the timber. The time was early September, not yet cold. This sort of Huckleberry Finn life was nice. He didn't know that Tilghman was on his trail.

Tilghman crept up and hid behind the hen house and waited. Soon after sundown Little Bill came out of the timber and started through the feed lots. Suddenly Tilghman stepped from behind the hen house, shotgun in hand. "Throw up your hands, Bill!"

Little Bill did what so many of the outlaws of Oklahoma practiced—ducked sideways to dodge the bullets. At the same time he fired. The bullet knocked Tilghman's hat off. Raidler did not run, for he was a man of courage. While Little Bill was shooting, Tilghman brought his shotgun up and hit Little Bill; even this did not stop Little Bill from firing. And he kept firing until his six-shooter was emptied. Then he fell.

Tilghman went to him and bent over him. "Let me die," Little Bill said. "I don't want to go to prison." Mrs. Moore brought water and cloths for bandages and washed and bound up Little Bill's wounds as best she could. Little Bill looked at her gratefully. Once he turned his eyes to Tilghman and said, "Please don't take me to prison."

It was not long until Sam Moore arrived at this scene of an Oklahoma tragedy—so common in these territorial days—and he and Tilghman put straw and quilts into the spring wagon. Moore drove; Tilghman sat in the back of the spring wagon, holding Little Bill's head on a pillow. They got to Elgin, Kansas, at daylight, a distance of sixteen miles. There Little Bill was taken to a doctor's house and treated. During all the probing, Little Bill did not once groan. His courage and fortitude were amazing.

Shortly before noon the train came. Tilghman borrowed a cot from the doctor and with Moore's help carried Little Bill on the cot to the baggage car and there, beside him, Tilghman sat, giving Little Bill water from a jug Tilghman had brought and the medicine that the doctor had prepared. Tilghman took the Missouri Pacific to Arkansas City, transferred his prisoner, and took the south-bound Santa Fe to Guthrie.

Bill Tilghman received a reward of one thousand dollars for capturing Little Bill. Little Bill recovered from his wounds and, when better, was tried at Kingfisher, Oklahoma, for robbing a mail train at Dover and was sentenced to ten years in the federal prison at Columbus, Ohio. After he was released from prison, he returned to Oklahoma, where he operated a tobacco shop. But that day, on the Moore farm, had been too much for him. He was crippled for life, and there in Oklahoma he died.

Meantime, Red Buck was roaming the country, holding up travelers, swooping down on post offices and making a nuisance generally. Finally he killed a man, and Chris set out after him. Chris and his posse cornered Red Buck in a dugout near Cheyenne, Oklahoma, March 5, 1896. They ordered him to come out. He came out shooting, but Chris was a trifle better shot and soon Red Buck was on his way to potter's field. There were no mourners. Chris would never admit that he had killed Red Buck. All he would say was, "Red Buck vas killed dot day."

An earlier member of the Doolin Dodgers whom Chris had tracked down was Ol Yantis, a tall, swallow-complexioned cotton farmer with upper teeth that bit down over his lower lip. He had taken part in the Spearville, Kansas, bank robbery. Yantis was as slippery as a catfish in August, but he had been recognized as one of the robbers. Sheriff Chalk Beeson (born Chalkley) learned that Yantis had gone to a sister's farm three miles southeast of Orlando, Oklahoma, and sent a man by train to find if Yantis was there. The man wired back that Yantis was indeed there. Beeson took the train to Guthrie, where he told his story to Grimes and Chris. Beeson had no authority to make an arrest in Oklahoma, so he requested help from Grimes. Chris and Deputy Tom Houston were sent hotfoot after Yantis. The posse arrived during the night and found a spent horse in the corral lot. The officers hid their own horses, then concealed themselves behind a hogpen. At sunrise Yantis came out of the house carrying a sack of feed for his horse in one hand, in the other a revolver. Chris waited until Yantis was near, then rose and called, "Throw up your hands, Ol. We're officers."

The speed with which an outlaw could react to the call of "hands up" was remarkable: before Chris could finish a bullet whizzed by him. Chris was carrying a .38 caliber saddle gun that had been given him but which he had never tested. Instantly Chris fired; Yantis swayed and Chris knew he had hit him. But it was a strange shot. The bullet went through Yantis' clothing, passed through a roll of bills Yantis had in his pocket, and lodged in Yantis' body, making a blood-smeared mess of the bills. Yantis kept firing; Tom Houston fired in reply. In a moment Yantis, grievously wounded, fell to the ground where he kept trying to pump his pistol. Chris called to Yantis' sister who came running out: "Get his gun, or we will have to kill him."

It was the old story all over again: straw in the bottom of a spring wagon, quilts, and off to town with the wounded man. This time it was to Orlando, Oklahoma, a town that did quite an outlaw business. Yantis died at one o'clock that night.

An example of what a deputy had to do in these stark days happened now. Chris took Yantis' measurements, went to Guthrie, and bought a coffin for him. This he had sent to the sister who buried the riddled body. There was fifty-five dollars in Yantis' pocket; this was returned to the bank. (The dates: The Spearville bank was robbed November 1, 1892. Yantis was shot twenty-eight days later.)

Memo: Chris never used his .38-caliber saddle gun again. Not enough power.

A peculiarity about Chris was that he would never admit his was the shot that had killed anyone. In this instance he said it was Tom Houston's shot that ended Yantis' career. Chris never wanted to be known as a killer and always kept away from the subject in conversation. When anyone asked him if he had ever killed anyone he would say, "Mebbe yes, when I fight mit de Indians."

Here's a letter to Reno from Chalk Beeson's daughter-in-law, Mrs. Merritt L. Beeson:

Dodge City, Kansas
Nov. 12, 1956

Dear Reno Madsen:

We have in our museum a negative of the torn bills. The bills themselves disappeared, the way money does. I can have a photostat made of the bills—or is it against the law to photograph money? I sure don't want to get into trouble.

Mrs. Merritt L. Beeson

P.S. The receipt your father gave and the photo of the lacerated bills are on display in our museum here in Dodge.

The death of Ol Yantis checked another Doolin man off the list.

CHAPTER 22

The End Comes to Bill Doolin

BILL DOOLIN was still free and footloose. He gave out word that he would never be taken alive. Chris was equally determined to take him, and had those relentless bloodhounds—Tilghman and Thomas—on Bill's trail.

One of Doolin's greatest problems was his rheumatism—quite a handicap for a man who is being trailed night and day. At this time Eureka Springs, Arkansas, was a fashionable watering place. Here the rich and mighty went and left their aches at the bottom of the pool.

Tilghman learned that Doolin was there. Tilghman did considerable thinking and decided, of all things, to go disguised as a preacher. He bought a long-tailed coat, a tall hat, a stand-up one-ply collar, a black tie, celluloid cuffs, and put on a saintly expression, the last being the hardest of all to wear. Then he added two articles of attire that are not usually associated with the clergy—a shotgun and a pistol. Thus equipped, Tilghman went to Eureka Springs to begin his campaign to save souls.

Leaning over the counter, the clerk at the hotel pointed at the gun. "What is that, Reverend?"

The Reverend said, "That is a shotgun. I'm going squirrel hunting with one of my deacons." The clerk, not knowing the ways of the saintly, let Tilghman take his gun to his room.

It was plain that his shotgun was going to cause Tilghman trouble. He solved it in his own way. He went to a carpenter and told him he had a trombone; would the carpenter make a wooden box for it? Bill said, "It is about this long and this wide."

The carpenter made a box for Tilghman's trombone. The box was so constructed that by pressing a spring the box would fly open. In the flick of an eye Tilghman could then take out his instrument and play on it. It was a new idea in the musical world.

Tilghman slipped out the side door of the hotel, past the clerk, carrying his musical instrument. He sat down on a bench in a little park where there was a spring of mineral water. People would take a tin cup fastened by a chain, fill the cup, and drink the health-giving waters. Tilghman sat patiently waiting for Doolin to come up to restore his flagging health. But Doolin didn't come.

Tilghman took his trombone back to his hotel, put it in the closet, then locked the closet so that no one would purloin his rare instrument. Then with his pistol tucked in his long-tailed coat, Tilghman went to the Basin Spring Bath House where the rich and fashionable were restoring their health. He opened a door which he thought led to a steam room, but it turned out to be a kind of waiting room for those getting ready to go to the steam room. There, to his astonishment, he saw that one of the rich and fashionable was none other than Bill Doolin, who glanced up from his newspaper but did not recognize Tilghman in his preposterous garb.

Tilghman backed away as fast as he could, mumbling to an attendant, "I want a bath."

"Go into the booth and change your clothes," said the kindly attendant.

Going into the booth, Tilghman made a simple change.

Taking the pistol from his pocket, he leaped back into the room and pointed it at Doolin. "Put up your hands!"

Doolin stared in astonishment, for he had never seen a preacher conduct himself in that way. But Doolin wasn't going to throw up his hands for anybody, low church or high church, and tried to get out his own gun. Tilghman seized Doolin's wrist and the two struggled. Not one person tried to help the preacher in his good work.

The place was in an uproar. Men who had been crippled by rheumatism for years got out of there like clay pigeons. At last Tilghman had Doolin down and told the proprietor—who had rushed in—to reach into Tilghman's long-tailed coat and get out a pair of handcuffs that happened to be there. Up to then the man had not known that preachers carried handcuffs. In a moment Doolin's wrists were decorated with a set of handcuffs of simple design.

It was not long until the two men were in the train on their way to Guthrie, one with his wrists close together. Word spread that the unconquerable Doolin had been conquered, and crowds came to see the tall, high-cheeked, knobby-knuckled Bill Doolin who had terrorized Oklahoma for so long.

He was clapped into jail on January 12, 1896. He did not like jails and got out as soon as he could. It was not always easy to get out of an Oklahoma jail; sometimes it would take days.

The prisoner who opened the door for Doolin was a Negro named George Lane. Heck Thomas was put on the trail of Lane and soon found that Lane had gone to the home of a Negro who was living in a small town near Harrisonville, Missouri. But Heck was outside of his district and could not make an arrest, so he came to Chris in Kansas City to get Chris to help. Chris had been placed on the Civil Service rolls and assigned to duty as assistant chief deputy in the office of Marshal Jo Shelby. After getting a fugitive warrant for Lane, Chris and Heck got off the train at Harrisonville and hired a livery rig to get them to the little town—this so that Lane and his friends would not see the two getting off the train and recognize them as officers. Lane did not know Chris by sight, so Chris went to the post office to get information about Lane. The postmaster said that Lane had just been there but had started to the house where he was living, a mile from town. Into their livery rig again went Chris and Heck and down the road they rolled. They met a boy coming home from school who told them where Lane was staying. The boy said that Lane had been boasting how dangerous he was and declaring that he would never be taken alive.

Down the road again the two went. The house proved to be a long, one-room wooden affair, with a door at each end. Chris and Heck jumped out of the buggy, left the team with the driver, and ran to the house, Chris going to one door, Heck to the other. They kicked the doors open and there, sitting on a chair in the middle of the room, was the surprised Lane. He reached for his Winchester, but it was too late.

By the time the two got him to the depot, a crowd had collected to see the dangerous man, now as meek as a kitten. One of the men on the depot platform said, "I thought you said you wouldn't ever be taken alive."

"I did," said Lane, "but when I saw how big them holes in the Winchesters looked, I changed my mind." Lane knew nothing about where Doolin was. He was taken back to Guthrie and placed in jail.

Doolin had disappeared like a diving duck. As a matter of fact, he had gone to the ranch of Eugene Manlove Rhodes, the Rhodes of writing fame, in New Mexico. Doolin wanted to reform and become a farmer, just as his father had been. He had married a preacher's daughter, and a son had been born.

After a time Doolin left New Mexico and came back to Oklahoma to get his family to take them to New Mexico where he would start life over again.

Mrs. Doolin was living at her father's on a farm outside of Lawson, Oklahoma; Heck's men were watching the place carefully. One day she brought a team to the blacksmith shop of Charlie Noble, the husband of the Rose of Cimarron. Most horses at this time of year were unshod. But Mrs. Doolin wanted hers shod.

Heck Thomas and a posse were put on the trail.

Mrs. Doolin, with the help of her father, had bought a covered wagon and had loaded it with a plow, a cultivator, and a coop of chickens, all to be used in the new life Bill and his wife were to lead in New Mexico. On the evening of August 28, 1896, Mrs. Doolin told her father and mother good-by, carried her baby to the covered wagon, and started on the long journey to New Mexico. It proved to be a short journey. Two miles west of Lawson, Doolin came out of the night leading a horse. He walked behind the wagon in the moonlight, still leading the horse.

Suddenly Heck Thomas and his men rode out of the weeds. It was the end for Bill Doolin.

But let Heck Thomas tell about it in his own words. A few days after Doolin's death, Heck Thomas wrote Tilghman about the killing. Here, published for the first time, is Heck's version:

Guthrie, Okla.
Sept. 3, 1896

Dear Bill—

The day before I got last news of Doolin, I was 14 miles beyond Chandler, and drove through in one day. Next day I got a telegraph message that Doolin and four others were in the Ingalls country and I started for B. Dunn's—had Rufus Cannon and Albert with me.

[Albert was Heck's oldest son.] Made the drive by 2 o'clock and, after getting to Dunn's, got the news that carried me beyond Lawson. Met the Noble boys and some others with fresh news, and made a run of about four miles on "Limber Jim"—got to where two of the gang had been that night, and crawled up close enough to watch old Ellsworth's house with Bill Cook's field glasses. [Ellsworth was Doolin's father-in-law.]

We waited a long time without seeing anyone, although there was considerable stir about the store and dugout. Finally he came out of the stable and, to our great surprise, started down the lane, coming west. You know how the store is situated on high prairie. If he had wanted to have made his escape, he could have had open roads north, south, east, northeast, southeast, or northwest through the pasture to those high hills that you have seen many times.

He came straight down the lane, leading his horse by the bridle reins, walking in the bright moonlight, Winchester in both hands, well out in front of him, nearly in a position to shoot. He was walking slow, looking first on one side and then on the other. He was sure on the prod, and was looking for the neighborhood boys that had been spying on him, intending to shoot them up a little. When I hollered to him and had one of the boys on the other side of the road holler to him, right after I did, he shot at me and the bullet passed between me and Bee Dunn. I had let one of the boys have my Winchester, and had the old Number 8 shotgun. It was too long in the breach and I couldn't handle it quick, so he got in another shot with his Winchester, and, as he dropped his Winchester from a glancing shot on it, he jerked out his pistol. Some of the boys thought he shot once with it and the others twice. At about that time I got the shotgun to work and the fight was over.

HECK

The body had twenty-one bullet holes in it. It was buried in Guthrie Cemetery where the grave can be seen today. An old buggy axle is driven in the ground at the head of the grave. It had taken the combined work of the Three Guardsmen to bring in Doolin.

Here is a letter from Heck Thomas' widow—Mrs. Matie M. Thomas—which brings out points that have never before been published. The letter was written to Chris from Tulsa, and is dated January 19, 1939. Here it is considerably shortened:

Heck had eight in his posse with him. He had hired Tom and Charlie Noble, who had a blacksmith shop at Ingalls, to try to get any information they could about Doolin. It was a tip from them that enabled Heck to get Doolin. Charlie Noble afterward married Rose Dunn, the Rose of Cimarron. Heck took Albert and Rufus Cannon and left on Doolin's trail. On that night the following went with him: Bee Dunn, Dal Dunn, John Dunn, Charlie Noble, and Tom Noble. Heck had Albert and Rufus Cannon stationed at one road leading to Preacher Ellsworth's house. Then he had George Dunn and Hy Cotts [a brother of Mrs. Bee Dunn] stationed on another road. It was a bright moonlight night. Doolin came down the road, walking and leading his horse. Heck had cautioned his men not to make a sound until he gave the word to fire, but one of the men got nervous and clicked his gun, and Doolin fired. Heck called to him to throw up his hands, but he continued to fire, then stopped. Heck told the men to cease firing; they crept up to him as he lay in the road, thinking he might still fire, but he was dead. Mrs. Doolin came down the road, screaming, but Heck told her that her husband was dead and in the hands of the law and that she could not see him. Bee Dunn got a wagon and a team of black mules from a farmer and brought the body to Guthrie. The wagon and mules were put on a vacant lot next to our house. Maggie Murphy, a little Irish woman who worked for me, came to me and told me to have the men take the wagon out of the lot, as the hay in the bottom was covered with blood and the mules were eating it. The hay was taken out of the wagon and burned and the wagon washed. Now as to the reward. Heck got thirteen hundred dollars. Five hundred dollars was from Wells Fargo, five hundred dollars from the state of Missouri, three hundred dollars from the railroad, and there were the usual marshal fees. Heck divided the money between the men. Dal Dunn was dissatisfied and so Heck paid Dal money out of his own pocket. The two Cannons were not open to the reward, so Heck gave them some of his money. When the division was over, Heck was out of pocket.

CHAPTER 23

This Happened to Dynamite Dick, and This to Arkansas Tom

DYNAMITE DICK's number was about to come up, too, but he didn't know it. He had been in the Ingalls fight and he had been one of the men in the dugout's Pullman berths when Bill Tilghman had walked into that lions' den. The matter of the number coming up began very simply. Dynamite Dick was in jail in Guthrie waiting trial when who should be brought in but Bill Doolin. Soon the two were hatching up a jail break, and this they managed to bring about. It was not long until Dynamite Dick and Bill Doolin were leaving the jail behind them as fast as their feet would take them.

A problem presented itself. For some time Bill Doolin had been troubled by rheumatism, and now his left leg gave out. Eight men had been in the jail break and now, when Bill sat down to rest his leg, five of the men deserted him. But Dynamite Dick stuck by him, and so did one of the other men. Bill solved his foot troubles. A boy and a girl drove up in a buggy; the boy was taking his girl buggy riding. Soon Bill and his friends were riding in the buggy and the boy and the girl were walking. A feat of magic took place. The three men disappeared as neatly as a magician's canary; the horse and buggy were found in the next county, the men not anywhere.

Oklahoma buzzed like a beehive when a naughty boy has given it a kick. A tremendous man hunt was organized, for there was a reward on the heads of the men, dead or alive. The trouble was that the heads had disappeared and no one today knows where Dynamite Dick hid himself. He had escaped the day after the Fourth of July, and the hunt went on week after week. The newspapers of Oklahoma asked, "Why don't our law officers do something? Why don't they bring in Dynamite Dick?" They had an excellent reason: they couldn't find him.

The summer dragged by. No Dynamite Dick. But at last his luck turned against him. The first week in December an informer brought in word that the wanted man was hiding on a ranch sixteen miles west of Newkirk, Oklahoma. The posse closed in, and that was the end of Dan Clifton, known as Dynamite Dick.

A word about Little Dick West. He had a strange career, a stranger end. He was rightly named, a pert little fellow, with too much white showing in his eyes. He was a dishwasher in a restaurant in Decatur, Texas, when Oscar Halsell became interested in him because of his quick, humorous replies. Halsell brought him to his Oklahoma ranch to help the cowboys, quite a different life from what Little Dick had been leading. It was not long until he met Bill Doolin; he would follow Doolin around as loyally as a dog behind a boy. Finding that Doolin was organizing a new gang, Little Dick said, "Can I join up, Bill?"

"What can you do, boy?" Doolin asked, amused.

"I can ride as good as anybody and I'm not afraid of anything."

"You're too little to do anything."

"When I have a gun I'm as big as anybody."

Doolin took him to the Spearville lawn party where Little Dick was given the least consequential job of all—to hold the horses and terrorize anybody who came out on the street. Little Dick had a wonderful time popping his pistol and howling like a hydrophobic coyote. The robbery went nicely. Little Dick got his share. It shore beat washing dishes.

The gang decided to rob the bank at Southwest City, Missouri. Little Dick was again given the job of scaring the wits out of people. Things didn't go quite so well. Citizens rushed out with enough guns to take Fort Osage, and Little Dick barely escaped with his life. Not only that, but the irate citizens got out their horses and came pell-mell after the gang. The outlaws scattered like hail on a tin roof and finally escaped. But it had been a close call.

Little Dick now rode steadily with the gang and became a professional. No horse holding, no street howling. He had come a long way. He, too, was in the dugout when Bill Tilghman stumbled in that January day.

Little Dick made himself scarce. As fast as he could he got to New Mexico where he is supposed to have tucked himself away on Eugene Manlove Rhodes' ranch. After a time he untucked himself and returned to Oklahoma where he looked around for an opening for himself in his specialty. A new gang was forming —the Jennings Gang—the poorest excuse for a gang ever turned out by the great state of Oklahoma. The gang consisted of Al Jennings and his brother and two O'Malley boys, the bottom of the bandit barrel. Little Dick was the only one worth anything as a bandit.

The gang decided to go into action. On October 1, 1897, they held up the Rock Island train ten miles north of Chickasha, Indian Territory, at a place called Pocasset. (The details of this weird robbery will be given in Chapter 24, the chapter dealing with the exploits of the so-called Jennings Gang.) Little Dick was so disgusted with the affair, and with these poor imitations of bandits, that he got on his horse and rode sadly away.

Bill Tilghman and Heck Thomas were on his trail. The end was not long in coming. Little Dick hid away on a ranch south of Guthrie and there Bill Tilghman, Heck Thomas, and two possemen went. Bright and early on the morning of April 8, 1898, Little Dick, unsuspecting, rode up to the home of a rancher to get food for breakfast. The law was hiding behind the barn. Getting off his horse, Little Dick started toward the house. The matter was soon over . . . and that was the end of the little dishwasher who had come to a ranch in Oklahoma and fallen in with a band of outlaws.

Arkansas Tom was an example of too much religion in the home. His father and mother were extremely religious; two of his brothers were preachers. The family was constantly urging him to show more interest in religion. The boy had no leaning that way and felt he was being "picked on." Finally, at the age of fourteen, he ran away to be a cowboy. Soon he fell in with the Doolin Gang—very exciting, young Tom thought.

His real name was Roy Daugherty, but when he got to Oklahoma he changed it to Tom Jones for reasons he never bothered to explain. He was from Missouri, but said he was from Arkansas; the men began calling him Arkansas Tom, and under this name he has gone down in history. He was the dude of the desperadoes; some way or other he always appeared well dressed. Also he was a tough customer. At the battle at Ingalls, Oklahoma, he, with seven others, fought off a posse of eleven, killing three. He was captured and it was not long until he was languishing in jail in Guthrie. And soon he was languishing in the territorial prison in Lansing, Kansas, with fifty years hanging over him—a considerable bite out of anyone's life. But it didn't work out quite that way. Tom's preacher brother in Carthage,

Missouri, set to work and finally got Tom out, Tom having served only seventeen years. He walked out on parole November 26, 1910.

Tom was a model man for four years, then became a movie actor in Hollywood. Was this going downhill? He acted in a film entitled *The Passing of the Oklahoma Outlaws* produced by the Eagle Film Company. He played the part of an outlaw—played it with the air of a man who knows what he's about. After being a movie actor he came back to Missouri where he robbed a bank at Neosho. This was definitely a lowering of standards. He paid bitterly for this lowering, for he was arrested, convicted, and sentenced to eight years in the penitentiary in Missouri. He would have been better off in Hollywood.

After four years he was paroled, and once more was a free man. But not for long, for he held up another bank, this one at Asbury, Missouri. By this time he was credited with having killed eighteen men and was considered the most desperate man in America. A huge posse was organized, but he disappeared like a ground squirrel into its hole. So far he had won, but he was now an old man—at least in the outlaw world. He was fifty-four and was not so quick on the trigger as he had once been. His charmed life was coming to an end.

Word came finally to the police department in Joplin, Missouri, that he was living at the home of a friend, at 1420 West Ninth Street, Joplin. In the family was a baby and he had become fond of Arkansas Tom. Tom had never married and seemed to like the child, as if something had been left out of his own life.

On this occasion "Red" Snow, the friend, was not at home. Arkansas Tom was playing with the baby when Tom heard a noise, looked out the window, and saw the detectives. There were four of them; they were at the front door and the back door. Tom's pistol was on a shelf; he snatched it up and started to run into the next room. The baby thought Tom was playing with him and threw his arms around Tom's legs. Tom, not wanting to hurt the child, hobbled along as best he could. He shot twice but, handicapped as he was, he missed. The detectives fired and Tom, seemingly not wanting to harm the child, wobbled over to a bed and fell across it, dead. The room was closed off and the coroner sent for. When the pistol was examined, it was found that after the second shot it had become jammed.

There was an aftermath to the story. The next day the mayor of Joplin demanded the resignation of the chief of police—the man who was supposed to be heading the attack. The reason was an ample one. The chief of police was found hiding in a clump of weeds a hundred feet from the unpleasantness.

The funeral was something of a sensation. The body was put on view at the undertaking parlors. Missouri—the Mother of Outlaws—still had many men who would not talk. They came out of the Ozarks and from the border counties—silent men who stood a few moments in front of the body, then moved out into the street, got into cars, and rode away.

Thus ended the career of the man who had had too much religion at home when he was a boy. He was the last of the Doolin bandits to be brought in. The date was August 16, 1924. He had been an outlaw for thirty years. Jesse James himself rode for only fourteen and one-half years.

CHAPTER 24

Those Rank Amateurs— The Jennings Gang

THE DALTONS and the Doolins had been cleared away, but other gangs were growing like crab grass, and the number of outlaws was still increasing. It was becoming difficult to get deputy marshals—too many widows.

Many of the outlaws were taken to Judge Isaac C. Parker's court in Fort Smith, Arkansas, where there was a gallows that could accommodate twelve men at one time. But six was the greatest number that ever stepped on the little treacherous doors at one time. Five another time. In the twenty-five years that Judge Parker was on the bench, he convicted nine thousand, four hundred and fifty-four, almost all criminal prisoners, and hanged eighty-eight—a record in the United States. The average judge sends in his office tenure, possibly, five men to death. Judge Parker sentenced one hundred and seventy-two to be hanged; some of them died in prison, some escaped, some got presidential pardon, some were commuted by the president to life sentences, one was killed while trying to escape, and so on down the dripping roster. (Personal note: There is a book on the judge entitled *He Hanged Them High* that I can recommend.)

And now there sprang up an imitation outlaw gang that was downright laughable. It was headed by Al J. Jennings who was supposed to be a bold, bad man. His career lasted one hundred and nine days, and, with the assistance of his stalwarts, he got three hundred dollars. That was the gang's complete and total take.

Here was the gang: Al himself, its dauntless leader; his brother Frank, Morris and Pat O'Malley, and Little Dick West. We have already seen what Little Dick thought of them. When Little Dick, who was a real bandit, found out what they were like, he suffered deep and complete humiliation. His spirit was broken; he never shone again.

One midnight the fearful Jennings Gang rode into the slumbering town of Cushing. There was a small store there owned by Lee Nutter, who lived next door. Going to the proprietor's door, Al pounded until the man sleepily opened. "What do you want?" he managed to ask.

Al put on a lugubrious voice and said that a friend of his had died and that he wanted to buy some clothes for him to be buried in. The proprietor thought the order was a bit unusual, but when he got outside he thought it was even more unusual, for there were four other men to help Al buy funeral garments for his departed friend.

A bit puzzled, the proprietor opened the door to his store. In a moment he was no longer puzzled, for the men began pulling off their old battered rags and putting on clothes from the shelf. When they had on their new suits, one of the men went to the cash drawer and took all the money it contained—forty dollars. Going out, the men mounted their horses and rode off into the Oklahoma night. The proprietor, after this unexpected rush of business, returned to his home and went to bed, a wiser man, it is said.

This midnight foray was one of the high points in Al's stark career of crime. Did they give up? Not these determined men. They got their grain sack ready and held up a Missouri, Kansas, and Texas train at Bond Switch, twenty-two miles south of Muskogee. They did this by piling ties on the track and waving a red lantern. The engineer turned on more steam, knocked the ties off the track, sped on, and turned in an alarm at the next station. The men took to the hills, the grain sack as limp as an empty Christmas stocking.

The men decided to rob the Santa Fe at Purcell, Oklahoma, and put on their masks and got out the moldy grain sack. A night watchman discovered the men hiding in the switchyards and told the town marshal who raised a posse and started after the men. But the men got on their horses and rode away so swiftly that the posse didn't have a chance in the world.

Then things changed. The men made a haul. At eleven o'clock in the morning, October 1, 1897, five masked Jennings men rode up to where a group of laborers was working on the Rock Island track eight miles south of Minco, Oklahoma Territory. There was a side track called Pocasset. The indomitable five ordered the section gang to flag the train that would be along in a few minutes, then the five walked bravely behind the section house and hid.

When the train stopped, one of the fighting five climbed into the engine cab and covered the engineer and fireman. Another of the men went back to terrorize the passengers, and this he did by making enough noise for a Fourth-of-July celebration. The other amateur outlaws went to the express car, but the messenger said he could not open the safe. The men were prepared for this. There was a big safe in the car and a little one. They placed a stick of dynamite on the big safe, put the little safe on top, started the fuse, then, with fast footwork, got out of the car. *Whang*! went the dynamite. The small safe was blown off; the big one, however, stood like the Rock of Gibraltar. The robbers started to do the job again, but found, when they'd jumped out of the car, they'd left their dynamite and that the sticks had all been exploded.

The boys, plumb mad now, ordered the passengers out of the car and in no uncertain terms told them to shell out. Out came the grain sack and into this the passengers were told to deposit their money and be quick about it. The passengers searched their pockets but could not find much money, so they put in their jewelry, trinkets, and pocketknives. During the process of receiving the passengers' offerings, Al Jennings' mask slipped off. The conductor recognized Al.

Al hefted the grain sack. It was heartbreakingly light. Well, he wasn't licked yet, not with a fighting spirit like his. He looked around. He must get something. Then he saw a jug of whisky and a stalk of bananas. Picking these up, he said, "I guess that's all," and jumped out of the car. Then he got his men around him and they all headed for the hills to enjoy the whisky and bananas.

Bud Ledbetter was a deputy United States marshal. He had got tired of the monkeyshines of the Jennings Gang, so when they entered his district he determined to do something about it. Lone-handed, he arrested four of them at one clip. It must be said that his posse was near, and this the four knew, and decided to make no resistance.

Al was taken to Chickasha, Indian Territory, and tried for assault with intent to kill and robbing the United States mails. During the trial the prosecution put on the stand the news butcher of the train Al had robbed. The news butcher, as befitted his calling, always carried a pocketful of small change.

"Do you remember this man?" asked the prosecuting attorney, pointing to Al Jennings.

"I do," said the news butcher with great feeling.

"Why do you remember him?"

The news butcher almost choked with emotion. "Because,"

he said indignantly, "when he came to me he made me throw my money into the grain bag, then said, 'You're just a damned crapshooter,' and I never shot a game of craps in my life an' I go to church regularly. That's why I remember him!"

Al was sentenced to five years in the penitentiary at Leavenworth on the first charge and given a life sentence in the Ohio Federal Penitentiary at Columbus, Ohio, on the second charge. Sentence was passed on him June 4, 1898. Chris got ready to escort him to the Columbus prison.

A tremendous crowd gathered at the depot to see the now-famous bad man. A lady schoolteacher, sympathy written on her face, edged forward. "Mr. Jennings, may I ask a question?"

"Yes, ma'am. Certainly."

"Are you guilty?"

"You heard what the jury told the judge," said Al.

"But I still wonder if you were really guilty," persisted the earnest woman.

"They said I was, so you had just as well believe it, too."

On the train, captor and captive talked in the easy way they did in Oklahoma at this time. During the course of one conversation Chris remarked: "Al, you once said that if you could rob a train just once, you would be fixed for life."

"Well, I am," said Al.

But he wasn't, quite. In less than four years he was back in Chickasha, a free man, pardoned by the President of the United States. Chris was sleeping in the courthouse this night, when he was awakened by a rapping at the door. "Who is it?" he called out.

"It's Al," said Jennings.

Chris opened the door and shook hands with him. Al was in a prison suit and looked far from spruce. "Chris, could you let me have a quarter? I haven't eaten yet." Chris gave him the money, and Al stumped off to an all-night restaurant. When he came back, Chris gave him enough money to take a train to Lawton where one of Al's brothers lived.

Soon Al was in politics, running on the Democratic ticket for the nomination for governor of the great state of Oklahoma. And he almost made it. He was a pleasant little fellow. People liked him, and when he came out on the street they rushed up, eager to "visit." When they spoke of his outlaw days, he would say, "That's all over. I was just a small fry."

But as the years went on he began to expand his part as a bad man. In his days as an outlaw he had never killed anyone, and there is no evidence that he ever even wounded anybody. He "got religion" and traveled over the country saving souls. His own, he said, had been saved long ago. Then he went into the movies as an actor—a major crime, some of the actors said.

As these words are being set down Al lives at 18824 Hatteras Street, Tarzana, California, where he is regarded as an authority on the outlaw West. A clipping I have before me from the Los Angeles *Times* of March 10, 1957, relates how the actor playing the part of Wyatt Earp in television came to Al for advice on the draw. Al told him all about it. In the interview Al said: "I shot and killed a few men in my day. But I always killed them in a fair fight."

CHAPTER 25

Maggie's Death. Chris Joins "Teddy's Rough Riders"

As has been told, Chris received twenty-nine dollars a month as quartermaster sergeant; when he became deputy United States marshal he got two hundred and fifty dollars a month, a vast sum. He said, "I don't know how I vill spend it all." This proved to be not too much of a problem, for he had married and his expenses had jumped up. And then two children had come along. It was not long until he began to wonder how he could scrape by.

Each time Chris went out, Maggie's heart stood a little still. Would the children be fatherless? Pensions were not given to widows of deputies. . . .

The trouble, however, did not come from that quarter. Maggie had always been a delicate, frail girl, exceedingly gentle, admired by everyone on the post. Maggie Madsen—there was none like her, people said. Chris was proud of her. And he was proud of his American children. He would make a peace officer oud of the boy. It was nice to uphold the law. It vas a fine t'ing to get into.

Maggie's health began to fail; in addition, there was the fear of what might happen to him. The days for her were long and the nights filled with anxiety. It was too late now for Chris to take up another profession. Sometimes peace officers went into politics, but Chris was too honest and sincere for that crafty business.

In the midst of his troubles he was transferred to the marshal's office in Kansas City; the climate was worse for Maggie here than it had been in Oklahoma. During this time General Jo died. Chris wanted to go to the funeral and he wanted to take Maggie with him, as he did whenever possible. The funeral was held February 17, 1897, in Westport, a suburb of Kansas City; it was the scene where Shelby had won a victory for the South. The notables of the day were there; military men from as far as Wyoming had come. One of the men who was there was Frank James, Jesse's brother, a tall, thin-shouldered, hook-nosed man with a squeaky voice. Chris had met Frank, and now introduced him to Maggie. But Maggie was not impressed. She just didn't like outlaws.

The next day, in the little apartment in Kansas City, she complained of not feeling well. She'd had too much excitement. Later that day Chris realized this was not it at all. She had a hemorrhage. The doctor said she must be gotten out of the cold, raw days that afflicted Kansas City at this time of year. But Chris was working for Shelby's successor. What should he do? He compromised by taking Maggie to the much milder climate of El Reno; he remained with her a few days, then went back to Kansas City.

For a time she seemed to improve, then it was seen that she was not gaining at all. On March 4, 1897, Chris resigned his Kansas City job and returned to El Reno. Maggie said she wanted to go to their farm. She had been born on a farm in Kansas; the happiest, most carefree days she had ever known had been on a farm. Chris was no land man himself, but if Maggie wanted anything, then she should have it. He took her to the Madsen farm seven miles northeast of El Reno. She seemed to get better, then began to weaken. She must have the best of doctors, Chris said, and they must come out to the farm every day. He mortgaged the farm. And there, on the farm, she died, May 2, 1898, from consumption.

Chris had the care of a girl of nine, a boy of eight. It was a new job for him, an Indian fighter and outlaw tamer. But the short, thick-set man with the big hands started in to take care of the two children. He moved in a confused and bewildering world. He took the children to El Reno—the place where he had first lived after he was married. But he had no job, no way of earning money, and there was that mortgage gnawing like a rat in the dark.

Life moves in strange and unexpected ways, and so now it did with Chris. One day there was a knock at the door and when Chris opened it there was a man from the depot with a blue envelope. The telegram was from Colonel Leonard H. Wood asking Chris to come to San Antonio, where the Rough Riders were being organized, and to act as his quartermaster sergeant. Chris had to wire that he could not come because of the children.

The next morning the man from the depot was there again. Chris must come. Get the neighbors to take care of the children. Chris went to see former Governor A. J. Seay and showed him the two telegrams. "You must go, Chris."

"But the children..."

"I'll take care of them." This was just fine and dandy—except that Seay was a bachelor.

Chris took the next train, and the two wondering, big-eyed children moved into the home of Mr. and Mrs. William Redder, in El Reno.

Chris got to San Antonio as fast as he could. Hardly was he on the camp ground before he met Colonel Wood, who greeted him delightedly. "Madsen, I want you to go to the quartermaster's office and check all the invoices and receipts."

"Colonel Wood, I haven't been mustered in yet."

Wood was set back only a moment. "I'll muster you in here and now."

"But I have not been examined by a doctor."

Wood took care of this, too. "Here comes the chief surgeon. I'll have him examine you." When the doctor rode up on horseback, Wood told him what he wanted. The examination was one of the quickest ever made in military history. The doctor looked at Chris and said, "I find the applicant in excellent physical condition." Chris was in the army again.

Chris's duties brought him in contact with Colonel Theodore Roosevelt who, some way or other, succeeded in dominating everybody. His great fame was just beginning; he felt very confident of himself and did not mind showing it.

One day Chris came to Roosevelt's tent and told the orderly he wanted to speak to Colonel Roosevelt. The orderly was doubtful but finally took in the message. Roosevelt looked up from a small portable field desk and said briskly, "What is it, Sergeant? What do you want? Don't you know I'm a busy man?"

Chris said he had a requisition for him to sign.

"I do not sign requisitions," said the indomitable Teddy.

"Colonel Wood is avay. You vill sign, please."

"I told you I do not sign requisitions. Wait till Colonel Wood comes back."

Chris explained that some supplies had come in and that if this company did not get them, some other company would, and that Roosevelt's company would not be equipped to go to Cuba. "Undt it vill be all your fault. You vill sign." He thrust the requisition order before Roosevelt.

"All right, Sergeant, I'll sign," said Colonel Teddy meekly.

Things did not go well with Chris in the Cuban campaign—fever. When mustered in he weighed two hundred; when he got his discharge for disability he weighed one hundred and twenty. He was gone four months; he did not fire a shot. He had to stop in New York City to rest, so weak was he; also in Philadelphia, where he was in a hospital for eleven days. He had also to stop and rest in Kansas City and in Wichita.

When he got to El Reno, he hurried to the house where the children were being cared for. He was in uniform and was so wasted away that the children didn't recognize him.

Chris didn't want to be a burden, so the next day he went to the Madsen farm and got into bed. And there, alone, he remained for three months. The neighbors, from time to time, brought him food. His rugged constitution fought off the effects of the fever and slowly he began to improve.

The first of November he returned to El Reno where he moved into the house of a friend. As Chris got stronger, the children came each day to see him; once more he became acquainted with them. By the middle of December he was able to walk without help. He had held a commission under the United States marshal at Ardmore, Oklahoma, and now sent him word that he was able to work. These were anxious moments. In a few days a messenger came up the front walk and rang the bell. The telegram was from the Attorney General in Washington, and it said for Chris to report to Marshal John S. Hammer at Ardmore. Chris got on the train and went to Ardmore, once more a deputy United States marshal.

The Three Guardsmen were still friends and they were still bringing in the bad boys and they were still having trouble getting their accounts approved by the Attorney General's office in Washington.

In February 1909 Chris and Bill Tilghman set off for Washington to see if they coudn't hurry up matters. Some accounts had stood a year without having been paid.

Colonel "Teddy" Roosevelt was going out of office and was preparing to give his last big social function, an army and navy affair. He found that Chris was there and sent a special invitation for Chris and his friend to attend. The two were flabbergasted. Attend a big social function in Washington! Could two boys from the hay crossings get away with it? It'd be worse than bringing in the Daltons.

After talking it over, they went to a secondhand store and each rented an evening suit. Then they went to the reception, trying to act as if this was an everyday affair. But when they got among the military and navy great they became ill at ease and moved here and there like barefooted boys in a patch of sand-burs. They became conscious that a British diplomat was studying them curiously. Bending toward his lady, he said, "Look at those crude Americans. What a country to produce such men."

Bill Tilghman watched his opportunity, struck up a conversation with an American whom he already knew and then, with a wink, said, "I want to introduce you to the new ambassador from Denmark—Christian Madsen, who has just arrived in our country." The British diplomat heard the accent and was tremendously impressed. Chris carried off his part well; and so did Bill Tilghman who, now and then, called Chris "Your Highness" and pretended to treat him with immense respect.

And now the two men, having made the matter a joke, began to feel at ease and to enjoy themselves, no longer afraid of the high and mighty.

The next day the two turned in their ambassadorial suits and once more were everyday citizens. They used to tell the story with great glee—the story of how Chris was an Ambassador for a Night.

CHAPTER 26

The Story of Ben Cravens, Bad Man

(Author's note: Until now I've used much of Chris's manuscript as basic material, and have rewritten, or added to it as seemed best. In this chapter I will try a different method. His shortcoming was that he did not tell enough about an incident. As a result I've had to get material from other sources and add to what he has set down all too briefly. But in this chapter I follow his own account, for he has dealt with the subject at greater length than he has with any previous material. Chris's weakness was that he would get off the subject and hop around until he was hard to follow. But in this he has kept to the subject; it is the best writing in the manuscript. It tells the story of Ben Cravens. Now the story, partly rearranged.)

Ben Cravens was the last of the notorious Oklahoma outlaws. Certainly he was one of the meanest and the most dangerous. I don't think, in all my career in handling outlaws, I ever knew a man as heartless as this character. He was meaner than Red Buck, which is all I need to say on the subject.

He was born in 1868, son of B. B. Cravens, a farmer living near Lineville, which is on the line between Iowa and Missouri. He was ornery from the start. He did not like the schoolmaster, so he took care of that matter by going to the schoolhouse and breaking all the windows and knocking the stove off its legs. He was picked up and placed in the town jail. He broke jail in no time at all. In fact, of all the men I have handled, he broke jail more times than any other. I will make mention of them in this or a later chapter.

He joined some roving horse traders who were moving across the country and, after a time, landed in the Indian Territory where he took a course in horse stealing, doing better than he did in school. Soon he was a professional horse thief, adding to this by running whisky for the Osage Indians. He was picked up in Guthrie and served two terms in jail. As soon as he was out he went back to his specialty, horse stealing, and was soon inside gazing out. But not for long, for he escaped and headed for Kansas where he took part in a train robbery. He pulled for Oklahoma, but his trail was picked up and he was shot by the city marshal of Blackwell. He was so badly hit we thought he would not recover, but he did. I don't know why it is but if a good man is shot, he dies, but an outlaw will live.

When he got well he was tried and sentenced to fifteen years at hard labor in the Kansas State Prison, at Lansing, that state, January 18, 1897, being the date. He worked a nice dodge. He was assigned to work in the coal mines. He whittled out a wooden pistol, covered it with tinfoil from cigarette packages, held up the guard, got his gun, made him hoist him to the surface, where he expressed his thanks by killing him. He made good his escape. Near Emporia he met two men who had been prisoners but had escaped and who recognized him. So he killed them, one of them on a bridge near Emporia.

Now I will have to go back a bit in my account. While he was in the pen he made the acquaintance of a young fellow named Bert Welty. Welty was released before Cravens told the prison farewell, and so now Cravens decided to go to the boy's parents who lived near Kiel, a post office about eighteen miles west from

Kingfisher, Oklahoma. He went there and found the young boy and was entertained by the parents. He began to work his influence on the boy and finally got him to go with him "on a trip" which was the way Cravens put it to the younger man.

Welty was a small fellow and Cravens persuaded him to dress like a woman. He said no one would ever suspicion a man traveling in a buggy with a lady. He said, when the time came, Welty could take off the dress and that would throw anybody completely off the trail.

At Red Rock they found a place that suited them. It was a post office kept in the back part of the store. Alva Bateman was the postmaster. Cravens and young Welty entered the store and, seeing nobody present, started to help themsleves to whatever they fancied and to rifle the money drawer of the post office, Welty being the one who got the money. The postmaster peeped through an opening reserved for this purpose, saw the intruders, seized his pistol, and came in and fired a shot but missed. Cravens fired, killing the postmaster instantly, March 19, 1901, being that date.

Cravens told Welty to get in the buggy and, just as they did so, a severe thunderstorm came up and rained like all fury. They drove away as fast as they could under the circumstances, Welty doing the driving. He drove into a ravine and the vehicle upset. They at once unhitched the horses and mounted them. They hadn't gone very far until Cravens took the shotgun he was carrying, turned around, and shot Welty who fell off the horse in a dying condition. Cravens rode away, leaving the moaning and suffering man.

It was not long until a posse came along and picked up Welty and took him to the store he had just vacated. He was carried to the home of one of the townspeople and nursed, and, when well, was put in jail in Guthrie.

Our friend Cravens disappeared like a soap bubble; nobody knew where he was. As a matter of fact, he was working as a hired man on a farm near Oregon, Missouri, and, while thus engaged, courted a girl by the name of Christina Rickenbaugh, and led her to the altar, November 27, 1902, a piece of bad luck for the lady.

We will draw a veil over him for a minute. A man named Charles Maust was arrested for stealing hogs and put on trial at Savannah, Andrew County, Missouri, was found guilty, and whisked off to the Missouri state pen at Jefferson City, in the spring of 1907, the term of the incarceration being four years.

One day when he was being shaved, the barber became suspicious and reported to the warden that Charles Maust had been in prison with him at Lansing under another name. Wheels were set in motion and Bert Welty was sent for. It was a big moment for Welty when he peered through the bars and saw the man who had shot him that rainy night so long ago.

As soon as the term was up, he was to be brought to Guthrie on the much more serious charge of murder, hog stealing now seeming like a pastime. The day before he was to arrive, I received a telegram from United States Attorney Wickersham. I will copy it down to see if my readers can read it. Here it is:

Washington, D. C. Nov. 3

United States Marshal
Guthrie, Okla.

Unsex Missouri soloist pickpocket advises General Parodist that Charles Maust estuarial therein marquee overvalued Ben Cravens tradition that interdigitale may stage in getting impassionates if paraffize to try restrainer irrepressible from your extravasated en route inher especially if thermostatic is made through paraffinize at overlean take tufted presidens in tews irrepressible United States Attorney will translate.

WICKERSHAM

Uncoded it reads:

Washington D. C. Nov. 3

United States Marshal
Guthrie, Okla.

Warden Missouri State Penitentiary advises general opinion that Charles Maust confined therein is notorious Ben Cravens. Understand that he may succeed in getting friends in Oklahoma to try rescue him from your custody en route Guthrie especially if travel is made through Oklahoma at night. Take usual precautions in transferring him. United States Attorney will translate.

WICKERSHAM

After a time we landed him in the Guthrie jail which must have seemed familiar to him, he once having turned his back on its hospitality. We took the severest precautions he wouldn't escape this time. In spite of our watchfulness, he had cayenne pepper smuggled in which he was going to throw in the eyes of the guards. There was a bit of miscalculation here, for he got it into his own eyes, which delayed the trial four days because he couldn't see the witnesses, certainly a laugh on our Ben.

The trial commenced at the federal courthouse and there was assembled the greatest number of outlaws ever assembled together in one place in all the history of rip-roaring Oklahoma. Many of them had done time, some had money on their heads but, knowing others of their ilk would be there, they took a chance the officers wouldn't go looking for trouble. The officers thought there might be concerted action to free Cravens, but there was no such. Maybe they thought he wasn't worth rescuing.

Al Jennings had had his citizenship restored, after he had been pardoned, and was now Cravens' lawyer. Jennings was all flash and sputter and I thought to myself it looked bad for Cravens.

The trial was a great social occasion as well. Ladies brought their lunches so they could hold their seats during the noon recess.

One of the first witnesses was Bert Welty. Welty was now the man holding the shotgun. Cravens pretended he didn't know him, but that was all right. The court and the jury believed Welty.

A parade of witnesses filed by. At the conclusion of the trial, Al Jennings told what a fine man Cravens was. The jury promptly found him guilty. He was given a life sentence in the federal pen in Leavenworth and it fell my duty to escort him there. The Oregon boot was just coming into style as an article of male wearing apparel, and I locked one on his right foot. The Oregon boot has a heavy iron weight, carried by a frame attached to the shoe sole, so that when a man tries to run away he will run in a circle, pie for the guard.

Word was flashed over the country and people flocked to the depot to see Cravens, sometimes holding up their children. I have taken many men to prison, but none that ever attracted so much attention as he did. I got him to Leavenworth and they put him through the scrubbing exercises.

His registration number in Leavenworth was 7855-L. He was transferred to the Medical Center for Federal Prisoners at Springfield, Missouri, October 17, 1936, and later was paroled.

He was a strange man, hard to understand. He never joined a gang; he always operated alone. Sometimes he was peaceful and half likable. Then he would be utterly ruthless. Sometimes I think if he had not got into that school episode back in Iowa, he might have turned out a different man. In talking to outlaws I'm impressed by how they usually got started on the downhill path by some simple thing. It might have been the same with him.

He died September 19, 1950—the last of the great Oklahoma outlaws.

In 1906 or 1907 Buffalo Bill came to Guthrie with his Wild West Show. He was then at the peak of his popularity; he'd had his command performance before the Queen of England; he'd driven the Deadwood Coach with five kings as passengers; he was a world figure. When he arrived in Guthrie to him it was just another place where he had to put on a show and he was not much interested. Chris went to the performers' tent, and there was Buffalo Bill sprawled out on a couch waiting to go on.

"Is Scout Cody here?" Chris called, keeping himself out of sight.

"Yes," said Buffalo Bill casually, for everywhere he went he was plagued by people who wanted to talk to him in person.

"I mean Scout Cody from War Bonnet Creek," said Chris.

Buffalo Bill sat up with interest. Who would know about War Bonnet Creek? "Come in. Who are you?" called Buffalo Bill, all interest now.

For a moment he did not know Chris. And then he recognized him and grasped his hand delightedly. "Come in, Sergeant. You're the only one I can talk to about what happened that day. Captain King is still living but I never see him."

Buffalo Bill shut himself off from everybody, and as they recalled their days together they talked and laughed, enjoying themselves thoroughly. "My enemies are now saying I didn't kill Yellow Hand, but you saw it and you can blow them down for me."

"I vill," said Chris, for he was an ardent supporter of Buffalo Bill.

He asked Chris about Chris's work and listened as Chris told of his life—guns, shooting, adventure—they all interested

Buffalo Bill profoundly. "You're doing more important work than I am," he said when Chris finished.

That night, when the show had to depart, Chris was the last man Buffalo Bill shook hands with.

In 1915 or 1916 Buffalo Bill came to Oklahoma City with his show. Chris tore around to see him. Buffalo Bill looked at him uncertainly, for he was going blind. The two talked briefly. Buffalo Bill seemed so tired and dispirited that Chris was not always sure that Buffalo Bill was following the conversation. When time came for the show to begin, a man came out and helped Buffalo Bill on the horse. When the performance was over, Chris went around to see him, but Buffalo Bill was so tired and weak that he could not talk. It was the last time the two ever saw each other.

The years went slipping by like ghosts at night. Chris was getting older. Not so spry now. Liked to talk about the past. And then, in 1917, the United States entered another foreign war. Hardly had we entered before Chris marched off to the enlistment station to tell 'em he was ready to fight his fourth war. He was sixty-six; a trifle old, they said. But something else happened that put salve on the wound. Son Reno marched off to the wars. He was a railroad man and enlisted in Chicago, July 7, 1917, and was in the first contingent to arrive in France after General Pershing and his staff. Says Reno:

"I was in the 13th Engineers, in the railroad end. It wasn't long till we were at Verdun. We started in with sixty-five French locomotives. Six were modern but in poor shape. Some dated back to 1854, with no cab, and had to be operated by hand brakes—not on the locomotives but on the tender. We were in hilly country; it required one brakeman for every seven cars to control the train when it was going downgrade. What a life! What railroading!"

The Americans were responsible for the capture of Sedan. Chris had reason to believe his son was one of them and was the most excited man in town. Why, he himself had fought there and now "the boy" he fight the same ole Germans. Then Chris read that thirty-four of the men were to be decorated. His son! His ex-posseman—his ex-deputy! But alas! things did not turn out quite that way. Reno was not one of the thirty-four. Chris was just plain mad. They were not treating the boy right.

Reno got back to the United States April 27, 1919, and soon was in Oklahoma. Chris met him proudly, wearing five of his own medals. One of the first questions Chris asked was, "How did it go at Sedan? I t'ink of that almost effry day since I hear you vas there."

CHAPTER 27

The Last Days of the Great Oklahoma Peace Officers. The End Comes to Chris.

It might be judged from what has been set down so far that all of Chris's cases were exciting. Most of them, however, were routine—the chasing of whisky peddlers, timber stealers, cedar haulers, fence cutters, post-office robbers. When a "case" came through, he got on his horse, or into the famous spring wagon, and set out, hot on the trail. His great, his outstanding belief in the sacredness of the law gave him wings.

He would be gone for days at a time. Maggie would not know where he was. Then a letter, addressed in that wonderful hand, would come. In the letters he always asked, "How are things at home?" Rarely did he write of his own plans, or the danger he was in. Then, suddenly and unexpectedly, he would turn up at the little white wooden house where he kept his family. Maggie never asked him where he had been or what he had been doing. Sometimes he told her; more often he didn't. Vould vorry her, he said.

One day, when the family was living in El Reno, he was shot at four times. After the prisoner had been taken, Chris came home, sat down in the living room with Maggie and the children, and began to talk casually about other things. A neighbor woman came excitedly in and commenced to tell about the "gun battle" that Chris had been in. He hadn't even mentioned it.

His career had been quite extraordinary—a career that could have taken place only in America. A Danish boy with an accent had had associations with three presidents: Chester A. Arthur, Teddy Roosevelt, and William Howard Taft. He had served as a guide for President Arthur and he had hunted with Teddy Roosevelt in Oklahoma. He had gone to see President Taft, in Washington, on business connected with the Justice Department in Oklahoma. And he had known General Phil Sheridan, and General Leonard A. Wood, for whom he had served as regimental quartermaster sergeant in the Cuban campaign.

On New Year's night, 1911, Chris reached the top in his profession of law enforcement, for on that night, in the federal office building in Guthrie, he was sworn in as United States marshal for Oklahoma. For twenty years he had been deputy marshal—now he was to be marshal. The job usually was given to a politician; now it was given to one who deserved it, a nice departure. He was appointed by President William Howard Taft.

It was the custom, when a new marshal was sworn in, to have the deputies who were to be retained sworn in, too. Five took the oath of allegiance as soon as Chris had taken his. One of these deputies was Heck Thomas.

That night, after the swearing in, the men had a party—a very genial affair, 'tis said. Chris twitted Heck and called him by the name that the old-time deputies had used, Scissor Tails. Among the deputies who functioned in Oklahoma, Heck Thomas was the dude, the dandy. He wore a long Prince Albert; it was from this that the name Scissor Tails came. He even wore this strange outfit when he was out to capture someone. Under it and out of sight was something not quite so flashy—his six-shooter.

Six changes in law enforcement had come about:

1. Better transportation. The day when Chris had put his

posse's horses in a freight car and had jumped them off onto a bank was gone. Automobiles were coming in; in a few minutes after a robbery they were hot upon the trail.

2. The harboring places were gone. An outlaw could no longer tuck himself away in a remote section and lead the life of Riley.

3. The law courts were better. No longer did a judge say, "Order in the court! I haven't been able to hear a word said by the last two witnesses."

4. Railroads were using safes that couldn't be blown open with a few sticks of dynamite.

5. Banks had organized and were using their own system of crime detection.

6. Jails were no longer sieves. Prisoners experienced considerable difficulty in escaping. The day when Ben Cravens could escape from five jails was gone forever. Some prisoners never escaped from even one. It showed the changed conditions.

Something was happening that was profoundly to affect the life of Chris Madsen and the lives of all deputy United States marshals; in fact, it was to end their very existence. And this was the admittance of Oklahoma Territory and Indian Territory as a state. President Theodore Roosevelt signed a proclamation November 16, 1907, and lo! a new state was born.

With the coming of statehood, law enforcement was turned over to local authorities: police departments, sheriffs, deputy sheriffs, city marshals, constables, even to justices of the peace—that is, all except for violations of the federal law. It was the Day of Doom for deputy United States marshals.

Once the Territory had had ninety deputy United States marshals roving over it, now it had six. What were the old marshals to do? Many of them had spent their working lives as deputies; they had not saved their money, they were just plain hard up.

The great, the mighty Bill Tilghman got a job as chief of police in Oklahoma City—a comedown indeed. But Ledbetter, who had "brought in" so many outlaws, got a job as sheriff of Muskogee County.

Chris's story was really the story of Oklahoma. He had seen it turn from villages of prairie dogs into skyscraper cities. And he had seen man hunting change from one lonely deputy straddling his horse and going out alone, or joining a posse and riding hard upon the trail of a felon. Law officers now worked in pairs, or in groups. There was now no such thing as a posse of ranchers riding like mad to bring down a horse thief. Law enforcement had taken over all that. Not only this but thieves were now being chased in cars. Chris could hardly believe it.

But the best thing—the most exciting—was that law and order were being brought to Oklahoma. How far away they seemed when he had gone to Beaver City and shots had been fired through the floor of his room. And how long it seemed since Guthrie had been the wildest, the toughest town in the United States. One fourth of the business houses then had been saloons; and there had been houses that one always spoke of with lowered voice. The old days were gone. Guthrie was now dull. There was no other word for it—a town without a saloon and with a revival service going on under a tent. Could this be wild, wicked Guthrie which had once been the capital of Oklahoma? The town where Chris had led Bill Doolin down the street from the jail to the courthouse?—Bill Doolin who loved his family so devotedly.

Heck Thomas—the mighty Heck Thomas who had killed Bill Doolin and had helped bring in Cattle Annie and Little Breeches —was not doing well. He could not adjust himself to the changed conditions. He said he felt as young as ever. But who does? What a pit that leads into! And soon the matter began to tell on Heck. But when a work call came, the old firehorse made another run. He walked unsteadily on the street—but jauntily. And he still was debonair.

Five days before he died he sent Chris a pitiful and touching letter:

Lawton, Okla.
August 5, 1912.

Dear Chris,

This malady is troubling me again, and I know I have not the strength or the inclination to resist it, so no matter what happens I do not want you or Tilghman to come over here, and no flowers. If I had got work, I would have paid you that $25.00.

Give my love to Reno, the best boy in the country to whom I owe a letter. Remember me to Marion—the dear sweet little girl—and tell her she knows we always loved her. Tell them life is a constant burden and misery and I hope I will not be here long. Love to all and good-by forever.

Your friend, Heck Thomas

He died six days after this letter was written. He was sixty-two. His correct name was Henry Andrew Thomas, but he had been called "Heck" since boyhood, and as "Heck" will go down in Western history. The "malady" that was troubling him was Bright's disease, complicated by a heart weakness. It is touching to know that this great peace officer died so poor he had to borrow twenty-five dollars from Chris.

Memo: Heck Thomas was buried in what was known as the Lawton Cemetery, on the lot of his brother-in-law John F. Lantznester. A stone has been erected by his youngest daughter Beth Thomas and his son Albert Thomas (now living in California). The stone is of native Oklahoma pink mountain granite. The inscription reads:

Henry Andrew
"Heck" Thomas
1850-1912

(As I write, plans are on foot to erect a memorial to the great Heck. I hope they go through.)

(Personal note: I think I'll stop the pace of the story for a moment and put in an item about Bill Doolin's son. He was a year old when his father was shot and killed by Heck Thomas that tragic night south of Lawson, Oklahoma Territory. The baby disappeared. What became of him has been one of the mysteries of Oklahoma. I will now tell what became of him; this is the first time this information has appeared in print. His mother married again and gave the boy an assumed name. He grew up with no one knowing who he was. He is living in Oklahoma, and is an honorable, upright citizen who has never been in trouble with the law in his life. I have talked to him. He has requested me not to reveal his name, and this wish I am pleased to respect.)

Bill Tilghman was not doing well—Bill Tilghman who had once been a buffalo hunter and later city marshal at Dodge City. Bill Tilghman who had once captured singlehanded the uncapturable Bill Doolin. Bill Tilghman who had spent so many years as a deputy United States marshal. One day he told Chris that he had been offered a job in Cromwell, Oklahoma, as city marshal. Cromwell was a rugged boom town—oil. Many of the men who had once been outlaws and outlaw suspects had drifted into oil drilling. They were tough and they were rough.

"I t'ink I would not go, Bill," said Chris.

"Why not?"

"Because you are not so young as you used to was. You draw a leetle slow now."

"I need the money."

"It ees not a goot way to earn the money."

Bill Tilghman went to Cromwell and was shot down on the street by a drunken prohibition officer named Wylie Linn on the night of November 1, 1924. Chris was a pallbearer at the funeral of his friend. Thus one by one the old-time marshals were going.

Chris liked to think of the past and the old days, and talked about wanting to visit the battlefield of the Little Big Horn where he had helped bury the dead. In August 1927 his son and daughter-in-law put him in the family car and started West. He sat in the back seat; the movement of the car made him sleepy and he dozed. Then he would wake up and gaze about him. He recognized hardly any landmarks at all, time and the speed of the car doing strange things to him.

Between Sheridan and Rawlins, Wyoming, they saw a man standing beside the road, trying to flag a car. Reno, who was driving, drew up. The man was an Indian and he wanted a tire pump. As the Indian worked the pump, he began to talk, the way a person does when he wants to show appreciation. He said he had his father with him. There in the back seat was a deeply lined, picturesque southern Cheyenne. The son said that his father had been in the Battle of the Little Big Horn. The old Indian, hearing this, became alarmed and tried to silence his son. Fifty-one years had passed since the battle, but the Indian was still afraid.

"I was a member of the Fifth Cavalry and I came on the field a few days after the battle," said Chris. "The squaws had crushed the heads of our soldiers." Chris did not say it vindictively, but to add a detail. The old Indian became alarmed when he found that Chris had been there shortly after the battle, and urged his son to get the car started. But the car was not quite ready to start.

Getting out of the car, Chris went around to the old Indian, wanting to exchange experiences, but not so the Indian. He pretended he could not understand English and hastily got out of the car and started up the road. In a few minutes the car came along and he got in. The incident showed how the Indians felt after all the years.

When Chris got to the battlefield he wandered around, almost groping, it seemed. "It ees not t'e same. It ees along here I walk, I t'ink. The monuments change effryt'ing." He spoke of General Wesley Merritt who, he believed, was a greater general than Custer; and he spoke of his old captain—Jacob A. Augur, captain of the Fifth Cavalry, commanding Company A. They were both great men. He came to a big heroic monument commemorating the fallen. The names were arranged alphabetically and there, under the M's, he saw his own name!

Greatly agitated, he hunted up the superintendent. "I am Chris Madsen. Here is my serial number. I am not fallen yet. Peoples vill say I am an impostor. My name must come off."

"I cannot do anything about it," said the superintendent. "You will have to write to Washington about it."

"I vill," said Chris.

And he did, as soon as he got back to Oklahoma. The War Department answered that according to their official records he had been killed in the battle and he would have to stay killed.

Chris rarely ever mentioned this experience. To him it was a disgrace to pretend to be something you were not. And there his name stands today as one of the fallen.

At last Chris was home from the trip. It had been tiring.

Although Chris was too old to work, he enjoyed the acclaim that was his. He was made a member of Oklahoma's Hall of Fame, the first law-enforcement officer to attain the honor. He was pointed out on the street; tourists wanted to see him. He liked talking to them; and always he emphasized the respect that should be paid to law. People who didn't obey the law got into trouble.

September 6, 1934, a new honor came to him. He was asked

to go to Montrose, Nebraska, to help dedicate two monuments—one was on the spot where General Merritt, Captain King, and Chris had watched the approach of Yellow Hand. The other monument was placed on the exact spot where Buffalo Bill had killed Yellow Hand.

Of all the warriors who had been there that day, Chris was the only one now present. Buffalo Bill had died in Denver seventeen years before this. Captain Charles King (later General) had died six months before this dedication, in Milwaukee, at the age of eighty-eight.

But there was another warrior present—White Buffalo! He and Chris had become friends, in spite of the way Chris had hauled the old fellow off to prison, and they often talked together, but never about Custer. And so it was today when the two were to dedicate the monuments. The feeling White Buffalo had against the whites was so deep and so bitter that during the whole day, although some of the time Chris and White Buffalo had to stand side by side, White Buffalo did not once speak to Chris. Little actions showed that his Indian feeling was so deep in him that he, for the time being, hated Chris. Finally the dedication was over and Chris returned to Oklahoma. Later, in Oklahoma, Chris and White Buffalo once more became friends.

Chris lived in a white wooden house at 1517 West Noble Avenue, Guthrie—the town where he had marched so many prisoners through the streets. He was restless. He had always been active; now he was being put on the shelf. He liked to go downtown and talk to old friends, who were disappearing so fast.

He continued to drive his car. His daughter Marion tried to discourage him, but he was headstrong. "I can drive as goot as ever." One day, in driving his car, he had a crash due to his poor eyes. He came home and said indignantly, "Dis town is gettin' full of poor drifers." He began to have accidents. His car was constantly being towed off to the repair shop. The insurance company threatened to cancel his policy. Finally the old fellow gave up—at eighty-seven. This was a hard blow; he had more difficulty now than ever to fill in his time.

Now and then a reporter from Oklahoma City, or from Tulsa, would come to him to get a story. There, sitting in his rocking chair and slowly swaying back and forth, he would talk of his adventures. He began to talk more and more about his boyhood in Denmark, his battles with the Germans, and his days with the French Foreign Legion. "I have fought in four wars and I have always win," he would say, "but mebbe I don't this time." Sometimes in talking to a person his eyes would close and he would fall asleep. In a moment he would wake up and look embarrassedly at his guest. "I don't know what ees the matter wid me today," he would say. But it was that way every day, and increasingly so. But he was ninety.

He liked to talk of the days he had campaigned with Scout Cody, as he called him. He was Buffalo Bill's supporter and admirer. When critics began to question the tales that Buffalo Bill spun, Chris was there to defend him. "Mebbe Bill exaggerate a leetle but mostly it ees true." He himself never exaggerated his own stories. He had told them many times; he never forgot a date, or a name, or an adventure from his days with the Fifth Cavalry and his days in the Indian wars. Sometimes he spoke of his first sight of the battlefield where Custer had fallen and where he had helped bury some of the dead. The thing that distressed him most was that the squaws had spitefully beaten in the heads of our soldiers. This he had not seen himself, for he had not arrived until after most of the dead had been buried; the bodies of the men he had helped inter had got some distance away from the battlefield and had been lost in the weeds and grass. He always said that a kind of fear had come over the Indians after the battle, as if they realized the enormity of what they had done; and as a result would not, after the first few days, come back to the battlefield.

More and more he took the side of the Indians in their struggle with the government of the United States. There was not, he said, one tribe that we had not at some time or other broken our word with. Sometimes he would talk about Custer, but he was no great admirer of that flashy individual. General Wesley Merritt was the greater general. . . .

He was restless when he got back, Chris who had always been so active. He began writing his autobiography. It is on this that the author of this book has depended for much of the material. He would write a piece for the Guthrie *Daily Leader* and proudly bring it in. He insisted that the editor read it then and there. And as the editor read, Chris sat watching his face. When the editor had finished, Chris would lean forward and eagerly ask, "Is eet goot, yes?" Then his eyes began to fail; he could no longer use a typewriter. He tried dictating the rest of his story, but he did not do well.

Each day his round, portly figure would march downtown in Guthrie, the scene of so many of his triumphs. He liked to go to the sheriff's office and sit and talk; after a time he would get up and go to the city marshal's office and sit and talk. Sometimes an officer from another county would come in, sometimes from another state. Chris would sit and talk to him, delighted to have a new ear. Sometimes the person would ask to see Chris's guns. Chris would take him home and show him the guns for which he seemed to have an almost personal affection. He especially liked to show his Krag-Jörgensen, the one that shot the steel-jacketed bullet. "Dis is the one that shoot Bill Doolin in the foot, undt here is the bullet he give me." Then with pride he would exhibit the bullet.

Something happened to the bullet; in some way it became lost. He was greatly upset, and time after time hunted high and low for it. Sometimes when he came from a walk downtown he would say, "Marion, you find it?" But it was never found.

This was his daily life until one morning he stooped to turn off the small heater in his room; in doing so he lost his balance and fell. Frank A. Derr, his son-in-law, heard him, hurried in, picked him up, and put him on the bed.

"It ees nutting. I vill go downtown as soon as I rest a leetle." He would not let them call a doctor. But that afternoon the pain became so great that he consented. The doctor found that Chris had broken his hip. He was taken to the Masonic Hospital, which was a part of the Masonic Home for the Aged, where he was a pay patient. When visitors came to see him, he would peer at them through his dim eyes, not really seeing them; but it was nice to have people come in and ask about you. Finally, in January 1944 he died—he was almost ninety-three. The funeral services were held in the Masonic Temple in Guthrie; he was given the Rose Croix rites.

The snow was so deep that the body had to be held nine days before it could be taken to the Frisco Cemetery, near the tiny town of Yukon, which is halfway between El Reno and Oklahoma City. And there it lies today, with his name and the date on the stone; and beside him lies the body of his beloved Maggie.

He left an estate of ten thousand dollars and his farm—small reward for one who had done so much for his country. And thus came to his end the last of the great peace officers of Oklahoma.

TIME CLOCK

1851, February 25—Chris gets himself born.

1876, January 21—Enlists in the United States Army. Things begin to happen.

1876, August—Helps bury the dead on the Custer battlefield.

1887, December—Marries Maggie Morris.

1889, April 22—Makes the "run"; gets a homestead seven miles northeast of El Reno.

1891, January 20—Quits the army.

1891, January 21—Appointed deputy United States Marshal under William Grimes.

1892, May 26—Appointed chief deputy to William Grimes.

1892, October 5—Dalton Gang wiped out at Coffeyville, Kansas.

1892—Ol Yantis killed near Orlando.

1893—Chris goes to Beaver City in No-Man's Land. Judge Dale's famous order: "Bring 'em in dead."

1894—Rock Island train robbed at Pond Creek by the Hughes Gang.

1895—Rock Island train robbed by the Doolin Gang at Dover. Chief Whirlwind dies.

1896, March 5—Red Buck killed by Chris's posse. July 1 Chris is transferred to the Kansas City marshal's office. Bill Doolin killed by Heck Thomas near Lawson.

1897, March 4—Chris resigns his commission at Kansas City and returns to Oklahoma, because of his wife's ill health.

March 6—Chris reappointed field deputy under John C. Hammer of Ardmore, for the southern district of Oklahoma, with headquarters at Chickasha. (Does not take up work until he returns from the Spanish-American War.)

1898, May 2—Maggie dies.

1898, May 21—Enlists in the Rough Riders.

1898, August 26—Discharged.

1899, January 1—Tranferred to duty at Chickasha, Indian Territory. Takes Al Jennings to the penitentiary, Columbus, Ohio.

1901—Beanblossom murder. Chris captures George Moran.

1903—Chris, singlehanded, arrests Jim and John Black and Murphy. The jail where Chris tucked them away is now a Girl Scout hut.

1906, April 1—Chris appointed chief deputy marshal at Guthrie. Chris's informer is killed by the Casey Gang.

1909—Chris and Bill Tilghman attend a White House reception.

1912—Chris takes Ben Cravens to the federal prison at Fort Leavenworth, Kansas.

1916, April 30—Resigns as chief deputy... when the Democrats find they've got a man who wants the job.

1916, 1917—On the road helping to exploit a motion picture dealing with Oklahoma outlaws.

1917, April 5—Becomes auditor and, later, clerk of the police court in Tulsa.

1918, August—Becomes special investigator for Governor J. B. A. Robertson; this continues until July 1, 1922.

1923—Appointed a trustee of the Union Soldiers' Home in Oklahoma City. When he was seventy-six he decided to retire; this lasted about two months. Went back to work which, he said, was the only way a man could be happy. Held several small court jobs.

1933—Started to write his life story; worked at this until three months before he died, when his eyesight failed him.

1944, January 9—Dies in the Masonic Hospital, in Guthrie—last of the great frontier marshals. He lacked a few days of being ninety-three. He was buried besides Maggie in the Frisco Cemetery, near Yukon, Oklahoma. The cemetery may be reachd by traveling north from Yukon four miles on State Highway No. 4, then west on a section line road three miles. The graves are in the Morris lot, parents of Maggie.

SOURCES

Chapter I

Chris's manuscript covers his arrival in New York. There are thirty-three pages of this manuscript telling of his birth in Denmark, his early days, and his first military service.

Miss Dorothy D. Richards, of the Hays Free Public Library, writes me that Boot Hill was located in the vicinity of the present Eighteenth Street and Fort Street intersection—then a quarter of a mile from town. The last of the bodies from old Boot Hill were moved in 1937 when this section was being graded and excavated.

Additional material is extant in the personal story which Chris wrote for *Winners of the West*, a military newspaper published in St. Joseph, Missouri.

Yellow Hand's scalp was not all that Buffalo Bill sent to his wife. Here's the list as made out by the Rochester *Democrat and Chronicle*, of July 28, 1876, page 6: Headdress, war shield, blanket, girdle, bowie knife, whip, bridle.

"The shield has the ghastly ornaments of several Indian scalps, thus showing that the death-dealing hand had been felt by only those in whose veins the blood of the red man runs. The headdress is five or six inches wide and about five feet long, and is made of buffalo skin." (Note: This would seem to indicate that Robert Lindneux was a little too dramatic in his depiction of the headdress. His picture shows that it was about eight feet long.)

It is usually written that Yellow Hand was a Cheyenne chief. He was a Cheyenne, but there is no evidence that he was a chief. Chris always said he was a "sub-chief."

One war correspondent died with Custer—Mark Kellogg. He was with the Bismarck *Tribune*.

The details of the making of the map do not appear in Chris's manuscript. They were told to Frederick S. Barde, who wrote them down and preserved them.

Chapter 2

In his manuscript Chris pretty well covers his winter campaign and his campaign against Dull Knife. In later life Chris often spoke of Dull Knife who so successfully eluded them. He could not understand the wily old chief. Dull Knife certainly wasn't like the dumb Indians the boys back in Denmark had talked about.

Dull Knife's camp was destroyed by Colonel Mackenzie's troops on November 25, 1876. It was located about forty miles west of Old Fort Reno, on Bates Creek near North Fork of Powder River, Wyoming.

In his manuscript Chris tells in more detail than I have here his experience with "contract doctors." They were one of his favorite hates.

Chris always spoke with great glee of his days as a dancing teacher. His son passed the story along to me. And the olive story.

Chapter 3

Comment from Reno: "You do not tell enough about William Grimes. The other day I stopped at Kingfisher, his former home, and there found a write-up of him. The article said that he had been a sheriff in Nebraska before coming to Oklahoma. He was the first United States marshal of Oklahoma Territory, because Warren S. Lutty, who was appointed first, did not make the necessary bond and hence did not qualify for the job."

The name of the railroad where Heck Thomas had his little adventure was at that time the Houston & Texas Central Railroad. It is now part of the Southern Pacific System. The Interstate Commerce Commission calls it the "Southern Pacific—Lines East." Reno worked on this road, before his retirement, as locomotive inspector for the Interstate Commerce Commission, and many times has passed the scene of the holdup.

It is usually written that Heck Thomas was born in Atlanta. His youngest daughter, Beth Thomas, now Mrs. J. B. Meeks, of Purcell, Oklahoma, writes that it was Athens, Georgia.

The account that Heck dictated about the Sam Bass affair is owned by Heck's daughter, Mrs. J. B. Meeks. Heck was appointed a deputy May 2, 1891.

A query to Mrs. Zoe A. Tilghman brought back the information that Bill Tilghman was appointed a deputy under Grimes on May 26, 1892.

The title of the "Three Guardsmen" was given to them by John Golobie, a Czech newspaperman, in Guthrie.

Chapter 4

Comment from Reno about the Dutchman's slug:

"It is most unusual for a gun to miss fire twice in succession. When I was serving with my father, I took a revolver from the hand of a dying bank robber and found that it had snapped once. The cap was dented but not deeply enough to fire the cartridge. You will recall I showed you the gun. I have fired it many times but have never had it fail to go off. Maybe the Lord was not ready for me or my father to die."

The Palace Hotel was owned by Dave Brumbaugh and Neal Brown. The Reeves Casino was owned and operated by Bill and Dick Reeves. Today, when you pass the historical corner, you can hardly believe it was once the toughest in the United States. Out-of-town people call it dull... a fighting word to the loyal citizens of Guthrie.

Chapter 5

Statements about Beaver City have been checked against the writings of Mrs. Maud O. Thomas who for twenty-one years was publisher of a newspaper in Beaver City. This paper is now known as the *Herald-Democrat.*

Some of the material in this chapter about the opening of court in Beaver City is from an Associated Press interview with John H. Cotterell, appearing in the Denver *Post* on July 25, 1932. Some of the material was supplied by Reno Madsen, as he remembered the story as his father related it to him. The official court records of this remarkable session of court have been lost.

Judge John Henry Burford was regarded as one of the eminent jurists of the Southwest. In 1907 he went into private practice with the firm of Burford, Miley, Hoffman & Burford. The latter was his son Frank E. Burford.

Chapter 6

The story of the hotheaded Peter Schneider is from Chris's manuscript.

Chris tells the whiskers story in his manuscript. The story is also covered in the spring issue of the *Chronicles of Oklahoma*, 1956, Volume 34, Number 1, page 89, in an article by B. B. Chapman. Foreman could, with some justice, be called "The Father of El Reno."

Arrington is known as the first and the greatest peace officer in the Texas Panhandle. His papers are preserved in the Panhandle-Plains Historical Museum, in Canyon, Texas, about twenty miles south of Amarillo. He died on his ranch on the Washita River, fifteen miles from Mobeetie, in 1923.

Chapter 7

A note from Reno: "You've poured it on a bit thick about handling a bale of cotton. An average bale (they vary) measures 30 x 48 x 60 inches when it comes from the gin, weighs five hundred pounds. There are tricks in handling a bale of cotton. A hook, like a hay hook, is used to get a grip on a bale of cotton. A man can rock a bale, pull it over onto his knees, and place it on a platform truck, but that isn't lifting it, like you say. It's handling it. A man can roll a bale over and over, like a baggageman did your old trunk, by tilting and rolling it on its corners. He could rock a bale to get the nose of a two-wheel truck under it, then pull it back, balance it, and get it moving. I am confident that Jim Bourland was as strong as an ox, but I doubt if he could toss a bale of cotton around the way you say. Be conservative, son."

The duel between Big Jim Bourland and Fred Hudson is covered fairly well in the *Daily Oklahoman*, of May 24 and 25, 1906. However, most of the details in my account are from Chris's story as related to Reno.

The Chris-Felix Young story is dealt with in the El Reno *Democrat*, of May 17, 1894 and in the *Daily Oklahoman* for May 16 that year. Also there is a short account in the *Canadian County Republican* for May 18.

Chapter 8

Zip Wyatt's real name was Nathaniel Ellsworth Wyatt. Zip's brother rejoiced in the name Nim. The boy's father had the old-fashioned name of William.

Chris tells the story fairly completely in Chapter 21.

Here are newspaper references dealing with Zip and his troubles: *Oklahoma State Capital* of August 9, 1894. Also July 30 and August 12, 1895. Kingfisher *Free Press* of June 27, 1893. Enid *Weekly Wave* of August 8, 1895; also September 5, 1895.

The town of Whorton no longer exists; it's now Perry, Oklahoma.

Chapter 9

The author has a photostat of the expense sheet that Chris filled in after chasing White Buffalo. It is signed by both Chris and Alexander Yellow Man.

This Chief Whirlwind incident is based on the story as Chris used to relate it to his family and friends.

Chief Whirlwind died in 1895.

Chris kept the pipe for years. Reno now has it.

Chapter 10

Chris left copious notes on the subject of trailing outlaws. This was supplemented by material given me by Reno Madsen who often rode with his father. Also Reno says he often heard Bill Tilghman and Heck Thomas discuss how they pursued outlaws.

Chapter 11

The story of the Walnut Creek Boys is from Chris's manuscript.

Chapter 12

The material in this chapter is from Chris's manuscript or from Reno's memory.

Chapter 13

The material about taking prisoners to Fort Leavenworth came from Reno Madsen, who served as one of the guards.

Also he went along on the Jo-Jo expedition and is my source.

The smallpox story was told by Chris to his son who passed it along to me.

The same holds for the Chinese prisoners' story.

From the indomitable Reno: "Metcalf was more of a man than you choose to indicate. I talked with him when he was laid up with his broken leg. Once he was on the trail of an outlaw named Gentry. He came upon him at the Marlow railroad station. The outlaw thought he had caught Metcalf unarmed and ran toward him prepared to kill him, then discovered that Metcalf was armed. When he discovered this, the outlaw was so frightened that he almost collapsed. Turning, he started to run away as fast as he could. Metcalf fired at the running man six times—and hit him each time. The outlaw died on the railroad track. This, Mr. C., gives you a little idea of what Metcalf was like as a determined peace officer."

Chapter 14

Most of the material in this chapter is from Chris's manuscript, or from stories he passed on to his son.

The Judge Vaught material came from an interview the author had with the judge.

Frank Dale—the famous "Bring 'Em in Dead" judge—was appointed by President Cleveland as Associate Justice of the Territorial Supreme Court; later he became its Chief Justice.

Chapter 15

Chris tells this story in detail in his autobiography. I have cut the story down, and have left out some details that did not seem necessary. The story has been added to by Reno Madsen who saw some of it happen with his own eyes, and who told me some parts that his father did not set down in the chapter.

The two men in the surrey with Dr. Beanblossom were Herbert Beanblossom and Harry Darnashear.

Chapter 16

The story of how Chris saved his superior's life is from Chris's own manuscript, enlarged by the additional material he passed along to his son.

There is a version of the story in the St. Louis *Republic* for January 8, 1911. But this version is not true. Pay no attention to it.

William Grimes was marshal from August 22, 1890, until June 30, 1893.

Chapter 17

Most of the information in this chapter came from Chris's manuscript and from the stories he told Reno.

There is no record of Odem's real name.

Henry Starr was killed while trying to rob a bank in Harrison, Arkansas, February 18, 1921.

Chapter 18

Most of the material in this chapter has come from Chris's own writings.

Note: The fight at Coffeyville has not been detailed, for it has been told a thousand times; and Chris was not there. He went to Coffeyville the next day, but was not there when the fun was on.

The newspapers of Oklahoma are replete with stories of the Daltons. Some of the more detailed accounts are:

The Stillwater *Gazette* for June 17 and July 16, 1892. The Fort Smith *Elevator* for May 8, 15 and September 18, 1891. *Indian Chieftain* for August 27, 1891. *Daily Oklahoma State Capital* for February 29, 1920. The Coffeyville *Journal* in days following the raid.

In fact, the papers of Oklahoma, Kansas, and Arkansas battened on the doings of the Daltons.

The first week in May 1931 Emmett Dalton returned to Coffeyville to revisit the scene of the Dalton Disaster. A reporter from the Kansas City *Star*, A. B. Macdonald, accompanied him to the graveyard where two of Emmett Dalton's brothers are buried. Emmett stood meditatively in front of Grat's grave and said, as if to himself, "Poor Grat! He was the hothead of the family. He was an unhappy, discontented boy who grew into a fierce fighting man. He never knew what it was all about."

Chapter 19

Most of the material in this chapter is from Chris's writings.

The exact number of days that Chris chased the Daltons is shown in one of his account books. It reads:

Pursuit of Daltons
August 23 through September 2, 1891

November 4 " 9, 1891
All of December, 1891.

In fact he pursued them until they were wiped out at Coffeyville.

Nix in his book deals with some of this general material. And so does Mrs. Zoe A. Tilghman in her *Marshal of the Last Frontier* and her *Outlaw Days*. The following papers have material: Guthrie *Daily News*, June 6, 1893. Guthrie *Daily Leader*, July 2, 1893. *Daily Oklahoman*, August 18, 1912. *Daily Oklahoma State Capital*, August 26, 1893.

In fact every paper in Oklahoma carried stories about the Doolins and their doin's.

Inkanish was killed September 12, 1894.

CHAPTER 20

The story of the Dover train robbery is based chiefly on two chapters in Chris's autobiography—Chapters 4 and 20. In addition I have used material he told his son in person and which does not appear in the two chapters.

The chapter has been read by Mrs. Zoe Tilghman to authenticate the part played by her husband.

The state papers bristle with accounts of the sensational robbery and pursuit. The following papers for April 4, 1895, have accounts—some in detail, some fragmentary: Hennessey *Clipper*, Enid *Daily Wave*, Kingfisher *Free Press*. The following day the *Daily Oklahoma State Capital* carried the story.

The next day (April 6th) the Guthrie *Daily Leader* featured the story. This paper had developments in its issues of April 10 and May 3 (the latter an especially good account).

El Reno *Globe*, April 12, 1895.

E. D. Nix deals with the robbery in his book *Oklahombres*.

The *Daily Oklahoma State Capital* has material about it in its issues of May 16, 1895, and November 7, 1896.

Note: The author wants to pay a compliment to the Newspaper File of the Oklahoma State Historical Society. Here is to be found the best coverage of newspapers of any state in the Union. Elmer L. Fraker modestly tells me if this be true, it is because Oklahoma is a young state and the bigwigs got immediately to work preserving its papers. Anyway, it's a fine newspaper collection.

A note from Mrs. Zoe A. Tilghman: "I'm glad to see you didn't fall for the story of George Newcomb drinking from an alkali creek, sputtering out in surprise, 'It's bitter!' and thus acquiring his nickname. Young Newcomb knew the country and the water as well as anybody. I once met the widow of Little Bill Raidler and she told me the Doolin men always called him Bitter Creek.

"My husband told me that when they first started on the gruesome journey they slung the body over a saddle on the outlaw's own horse. As soon as the officers could, they procured a spring wagon, as you have it in your story.

"You might add that the Dunn Ranch was eighteen or twenty miles east of Ingalls, in an area that in the early days was called 'Cross Timbers.' It's mentioned by Washington Irving in his notes."

A sidelight on the character of Bill Doolin is given by E. Bee Guthrey in *Chronicles of Oklahoma*, Volume 3, Number 1, for April 1925: "I knew Bill Doolin in a rather different way. I was editor of a weekly newspaper in Stillwater. One day I was on horseback going from Stillwater to the Pawnee agency and was about three miles east of Ingalls when I met Bill Doolin and three of his pals. Each had a Winchester in the scabbard of his saddle. Also each had a pair of shot sacks swinging from the pommel of his saddle. Each shot sack was pulled down by something heavy within it.

"Bill drew up his horse, and so did the others. Then Bill, calling me by name, asked if there were any deputy marshals in Ingalls. I said I hadn't seen any as I had come through. After talking a moment I said, 'What have you men got in those shot sacks?'

"Bill ripped out an oath and said it was none of my business. No man was ever more right. As I started to ride on, Bill turned in his saddle and said, 'Bee, are you still running that one-horse newspaper at Stillwater?'

"'Yes.'

"'How much a year is the rag?'

" 'One dollar.'

"Reaching down into one of the sacks, he pulled out a handful of its contents and tossed it over to me. It fell at my horse's feet. I got down and picked it up, Bill watching me with an amused smile. When I got the thing up and separated from the dust, I found I had eleven silver dollars.

"I told Bill this would pay for a subscription for eleven years. 'That's what I want,' said Bill.

" 'Where do you want it sent?'

" 'I hadn't thought of that,' said Bill. 'Send it to Ingalls till you hear I'm dead, then send it to hell.'

"The key to all this was that there had been a bank robbery in Clarksville, Arkansas, in which a great many silver dollars had been taken. I never tried to find out who the robbers were.... I sent the paper faithfully to Ingalls until the telegraph keys began to chatter. I did not try to forward the paper, as I had no mailing privilege to the address he'd given me."

Another glimpse of Bill Doolin is given by Jim Williams, Guthrie, Oklahoma, in an interview appearing in *Indian-Pioneer History*, Volume 49, page 521: "I knew Bill Doolin when he was just a big-hearted cowboy and we worked on adjoining ranches. I did not witness the following incident, but my uncle and my cousin were there and described it to me. There was a big three-day celebration in Coffeyville. The ranch hands decided they would have a celebration of their own in a pasture about a quarter of a mile from the town. They sawed some barrels in two and filled them with beer and ice. Everybody could have all they wanted, free. While the cowboys were drinking, two constables came out from town and asked who owned the beer.

"Bill Doolin spoke up. 'Nobody owns it. It's free. Help yourselves.'

"The officers said, 'It is against the law to drink beer in this state and we are going to pour the beer out.'

"Bill, who had a quick temper, said, 'If you pour our beer out, you're going to get hurt.'

"The men started to roll a barrel away. Guns were whipped out and the two officers were killed. It was never known who fired the shots, but Bill was in charge of ceremonies and was considered responsible. He left the ranch and from that day on was on the dodge. We always thought that was the beginning of his criminal career."

Bitter Creek and Charlie Pierce were killed July 20, 1895.

Reno at work: "You pass over very glibly the matter of rewards. A deputy working on a fee basis and possemen working the same way were able to collect rewards. However, there was a joke in this rewards business—the money was offered for arrest and conviction. If the reward was offered for a criminal dead or alive, there had to be positive identification of the corpse. Once my father arrested a man named Simpson who was charged with the murder of two deputy United States marshals. There was a reward of three hundred dollars for arrest and conviction. My father was field deputy at the time and would have been eligible to collect the reward, but when Simpson was tried he pled guilty and was acquitted on the grounds of justifiable homicide. My father had risked his life to make the arrest; all that he got was his fee for serving the warrant."

When Judge Dale retired from the bench, he joined with A. G. C. Bierer; the firm continued until 1926. Judge Dale later joined the firm of Dale, Brown, and Hoyland, in Guthrie, where he continued until his death.

The *Daily Oklahoman*, of February 2, 1930, retells the Bring 'Em in Dead story.

Note from Reno: "I do not accept the Frank Canton story as to the shooting of Bitter Creek. I have correspondence between my father and the United States Attorney General that Canton had been 'the lone highwayman' in Texas before he ran away to Alaska. Canton tried several times to get a commission as deputy marshal but was turned down by the Attorney General."

Chapter 21

The story of Tilghman in the dugout was told to me by Mrs. Zoe A. Tilghman, who said she had heard her husband relate it many times; in fact, she said there once was a motion picture depicting this scene and he had traveled with the picture for a short time, and, from the stage, told what had happened in that outlaws' haven.

Tilghman got the award money September 7, 1895.

E. D. Nix wrote that in the Yantis pursuit Heck Thomas was the other deputy marshal. The deputy was really Tom Houston. Nix, in *Oklahombres*, is not a reliable source of information. After he had to resign his office, he rarely came to Oklahoma. And he wrote from memory, thirty years after the events he was telling of. The writing was done by a hired assistant; the two did not get along well. After the book was out, Nix said that he had not got to read proof and he regretted the errors that had gone into the book.

Material dealing with the life and death of Little Bill can be found in the *Daily Oklahoman* of September 12, 1895, and in the Fort Smith *Elevator* of September 13, 1895. Also in the Kingfisher *Free Press* for April 9, 1896.

My thanks to Mrs. Zoe A. Tilghman for going over the part dealing with her husband and Little Bill. From Zoe: "You ask me the correct spelling of Red Buck's family name. Most writers set it down as Waightman. This seems to be wrong. My husband copied it down from court records. There is no known signature of Red Buck's so I think we can accept the court records; here it appears as Weightman.

"P. S. Bill was an exceptionally good speller. I never knew him to misspell but one word and that was ecstasy, a word that will rope and tie almost anybody."

Author's comment: How illuminating this is! Most people think of the frontier marshals as lacking in education. Here, however, is one of the most famous who can spell like a champion. But that was Oklahoma at the time I am writing about: all sorts and kinds mixed up into a wonderful, a fascinating cross section of America.

Ol Yantis' name is often misspelled; sometimes it is Yontis, sometimes Yountis. His sister said the family used *a*.

Reno says his family used to have the bullet that ended Yantis' career, but it disappeared and all the hunting has not brought it forth.

CHAPTER 22

The Doolin information is from Chris's manuscript and from notes that he did not get to write out in full. The letter from Heck Thomas is owned by Mrs. Zoe A. Tilghman. All the papers in Oklahoma carried stories of how the end came to Doolin, no two of them agreeing. He was the most famous outlaw in the United States; the papers had a wonderful time. Mrs. Zoe A. Tilghman, Bill Tilghman's widow, has gone over the part played by her husband.

CHAPTER 23

The Spearville cashier, J. R. Baird, later said that the amount the boys got from his bank was $1,697.

The shooting of Dynamite Dick was covered by practically all the papers in Oklahoma. The best account appears in the *Daily Oklahoma State Capital* of December 4, 1896.

Little Dick's association with the musical-comedy Jennings outlaws is covered at some length by nearly all the Oklahoma papers. The shooting down of Little Dick appears in them under the date of April 8, 1898. The best account is in the *Daily Oklahoma State Capital* of that date. Zoe A. Tilghman also deals with Little Dick in her *Outlaw Days*.

There is much newspaper material dealing with Arkansas Tom and his wild ways. The best accounts are in the Joplin *Globe* for August 17 and 18, 1924. In some accounts his name is spelled Dougherty; in the records of the Missouri State Penitentiary it is Daugherty.

My thanks to J. T. Lamar at the Missouri State Penitentiary for digging up the official records for me.

CHAPTER 24

The incident of the burial clothes is dealt with at greater length by E. D. Nix in his book.

The incident of the alleged dice thrower was remembered by Reno Madsen, who was present.

The matter of the whisky and the bananas is handled nicely by the Guthrie *Daily Leader* for October 5, 1897.

Frank Jennings and the O'Malley brothers served their terms and returned to Oklahoma where they "settled down" and became respected citizens.

Jennings was released from the Columbus prison November 13, 1902.

Chapter 25

Most of the material in this chapter is from Chris's manuscript, and from the memories of little Reno.

Chapter 26

Cravens made the following prison escapes:

Lineville, Iowa —
Corydon, Iowa —September 8, 1890
Guthrie, Oklahoma —Christmas Day, 1894
Tecumseh, Oklahoma—1896
Lansing, Kansas —November 16, 1900

When he was in hiding he worked for the following farmers in Mound City, Missouri: Robert Gillis, John Norman, Henry Alkire, and a Mr. Melvin. He also worked on the Rankin Number 4 Farm, Tarkio, Missouri, then rated as the biggest corn farm in the world. His theory was that no one would look for him on a farm doing hard work. And no one did, but he made the mistake of stealing some hogs, then was arrested under his assumed name of Maust.

Chapter 27

Much of the material in this chapter was supplied by Chris's son. This I added to by interviewing six people in Guthrie who had known Chris and who saw him in his declining days. The papers of Oklahoma carried detailed obituaries.

INDEX

Index

Y

Z